THE MYTH OF CHRISTIAN SUPREMACY

THE MYTH OF CHRISTIAN SUPREMACY

RESTORING OUR DEMOCRATIC IDEALS

BURTON L. MACK

Fortress Press
Minneapolis

THE MYTH OF CHRISTIAN SUPREMACY
Restoring Our Democratic Ideals

Original edition copyright © 2017 by Burton L. Mack, published under the title *The Rise and Fall of the Christian Myth* by Yale University Press, New Haven, CT.

Cover image: Photo by Dan Cristian Padure on Unsplash
Cover design: Brad Norr

Print ISBN: 978-1-5064-8213-2

CONTENTS

THE MYTH OF CHRISTIAN SUPREMACY

INTRODUCTION

Early readers of this project have suggested that I tell how I journeyed from the spirit-centered evangelical Christianity of my youth to the view I present in what follows, deemed "radical" and "controversial" by some as it has evolved.

This book is about the cultural influence of the Christian myth. As a boy in the Church of the Nazarene, where my father was a pastor, I had no concept of what I now call the Christian mentality, but I did know about the pervasive aura and influence of what the Nazarenes referred to as the Holy Spirit. The Nazarenes had emerged from Methodism toward the end of the nineteenth century. They cultivated the personal experience of "sanctification" and the quest for "purity of heart," having rejected the "formalism" of the Methodists and other mainline churches. They knew that they were Christians, but had no concept of Christianity as a religion concerned about society as did other Protestant churches. Their view of the world beyond the borders of the church was that it was dirty and dangerous. Their focus was upon the cloistered community of the Holy Spirit. I experienced this atmosphere as suffocating, an encompassing environment demanding obeisance without any clarity about the reasons for being obedient. I raised some questions about the cluster of prejudices used to mark the world outside, only to find that my Christian community did not have rational reasons for their attitudes. In high school I had friends like Bob Lacanale, a paraplegic whose father brewed homemade beer (a no-no for the Nazarenes), and Zek, a Syrian Muslim with whom I played chess, sometimes at his home in a curtained-off room (about which my parents raised their eyebrows). Neither of these friends was dirty or sinful in my view, but my Nazarene Christian elders looked down upon them, and I did not know why.

High school in Portland, Oregon, was a wonderful change of atmosphere. Math and science opened up large and exciting worlds to explore that called for curiosity and critical thinking. When I graduated I was offered the Bosch and Lomb scholarship to Yale University. I was quite proud of it. But when I told my father about it, he said that I could not go to Yale because it was a worldly and sinful school. I would be going to Pasadena Nazarene College, where I could learn about Holiness Christianity from H. Orton Wiley, one of the founders of the Church of the Nazarene. I did that, of course, dutifully, and managed to write a master's thesis on the concept of love (*agape*) in the New Testament. And because Pasadena Nazarene was a college that trained teachers and ministers, it was taken for granted that I should become a minister.

I was appointed to the church in Corcoran, California, where I found myself in the cotton country of J. G. Boswell, founder of what is still the largest private farm in the country. There Caterpillar D8s tilled the fields in sections, pulling harrows fifty feet wide behind as the tractor plied a straight line for a quarter mile before turning around. Mexican migrants lived in cotton camps outside of town. (The migrants were called "wetbacks" in those days.) The local Methodist minister befriended me, and we participated in the founding of the Kings County Migrant Ministry, my first experience of social and cultural inequalities in the big world outside the church. The cotton camp was close by and needed water and toilets. We waited upon J. G. Boswell, who gave the ministry $5,000 to make some improvements, and the Tulare Migrant Ministry visited our congregations to tell us that Jesus wanted us to care for "the least of these." I was not sure what I thought about the situation, but I had some encouragement from the Ministerial Association and the leaders of the Migrant Ministries in other counties of the San Joaquin Valley to begin thinking of Christianity as having concerns for the well-being of migrant laborers. The Church of the Nazarene, however, was not able to think with me about such a project, much less allow me to use the resources of the church to address the physical needs of the cotton pickers. As H. Orton Wiley was remembered to have said, in relation to the storefront churches in downtown Los Angeles in the 1930s, you have to decide whether to be a mission or a church.

I was transferred west to the Nazarene church in Santa Paula (self-described Citrus Capital of the World), where, fortunately, the local Episcopal and Presbyterian ministers understood my quandaries and let me discuss with them the Christianity they thought we all shared. They had no idea how little I had learned about Christianity from the Nazarenes, and how completely dependent upon them I was for this intellectual introduction to what later might be called the Church in the World. They said I had three choices if I wanted to transfer membership to a church that had a social ethic: the Methodists, the Presbyterians, or the Episcopalians. When Ted Gill, a newly installed president of San Francisco Theological Seminary, was invited to address the local Presbytery, I was invited to attend. After an informal get-acquainted lecture about his family's place in the economy and his own participation in Martin Luther King Jr.'s Selma march, I was introduced to him as a Nazarene considering the Presbyterian Seminary. He looked me in the eye, smiled, and said I would be welcomed. I decided to go to San Francisco in order to pursue my education in Christianity and the world.

The seminary experience turned out to be my enlightenment, what with the learning of Greek, Hebrew, and a bit of Aramaic, as well as my first serious review of the history of Western civilization (it was actually "church history"). The Bible was central. Theology provided the intellectual system for thinking about Christian beliefs. And social history was the arena within which the Presbyterian Church had its place and mission in the world. A bigger picture was in the process of forming as my introduction to the church as a social institution. My enlightenment had a profound effect upon the aura of the spiritual environment I had experienced in the Church of the Nazarene. The Nazarene "worldview" did not have a big picture of the world around it, or any indication of the structure or logic of its own world. It was actually not more than a bubble of sensibility that kept Christians worried about the purity of their souls. But now, in the Presbyterian Church, it was no longer the Spirit, but a certain placement of the Christ, the Gospel, the Bible, and history that expanded the horizons of the Christian's worldview and gave it some rationale.

Some of the professors were at work on the teachings of

Jesus, thinking them key to the origins and theological significance of Christianity. I was put to work learning the language tools for the translations needed to determine the original words of Jesus. I still have the Syriac *New Testament and Grammar* on my shelf. But then Neal Q. Hamilton returned from Germany, where he had been studying with Rudolf Bultmann. It was not just the teachings of Jesus, but the *proclamation* of Jesus' death and resurrection (Paul's *kerygma*) that mattered. So now there was a theological debate about Christian origins to consider if I wanted to find the answers to my questions about the reasons for Christian beliefs and their significance. Bultmann called Paul's *kerygma* the "Christ Myth" and said that modern-day Christians were not able to believe in myth, even and especially the Christian myth. Thus the Christian message had to be *demythologized*. An extremely rich period of discourse had developed. There were Kierkegaard, Jaspers, Sartre, and the list of books on "Jesus Christ and Mythology," "Kerygma and Myth," and "Christ without Myth." I did my best to comprehend this discourse, a brand new way of thinking for a culturally deprived erstwhile Nazarene. But then I wore out my professors with my questions about the significance of certain theological propositions for understanding the human situation in general. Ted Gill, Arnold Come, Neal Hamilton, and James Robinson (who had come up from Claremont to lecture on Bultmann) said I should go on to Germany to study with Hans Conzelmann, who was dealing with the questions of myth, meaning, and history.

I arrived at the University of Göttingen in 1963. By then the Germans had learned much about myth and the history of religions. Conzelmann was a student of Bultmann, but more interested in the ways Ancient Near Eastern myths had become intellectual traditions that influenced early Christianity. His essay on Sirach 24 caught my attention, because he established some links between Sophia, Chokma, Isis, and Maat, each of whom was being treated as a personification of "wisdom" in the literatures of the times. This brought the several cultures, Greek, Hebrew, and Egyptian, together as if their mythologies were modes of social thought. My assignment was to see whether the *logos* (word) in Philo and the first chapter of John's Gospel also followed a mythic grammar indebted to the mythology of Sophia-Chokma. The notion of seeking Sophia-Chokma, a mythological figure that had taken flight because of her rejection by society, but would return and/or could be found if pursued, was being discussed in Göttingen, along with the Ancient Near Eastern "Anthropos Myth." So my task was to track down the wisdom myth and the anthropos myth and to see whether the Prologue to John was indebted to them. I spent two years researching the literatures of the Ancient Near East looking for traces of these myths. Then Carsten Colpe found that the anthropos myth was a scholarly fiction; there was no such thing in Antiquity. And I, finally, told Conzelmann that the wisdom myth was hardly to be found in the Ancient Near Eastern literature, but that he had been right about the Egyptian mythologies of Maat and Isis as models for the figure of wisdom in Sirach 24, as well as for the wisdom poetry in the Wisdom of Solomon, and that Philo knew about this configuration but clearly preferred the figure of the *Logos* to that of *Sophia* for explaining the wisdom of the written books of Moses. Conzelmann encouraged me to write it up. Well, they gave me a doctorate for it, but I never did get back to the Gospel of John.

Then I was back in the United States at Rutgers University, with the responsibility to teach courses in the New Testament, even though all I knew was the literatures of Greece and the Ancient Near East as the "background" to the New Testament. It was toward the end of the sixties, when students wanted to know what had gone wrong with Western civilization and the Christian tradition, and why our nation-state thought it could spread democracy by dropping bombs on Vietnam. All I could do in New Jersey was introduce English majors to the literatures of Christian origins as I had learned to read them. The students thought it was interesting, of course, that they could read these texts "in social-historical context," as they said, without having to deal with the Christian "belief system," as they called it. But of course, none of us could say why Christians thought the New Testament and the literatures of Antiquity were so important, why I had to spend so much time studying them, why a college needed to offer a course in them, or what difference that knowledge made for the way the world was working in the present. My students were becoming my teachers. And because most of them were raised much differently than I, their knowledge of the world around them continued to be my most relevant academy.

Then some New Testament scholars who found my work on wisdom and Philo interesting asked for a lecture or two. There was the Society of Biblical Literature (SBL), the Jesus Seminar, the Institute for Antiquity and Christianity (IAC), the North American Association for the Study of Religion, and eventually the SBL Seminar devoted to "Ancient Myths and Modern Theories of Christian Origins." By then I had moved, first to the Methodist Theological School in Ohio, where everyone had more answers than questions, and then to Claremont, where James Robinson, Hans Dieter Betz, and Robert Funk took me in as a junior colleague and project director at the IAC. I wrote *A Myth of Innocence* because Funk said I couldn't have New Testament credentials on the basis of writing only about Old Testament texts and authors. So I took the Gospel of Mark as my New Testament text and analyzed it the same way I had written about Sirach, the Wisdom of Solomon, and Philo. When Ron Cameron, Merrill Miller, and Jonathan Z. Smith read the Mark book, they looked me in the eye and asked about my social theory of religion. They said I had written the book to explain the mythology of the Gospel of Mark, but without referring to its Christian theology or meaning. How did I do that? Did I have a social theory of religion that called for a rational explanation of myth? When I said that I did not know what my social theory was, they told me we would have to form a seminar on the Mark book to find out. They said that my description of Mark's text sounded like Smith's method of redescription, and he might help us (me) with his theory of myth and ritual. Oh my, I thought. Smith represented yet another area of research and disciplined thought for which I had absolutely no academic preparation.

But Jonathan did join us, and we had a marvelous go of it. The seminar had to struggle with a redescription of the several groups that produced the early myths, all of which New Testament scholars (and I at that time) had called "communities." Now there were instead the Q people, the Thomas people, the Hellenic schools of philosophy, Mark's picture of the disciples in synagogues, Paul's *ekklesiai* (which was traditionally translated "churches" and thus sounded Christian, even though the Greek word means simply groups or gatherings), and so forth. It was tough going, however, and we were not able to find the attraction for any of these social formations that called for the myths they came up with, and none that fit with the eventual pictures of Christianity or Christian congregations that all of us still must have had in mind. So our papers stayed pretty much at the level of social-historical description without being able to clarify the link between "mythmaking" and "social formation."

The seminar served as my induction into the guild of biblical studies and provided me with friends, colleagues, and conferences. I was able to accept some invitations for papers that gave me opportunities to continue to write. James Robinson asked me to do a social history of the Q people similar to what I had written about Mark, and John Loudon said he wanted to publish it at HarperSanFrancisco. When it appeared and Loudon thought it looked good, he encouraged me to think of writing the next book on the question of who really wrote the New Testament. I thought I could do that because the subject was the authors of the literature, not their theologies, and my students at Rutgers had taught me that the significance of a writing required asking about the social situation and intentions of its author. But *Who Wrote the New Testament? The Making of the Christian Myth* turned out to be an introduction to all of the authors of all of the writings in the entire New Testament corpus. When Loudon gave its publication a reception at the annual meeting of the SBL, I discovered I was on my way to being regarded as a New Testament scholar without needing to think of it as the Christian's word of God. Obviously, my studies of the New Testament had not answered my own questions about the Bible as the Christian myth and how it could be that Christians believed in such a fantastic story. It finally dawned on me that most of my colleagues in the Christian Origins seminar had become biblical scholars by some other route, because of a familiarity with Christianity and the Bible based on the way they grew up in their Protestant churches. The categories we were using to redescribe Christian origins were indebted to that familiarity. And that was why these categories did not work for Christian origins, because the Christianity everyone had in mind was actually not there at the beginning. We said we knew that, of course, but thought to analyze the separate ingredients that were there, thinking to discover how and why they were put together to form the religion that eventually appeared as that of the Christian Roman Empire and Christendom.

When it became clear that the first major formation of Christianity was the result of Constantine's creation of the Holy Roman Empire, and that it drew upon the model of the Ancient Near Eastern temple-states and aristocratic empires, I decided to start reading in the history of religions, searching for models and theories of religion that might be used as a theoretical frame of reference for understanding Christianity. By then Jonathan Smith had joined me in another conference about ritual, asking historians of religion to discuss René Girard's *Violence and the Sacred*. This gave me a fairly clear picture of Smith's theory of both myth and ritual, as well as his method of working with cross-cultural comparisons. I was intrigued with his use of ethnography for comparisons, several examples of which found their way into the papers and protocol of the Christian Origins seminar. I realized that ethnography was producing more or less complete pictures of tribal societies and the ways in which their myths and rituals fit right into their social structures and practices. Because I had never been clear about the place and function of Christianity in Western societies and cultures, I decided to investigate the theories of religion by ethnographers. I had the works of Durkheim, Lévi-Strauss, Malinowski, and Sahlins in mind as a place to start. So I went to work on a social theory of religion in which myth and ritual functioned as the primary components of religion and culture in ethnographical societies. It became an important chapter in my scholarly quest. I discovered that my questions about Christianity stemmed from my own rationalistic sensibility, a mind-set that was not shared by others satisfied with other modes of meaning and making sense of their social worlds. When Lévi-Strauss explained his work with the myths of indigenous tribes of South America that he found to be reasonable, he said that all peoples were intelligent and all myths the products of thinking. It was the same with Durkheim, Malinowski, Hultkranz, Boas, and Jonathan Z. Smith. What a relief. I had been castigated by New Testament scholars since *A Myth of Innocence* for being too "rationalistic," and when I started talking about a "social theory of religion," Hans Küng, on sabbatical in Claremont, said, "Okay, but it has to be *religion*, not sociology." And so my ethnographic project taught me more than myth theory. It told me about cultures and mentalities, and that the categories of a particular discipline, beholden as they are to its own culture, may not be able to describe another's myth and ritual without putting its own categories on the table to be analyzed in the process of seeking a common understanding. The rub, of course, is the need for both sides of the table to be interested in such a negotiation.

Along the way I developed the concept of "social interests" to relate myths and rituals to the social practices and productions of ethnographic societies, and thought to use it as a category to advance the Christian origins project in its quest to theorize the link between "social formation" and "mythmaking." There are now two volumes of seminar papers in print, and a third volume recently submitted for publication. And even though we all now knew that there was no Christian religion there at the beginning, not even the Bible that eventually became so important as a ritual and historical document for Christianity, my ethnographic theory did help to make some sense of some of the early (pre-) Christian experiments in mythmaking that were later taken up by Christendom. That should have been reward enough for one scholar's investment in biblical studies.

But then we were all shocked out of our academic ease by the 9/11 event that the Bush administration called a "terrorist attack," calling for war. This response was complicated by the administration's references to the concept of the "Christian Nation." Putting the two together made it appear that we had a social crisis and a cultural conflict on our hands. When it became known that a pseudointellectual cabal of the Bush administration had been talking about the United States as the Christian Nation for some time, the social and cultural confusion was made much worse. Behind this talk were Wolfowitz, Rumsfeld, Rove, Cheney, and others, who had created some white papers on "The American Century" (meaning the twenty-first century) incorporating the notions of "manifest destiny," the spread of the American way, absolute executive authority, financial power, and global military control, all justified by the concept of the

Christian Nation's supposed right to be the leader of the nations of the world. And the president, George W. Bush, cited the Prologue to the Gospel of John to describe America's role as a light to the nations, a "light shining in darkness, and the darkness did not overcome it." (What he meant was "would not be able to overcome it.") These conservative Christian politicians were obviously beholden to the big-picture mythology of Christendom, now applied to the righteous nation and its global military destiny of control over the world. Carl Schmitt's political philosophy had taken root in America, a defense of divine sovereignty on the model of Catholic Christendom, and for the absolute executive authority of a monarch in order to guarantee a society's unity and stability. This political philosophy was actually a theology that can be seen in the work and influence of Leo Strauss on neoconservatives, imperialists, and Christian fundamentalists. The development underscored Jeff Sharlet's insight about Christian fundamentalism erupting at the peak of power, destined to cover the entire world (*The Family: The Secret Fundamentalism at the Heart of American Power*).

I was stunned. The "Christian Nation" talk seemed to be grounded in the Catholic mythology of Christendom, but was being parroted by Protestant Christians as if what "Christian" meant no longer needed the authorization of the Christian church as a social institution. It violated the American rubric of the separation of church and state and posited "national and economic interests" as the reasons for "missions" abroad, in contrast to the traditional reasons for the Christian mission, namely the conversion of others to the Christian religion. The goal of the American Century was actually the "American Empire" of global economic and military control. The "gospel" was now the "spread of democracy" and "nation-building." So there was little left of what Protestant Christians had understood as Christianity except the archaic fascination with sovereignty, power, and authority which was now being transferred from the deity in his cosmic realm to the hands of the conservative politicians and financial institutions of the American nation-state.

Something had to be said. So I wrote the books *Myth and the Christian Nation* and *Christian Mentality* as my contribution to the questions that were raised about Christianity and the United States. What I found interesting was the presence of what I had been calling a mythic mentality as the way in which a people learned to think about their religion and society. Both books emphasized this feature of the conservatives' discourse about the Christian nation and emphasized the curious sense of self-evidence about the logic of the Christian myth of Christendom on the part of conservative Protestant Christians in the United States. When colleagues reviewed the books in panel discussions at the annual meetings of the SBL, they were worried not about my assessment of the social situation but about my theory of myth and mentality. Most of these colleagues were postmodernists, for whom the big picture of Christendom as well as the grand narrative of Western civilization had been consigned to the past and could no longer work persuasively as a myth or a mentality. This meant that I had to try again, to paint the picture not only of the current conflicts as social issues but also of the social issues as intellectual issues. The questions, then, had to be changed. It was not only how the Conservative Coalition could draw upon the logic of a Christendom that was no longer there except in the form of a cultural mentality. It was also, and especially, whether religion actually had anything left to say about the social and cultural issues of the present state of the world. This book is my meditation upon these questions. I ask the reader to join me in a novel cross-cultural and cross-disciplinary intellectual journey.

1 THE BIG PICTURE

Humans have always painted themselves into big pictures of their world. From the Aranda of Australia to the nation-states of modernity, these pictures of the world are as vast as the human imagination can reach. And because the worlds humans live in comprehend both a natural order and a social history, these converge to form an arena in which the interests humans take in their projects of living together make the picture dynamic. Thus the scope of the canvas on which humans paint their worlds can stretch to the horizons, including all of a people's imaginable time and space.

We call these pictures of an encompassing world myths. The edges may be as fuzzy as the horizon is far. But the foreground will have sharply profiled heroes and precedent events of a people's history, as well as some suggestion of the social formation they have constructed. Social formation is the major product of the collective human enterprise. I want to describe several of these social formations and their myths on the way to an analysis of our own big-picture canvas, a picture that is in danger of losing a coherent social design and logic. I want to emphasize the territory on which a people lives, their picture of themselves in their mythic world at that place, and the structure of their social formation as their accepted design for living together.

THE ARANDA

The Aranda, an indigenous tribe of Australia, live in the bush and tell stories about their ancestors. The ancestors lived in the time of the "Dreaming," a time when the bush was being formed into the shapes it now has. These ancestors wandered over the bush much as the Aranda now do, for the Aranda are what we call hunters and gatherers. When their ancestors came to the end of their lives, each was transformed into some feature of the topography. These events shaped the landscape, and the Aranda recall them with stories that took place there by the rocky precipice, here by the stream, over there in the bush, all with names for their places. The ancestors also introduced the flora and fauna, so that their stories mark the terrain as a land of memorials. The contours of the bush are therefore a constant reminder of the ancestors who created the land on which the Aranda now live. When the present Aranda die, they also return to the time of the Dreaming.

Western ethnographers have always been astounded at the Aranda for living in such a land, with a climate Westerners thought to be inhospitable. The Aranda were therefore said to be a "primitive" tribe without a history, technology, or culture. These ethnographers have been wrong about the Aranda as a primitive tribe without a culture, for the Aranda's stories are their history, and they do not think of the bush as inhospitable. It is their home.

THE WINNEBAGO

The Winnebago are a Native American tribe who lived in the lake and forest lands of what is now eastern Wisconsin. They settled in permanent camps, raised corn and beans, and hunted local elk, and bison farther away. Ethnographers soon discovered that their social system was quite complex. Twelve clans were divided into two moieties, each with a chief in charge of various tribal activities. The Thunderbird moiety was responsible for holding counsel, hunting, and defense. The Bear moiety looked after the village, farm, and working assignments. Each clan had some particular area of responsibility, and the picture they painted of themselves was sketched in the arrangement of the wigwams. Their camp was oriented to the coordinates of the natural world, arranged to facilitate the smooth operation of tribal activities, and marked for their festivals of the yearly seasons. Thus the design was also a thoughtful reflection of their social system.

The ethnographer Paul Radin was curious about the arrangement of the clans and what the two moieties said about the arrangement of the wigwams in their camp. Members of the Thunderbird moiety said that the wigwams were arranged in two semicircles that divided the camp in half, with the main lodges of both moieties set toward the center. This described a balance between the two moieties and the status of their chiefs. Members of the Bear moiety, on the contrary, said that only the Thunderbird chief's lodge was in the center and that all of the other wigwams ringed around it in concentric circles. Jonathan Z. Smith, historian of religion at Chicago, has explained that the Thunderbird moiety was dominant, for it had the power of executive functions, and from its perspective the two sides were equal and the camp was flat. From the perspective of the Bear moiety, however, the picture was that of a hierarchy of powers in which the concentric circles described degrees of subservience and dependence upon the single center of power. One knew one's place in the whole system by means of the hierarchy, but could accept one's place because of the balance. The logic involved was that of reciprocal centers. This social arrangement was designed to live in harmony with the natural orders on the one hand, and within the social orders and histories of the tribal projects on the other.

ANCIENT GREECE

Ancient Greece was a large peninsular landmass of broken terrain, divided into valleys where leading families established their estates for the control of a district. The people of their district farmed, hunted the adjacent lower ranges, and ran their herds of sheep and goats. The estate owner took responsibility for the defense and well-being of the entire district. His ancestors figured in the stories of old, providing a kind of family's genealogy and history of the major events of the past that marked its heroes with powers and honors. These stories gave the leading families their importance and prominence. Their status among the other estate families throughout the Grecian lands was also registered by their genealogies and histories traced to ancestral heroes. This social formation gave birth to the hundreds of hero tales we now take for granted as Greek mythology. Most of these heroes were what we call chthonic ("from the earth"), each tied to his district by means of a local tomb or shrine and understood as the progenitor of the leading family line. The hero's exploits made it possible to imagine the distinctive features of the family that gave it prominence. And in the case of a few who eventually came to preside over yet larger districts and their cities, such Aegeus of Athens (from which we have the Theseus legends), Laertes of Ithaca (from which Odysseus), Cadmus of Thebes (from which Oedipus), and Heracles of Tiryns in the Argos, their local legends were taken up by poets and playwrights time and again in the composition of national epics.

When a visitor entered the district of a hero, or approached some other place storied in a national epic, it was proper to make an offering (*thusia*, which Western scholars have translated "sacrifice") at the appropriate shrine or monument. This gesture served as a sign that the visitor knew where he was and whose family tradition was to be recognized. How did that practice come about? Professor Stanley Stowers, of Brown University, has worked out the social significance for the people of the district who celebrated an annual thusia at the shrine or tomb of the district hero. The thusia took place on the memorial of the hero, the protector and progenitor of the estate, at the time of harvest or when the herds would be sorted by culling for healthy reproduction. The father would invite all of the people of the district to the celebration and prepare a feast. An animal from the herd would be "sacrificed" and roasted, the meal cooked by the servants, the wine prepared, and a dash poured out for the hero. Then everyone would be served, in order, from the men and women of prominence in all of the families, through the skilled laborers, and to all those who performed the menial tasks. This in effect called attention to the gathering as an actual manifestation of their society as a structure of relations, and it reflected their individual places in the hierarchy of the district as well as their contributions to its well-being.

Stowers was especially curious about a constant refrain as he collected the histories and descriptions of the thusiai. It was the reminder that the father had asked one of his sons to "sacrifice with him." It finally came clear that asking one of his sons to "sacrifice with him" was the way in which the father's choice of an heir apparent was made public. Thus the thusia was a ritual occasion at which all the people were present in their various roles, and the estate family's past, present, and future were signaled to mark its history and importance for the well-being of the district. District hero, father, and son focused the big picture, and all the people saw themselves actually taking part in its social world, feasting together as an extended family.

ANCIENT NEAR EAST

In the ancient Near East the Tigris-Euphrates valleys provided lands for agriculture if only the waters of the rivers could be channeled out onto the fields for irrigation. Aristocratic estates emerged to organize the labor, build granaries for the surplus produce, and support scribes and supervisors to keep accounts, distribute the food supplies, and look after the workers. The estates soon became large, and the scribes had to keep the owners informed about their operation, the need for construction projects, and the times for public celebrations of the seasonal festivals. Modern scholars have called the scribes "priests" and the estate owners "kings" of a "temple-state" because they noticed the similarities to our own Western institutions of religion and empire. And it is true that the civic buildings of the ancient Near Eastern kingdoms eventually included grand "houses," as they were called, one for the patron deity ("temple") and one for the king ("palace"). And some of the scribal functionaries, having learned to keep accounts in writing as well as numbers, found that they had time to compose royal epics and histories for the celebrations. But the cluster of buildings and officers at the center of a kingdom was actually a complex administrative structure for aristocratic estates in the process of becoming empires. Thus the three thousand–year history of the Tigris-Euphrates valleys before the Hellenistic period is marked by kingdom after kingdom; now one king in this city, another in that one; and armies marching to defend the territory or take the neighboring lands in conquest. Thus there were the Sumerians, the Assyrians, the Babylonians, the Persians, among others. And from this period of warring kingdoms we have two major myths that were told and retold time and again. One is the Akkadian Creation Epic, an account of the creation of the world called the *Enuma Elish* ("When on high the heaven had not been named . . ."). The other is the Epic of Gilgamesh. Both are concerned with the nature of royal power.

The *Enuma Elish* is about a primal pair and their progeny before the world was formed. Apsu, the father, and Tiamat, the mother, found themselves unhappy with the first two generations of their boys, who were always quarreling, showing off, and making a racket. Each wanted to be the first and strongest among the others. Apsu wanted to do away with all of them and return to the calm before their generation. Tiamat said "No," but had no solution to the clamor. Thus the tensions and fighting increased. The sons took sides, some for the father, some for the mother, and went to war. Apsu was killed and Tiamat was cut to pieces to form the heavens and the earth, over which the warriors who won would rule. It is easy to see that the creation of the world was a projection of the court intrigues and military battles typical of the ancient Near Eastern kingdoms. It was a story that could be told to glory in the power of any contemporary king or emperor, and it was apparently recited at a New Year's festival. But the subtheme of civilization at the cost of absolute power and warfare was also clearly inscribed. Reading this literature in Pritchard's *Ancient Near Eastern Texts*, one often catches sight of the scribal priests tweaking their kings' sense of their divine authority and power.

The Epic of Gilgamesh takes up this subtheme as a very serious problem. The scribes cast Gilgamesh as an early king engendered by the gods who thought to make a name for himself as a mighty warrior. The gods take note and prepare for him a comrade, Enkidu, fashioned as a mortal. After they have many successful ventures together, such as encounters with the dragon of the dark forest, and with the bull from the sea, Enkidu finally dies. Gilgamesh is crushed and goes on a quest to find the gods face to face and ask for eternal life. He goes to the ends of the earth, the bottom of the sea, the heights of the mountains, and finally meets Utnapishtim, the guardian of the way to the gods. Utnapishtim tells him that no mortal can go to the land of the gods and have eternal life. So Gilgamesh finally returns to Uruk, his city, and there he sees that the brickwork and the ramparts are lovely. They are as lovely as if the gods had laid their foundations at the beginning of the world. He therefore carves the story of his quest upon a stone stele to make it clear that the quest brought him back to Uruk, where he found the answer. And so it is the city built by kings and their people that marks the glories of the life of mortals. One does not need eternal life if the city you build is glorious.

THE HEBREWS

Somewhat later, during the first millennium B.C., the Hebrews, a Semitic tribal people, wanted to build a city and a temple-state in the Levant. These lands had always been on the margins between the ancient Near Eastern empires and Egypt. There was no illustrious history of viable kingdoms centered in any of its small cities. The Hebrews found themselves in the midst of the sea peoples of the Levant, with foreign nations to the north, east, and south. None of these nations or peoples looked kindly on the attempt to establish a new temple-state in the Judean hill country. And the early history of these Semitic people and their attempts to build a temple-state in Jerusalem is murky and fraught with conflicts. The legends we have in the Hebrew Bible from about the fourth century B.C. tell of migrations from the Tigris-Euphrates valley, a promise by their patron deity to show them a land of their own flowing with milk and honey, an exodus from an enslavement in Egypt, a conquest of the land, an early temple at Jerusalem built by Solomon, King David's son, a subsequent history of tribal conflicts, defeat at the hands of the Assyrians, deportations under the Babylonians, a restoration of sorts under the Persians, construction of a second temple under the Maccabees, and a final destruction of the temple and a dispersion of the people under the Romans. Reconstructed mainly from the Hebrew Bible, this history is what we call the epic of Israel. It is all about a creator-god whose choice of the Israelites as his children was aimed at the construction of a temple-state in Jerusalem to be governed by the laws and instructions given to Moses, an early sage, whereby a people could produce a kingdom of peace and justice. That it did not work out marks the epic not only as a tragedy for the Hebrew people but also as a profound commentary on the consequences of civilizations bent on the conquest of other peoples.

CHRISTENDOM

The early Christians did not have a land where they lived or a country to which they belonged. They were not even citizens of the Roman Empire, across whose lands they were distributed, along with all the other people uprooted by the Greco-Roman age. Many of the older kingdoms, lands, and peoples had been crushed by Alexander the Great, and the Romans were in the process of dismantling what was left of their infrastructures. Some of the peoples from the older kingdoms, such as Egyptians, Phoenicians, Macedonians, Greeks, and Persians, took their cultural symbols with them as they moved or were moved to cities in other lands throughout the Greco-Roman empire. Athens, Alexandria, Ephesus, Syracuse, Rome, and others all had shrines, rituals, and other cultural artifacts from other countries and cultures. These cultural symbols kept diaspora peoples in contact with one another and their traditions. The early Christians had no homeland traditions. All they had to take with them were some teachings of a founder figure about another kind of kingdom, one they imagined might be possible were their god the king. Nevertheless, this seems to have been a heady teaching for the times, and it became a kind of metaphysical philosophy as various teachers and groups worked over what they may have called the teachings of Jesus. They discussed these teachings on the model of the Greek schools of philosophy, and formed networks of small groups on the model of what the Greeks called "associations." The intellectuals of these school traditions, many of whom were Jewish scholars bewildered by the tragedy of the Israel epic and troubled by the question of whether the Jesus teachings and associations could possibly be understood as working out a kind of sequel, were nevertheless producing a large literature to answer these questions. They attempted to link their teachings about this novel notion of a kingdom with the epic of Israel in the Hebrew Scriptures, then fit it into the big picture of the cosmos as imagined by the Greeks, and finally locate the Jesus schools and associations within the lands and powers of the Roman Empire. Meanwhile, stretching the time span into the second and third centuries, these "school" associations became local "social" groups, and their leaders found themselves taking care of the practical needs of their people, thus providing a kind of social service to peoples whose erstwhile kings and officials were no longer in power.

Eventually, Constantine took note of these Jesus schools early in the fourth century as the Roman Empire was coming to its end, its many would-be emperors fighting over its cities and lands throughout Europe and the East. The model of empire worked out by Caesar Augustus in place of the older Republic was running out of energy, ideas, and the control of its many peoples. Constantine, an unlikely successor of the office of emperor, with its Roman and senatorial notions of aristocratic dynasty, nevertheless succeeded to that office as a military man after an especially complicated period of civil war. Another odd feature of his credentials was that he apparently understood himself to be a Christian even though tutored in the court of Diocletian at Nicomedia, the Eastern emperor who unleashed the last of the persecutions of Christians in the early fourth century. Historians have not been able to explain how it was that Constantine had become a Christian or survived as a Christian in the court of Diocletian. But it does appear that there was some influence from other prominent Christians who by now may have been in evidence at the Eastern court. It is also the case that during this period of confusion about the Empire, there were many would-be emperors in the wings, several serving as generals in the armies throughout the erstwhile spread of the Empire, and all of them devoted to this or that deity or hero as their protector. In any case, once Constantine was secure in his position as the next Roman emperor, announcing devotion to Christianity at the Milvian Bridge, he apparently thought the networks of these early Christian groups might help as a kind of social glue to keep the pieces of the erstwhile Roman Empire together. Historians have sometimes thought it strange that Constantine could use the religion of a dislocated non-Roman people who sought to imagine God's kingdom on universal terms (one kind of big picture) in order to claim divine authority for the Roman Empire (another kind of big picture). But that is what he did.

Constantine installed Christianity as the official religion of the Empire and put Christians in charge of piety, welfare, and the instruction of the people. He convened councils of the leading Christian bishops to decide finally upon the dates for their major rituals, as a respectable calendar required. He encouraged Eusebius and others to come to some agreement upon the selection of their scriptures, and to work out a common credo, thus turning "belief" in the gospels into an intellectual judgment about myth and history that would distinguish the Christian mentality from both its Jewish and Greek precursors. And Constantine asked the bishops to supervise the designs and locations for the basilicas he planned to build for them as temples for the worship of their god and for the honor of the emperor. What a historic event, the installation of a "faith" as the religious institution for an autocratic empire. Constantine seems to have been impressed with this arrangement, of course, for the Christian Scriptures, now to consist of the Hebrew Old Testament and the early Christian writings as the New Testament, allowed the *Roman Empire* (soon to be a concept able to survive the dismantling of the Empire itself) to see itself in continuity with the epic of Israel, chosen by the universal god of creation and the cosmos to rule in his name as the supreme authority and power for civilizing the world of pagans. Christendom had begun.

Constantine's vision changed the course of Western history, but it did not work as the solution to the unification of the Roman Empire. Rome remained a "pagan city" soon to be set upon by the Visigoths (Alaric, 408), Attila the Hun (410), the Vandals, Franks, and others during the sixth century, up until the Norman sack of Rome in 1084, which was still seen as a dismantling of the "Empire." Then there was the conflict with Constantinople as the "capital" of Eastern power and the confused histories of the many wars and conflicts among the kings of various peoples throughout the Eastern, European, and Mediterranean lands for the next long chapter of Western civilization. Nevertheless, the combination of royal power and religious institution, a version of the ancient Near Eastern temple-state pattern, gave the church its curious role as the divine authority for Christendom. This institutional form of religion was a winner for the long period of Western civilization. For about fifteen hundred years no monarch among the European nations thought of ruling other than a Christian kingdom.

This means that Constantine and the *Roman* Empire were not the winners. It was Christianity and *its* empire that won. It was the big picture of Christendom that provided the mythic world and mentality for all of the subsequent kings and kingdoms. The mythic picture was all encompassing. It filled the vast expanse of cosmos and history with the stories from the Bible until there was no room left for other histories or peoples. The Christian god ruled the universe as a solitary sovereign from creation to a "final judgment" (eschaton). The world of this biblical epic (myth) stayed in mind as humans designed the shape of their cathedrals, palaces, and cities on earth. The monuments are obvious and familiar. The cathedral at Chartres and the Notre-Dame in Paris are excellent examples. The Christian world of cosmos and history was etched in the stones of the portals, columns, and the arches high above. The apse was packed with images of the father-god above in the clouds of heaven, his son ascending into heaven, and the figures of the pious from the history of Israel, the disciples from the Gospel stories, and the saints and kings of the subsequent histories. Later, the so-called passion narrative could be depicted on the sanctuary walls as the "stations of the cross" on the way to the altar, where the red candle light marked the presence of the divine spirit, and the ascending son of god was replaced with a crucifix. The cathedral was designed as a microcosmos, and the ritual within took place in otherworldly time. It was eternal theater. All art, philosophy, piety, vestments, and discourse from this long period of Western history reveal a sensibility for the divine drama of heaven and earth that Western civilization took for granted. The cultural manifestations of this Christian mythic world are a legacy still with us.

THE NATION-STATES

Christendom slowly came to an end. What we have called the Renaissance, the Age of Discovery, the Reformation, the Enlightenment, the Industrial Revolution, and the Colonial Age have all contributed to its demise. The church is still here as the common religious institution of the Western nations, but its fracture into denominations and state churches has determined that it can no longer think of itself as the conscience of a medieval kingdom or an aristocratic feudalism, much less a global world. Even the big picture of Christendom ruled by divine and human monarchs has faded into the background as nation-states have arisen. The center of power for both culture and society is now located in the nation-state, not in the Christian churches or kingdoms.

Anthony Giddens has studied the various ways in which the European nation-states brought an end to medieval feudalisms and their monarchies (*The Nation-State and Violence*). It was the Industrial Revolution that introduced a new organization of human energies, interests, and occupations. This eroded the feudal system and brought the serfs to the cities as workers. The surplus production of materials by factories created new markets. And taking advantage of the new markets gave rise to cap-

italism. Capitalism generated financial institutions and marketing organizations that changed the ways trading took place and
governments understood their purposes. Wealth would mark the
strength of a nation among nations, and a nation would be responsible for supporting and protecting its own businesses and
corporations, often at the expense of the well-being of the people
and relations with other nations. The control of the nation would
require a system of laws, surveillance, and intelligence agencies
quite different from those customary for Christendom. And now
there was a military that took its place as an essential part of the
picture. The nation-state did not need god or religion in order to
function.

Two features of this social formation stand out for Giddens.
One is that the ending of monarchies in the nation-states made
democracy possible. This was because the energies and powers centered in monarchy had been relocated to other agencies
and institutions within the structure of the state. This, Giddens
says, can be celebrated. The other feature, however, is that the
nation-state now needed total control over its people, borders,
agencies, and organizations in order to function as an organized
productive unit. This need for total control of its population on
the part of a secular organization of political power was new in
the history of the West, and it is scary. It is understandable, of
course, as the requirements for a nation-state to be strong, productive, and wealthy as a capitalistic organization. But since there
is no built-in guarantee to guard against an autocratic abuse of
executive powers, the total surveillance and control of the people can easily be abused, as several histories of fascism during the
twentieth century reveal. This threat seems to reveal a weak-

ness in the design of the nation-state, one that frustrates democracy. It means that the nation-state model is just now struggling to find a way to control power, wealth, and military might in the interest of a society that values common interests and the well-being of peoples. Toward the end of the nineteenth century we in the United States thought that we were all engaged in the constructive pursuit of ways other than war and wealth to find social existence rewarding. But in fact, the big picture we have painted is now filling up with a frightening stream of violent events and images. There is exploitation of natural resources, climate change caused by deregulated industries, the dangers of global warming, army bases everywhere, militias with guns throughout the world, massacres and genocides, and all of it sensationalized by our media and popular culture. The themes are power, violence, and fear. Apparently, our nation-state does not have the intellectual, philosophical, and/or legislative means to know what to do. In fact, the administrations in the United States have exacerbated such problems with their own employments of power, violence, and fear.

THE CHRISTIAN NATION

In Europe, the Christian mythic world that focused on the divine sovereign and its earthly rulers has now receded to a vague outline of the big picture once imagined by Christendom. The details of the biblical myth and its medieval worldview have faded. Not many angels are left. Only a sensibility of an environment partially transcendent, that has come to be called a "spiritual realm." The church's cathedrals have become monuments to and museums of their past glorious histories. The accoutrements of royalty now function as symbols in civic pageants. The public atmosphere created by the residual elements of the erstwhile Christendom is accepted by the citizens as a matter of course.

In the United States, however, the notion of a Christian nation is still rather sharply in profile at the level of personal and ethical expectations of public behavior and institutional responsibilities. This is curious, because the social functions of the churches in America have focused mainly on family rites of passage, personal religious experiences, and private devotions, not on attempts to think about the society, much less to cultivate any vision of a Christian society. Part of the reason for this difference from the European situation is that the United States started as trading company colonies, not as a monarchy. The federal union was the result of disparate colonies working out practical compromises on matters of rights, property, boundaries, taxation, representation, and citizenship. Only later were there larger cities, industries, road building, adding territories to the west, homesteading, railroads, cattle ranching, mining, lumbering, and developing the lands for farming, small towns, and the culture of rural America that lasted until the middle of the past century. All of these were matters of independent pursuits and bootstrap efforts that did not need the church or the Christian myth or the federal government to tell them what to do. So there was precious little about the society we constructed that had to be thought of as a Christian nation until very recently.

And yet, from the beginning, it was assumed that the United States was a Christian Nation. The reason for this was that the dominant class of immigrants in control of the original colonies was European. And the majority of the Europeans involved in forming the federal union of the United States understood themselves to be from Christian countries. It was therefore easy to assume that all Americans were Christians of some sort, just as were the European countries from which they migrated. Not much thought was given to this view of America as a Christian Nation, however, and to call it into question did not become a significant issue until recently. That was because religion was understood to be a private matter, not a national myth with a social logic of concern for living together constructively in the world of work and enterprise. Thus the outlines of the big picture of Christendom did not completely fade away in the minds of Americans. And that means that the narrative logic of the Christian myth was still there as the mythic grammar of the culture for thinking about the world at large and one's place within it. The fact that the mythic grammar of Christianity was not erased, even though not consciously cultivated as religious myth, makes it possible to reread the history and find many indications of a widespread Christian mentality that allowed for attitudes, motivations, policies, and judgments to correlate with the narrative logic of the myth. There was, for instance, the rationalization of the westward movement as "manifest destiny"; the various versions of America as the "Promised Land," the City on a Hill; the assumption of a link between righteousness and the work ethic; the claim to the lands because we were a superior people and righteous nation; the treatment of American Natives, African American slaves, Asians, Mexicans, and many others as second-class citizens, unworthy of citizenship, property rights, and civil rights because they were not (Euro-American) Christians. These and many other features of our history do correlate with the grammar of the Christian myth, as we shall see. The features tell us that during the nineteenth and twentieth centuries Americans did assume in some inarticulate way that the United States was a Christian nation, or at least a nation constituted by Christians, not by those of other religions.

Such a naïveté is no longer possible. There are now peoples from many other religions and cultures living in the United States as their country. And the recent history of conservative Christians and politicians coming into power at all levels of our society and government in the name of America as a "Christian Nation" has not produced a Christian nation. It has, in fact, led us into a series of obsessions with military power, demands for regime change in other nations, resistance to bilateral negotiations with other nations, policies of free rein for our corporations at home and abroad, failure to control exploitation of the natural resources of our country and other nations, failure to respond to the dangers of climate change, preemptive war in the "national interest" of our oil companies, failure to provide living wages, adequate education, and health care for all workers, and failure to regulate our financial institutions. These issues have contributed to a society and a world in duress. The big picture the United States has painted is not a pretty sight. It is a world of power abuse, violence, and fear.

So the questions to be asked at this point have to do with the Christian worldview and the social history of the Western nations since Christendom. How is it that the Christian myth of sixteen hundred years seems to have faded from our social scene and cultural history? Could it be that the Christian myth was interested mainly in the social institutions of church and empire, less in the social projects of the rural hinterland, villages, and cities? Has something gone wrong with our social projects to account for the worlds of power, violence, and fear we now have on our hands? Could it be that Christian thinking is somehow still implicated in the cultural and social changes that have produced this modern picture? Does Christian mentality persist now in the minds of the people only in support of power and authority, without being able to address social needs, issues, and formations? Or is it the case that there are social values still embedded in the Christian myth that might be called upon to create a vision for our multicultural world? Can a picture of a just, sustainable, and meaningful multicultural world be imagined at all? These are the questions that bring the histories of Christendom and the Western nations to a critical impasse.

This book is my attempt to address these questions. Chapter 2 will be about a theory of myth and ritual based on ethnographic studies. This theory will come to focus on the notion of "social interests" as a basic component for the constructive picture of tribal and other societies. It is a concept foreign to most Americans, but can be described and used to account for the interests that are driving American industries and the global scene today. Chapter 3 will present a description of the Christian myth and its history that has served the Western tradition as its mythic world. This will make it possible to continue with Chapter 4, a review of the social projects that have emerged in Western history since the Enlightenment and the Industrial Revolution. These projects developed out from under the totalistic cosmic canvas of the Christian worldview, thus producing bodies of knowledge, social formations, and interests about which the Christian myth had little to say. In Chapter 5, then, the current social issues about which there is a great deal of public discourse and concern, can be registered and analyzed as the conflicts among various social projects in our society that are pursuing their own social interests. Instead of producing a common myth (big picture of the whole), each of these major projects has evolved its own big picture of itself, and these big pictures are discordant. In Chapter 6, the analyses of our society on the part of academics and culture historians will document a sense of dis-ease at the level of the people caused by living in the dynamic created by the multiple projects and atmosphere of the consumer society. In Chapter 7 the failed "missions" of the administration and military to the Near Eastern peoples will be treated as the result of a residual Christian mentality. This will raise the question of a haunting cultural mentality in a nation that thought it was committed to the common good but has not been able to succeed. In Chapter 8 the need for a new big picture can then be spelled out, together with some thoughts about the kind of picture possible.

2 THEORY

We need a social theory of myth and ritual in order to understand their social significance and to explain what they do. There are very few theories available in the Western traditions of religious studies that explore the social significance or effects of the Christian myth and ritual. The Western notion of religion, beholden as it is to the Christian tradition, leaves the meaning of myth and ritual to the mystery and awe typically cultivated by the Christian sense of reverence and mystique. This will not do. It allows the double-deckered universe to stay in place while trying to translate the mythic world located in the transcendent realm into understandable terms, forces, and figurations of the empirical world. And since there is no way to turn the agencies of the divine (God and his Spirit, thought by Christians to activate the events encountered in Christian religious experience and worship) into historical or this-worldly subjects available for study, religion in America becomes a personal tryst or quest for contact with the supernatural forces of a transcendent world. Thus we do not have a *social* theory of religion among our many disciplines of religious studies. If we do not have a social theory of myth and ritual, we will not be able to answer the question about the big picture in Western traditions and what has happened to it.

There are many studies of myth and ritual in the archives of Western academies and the libraries of academics. And there is currently a huge outpouring of cultural studies exploring the social changes and their effects since the Enlightenment and Industrial Revolution. Unfortunately, not many of these studies sense the need for a social theory of religion based on a secular and scientific anthropology. All seem to accept the rule of tolerance with respect to religions and religious faith as being protected in the interest of decency and democracy, not to be questioned. The result is that a sense of mystery and mystique is automatically granted to myths, rituals, and religion. Thus there is no attempt to ask about their rationales or social logics.

This has not kept a stream of intellectuals from being fascinated with the mythic (otherworldly) agents of the Christians' transcendent realm. Many scholars have found themselves intrigued by the challenge of working out the relations between the two layers of the double-deckered universe. The transcendent world is imagined ontologically, of course, as a realm of reality that the Christian God and his Spirit inhabit, and from which their powers and agencies can be discerned in the "creation" of the world and the course of history. God and his Spirit are thought to activate the events storied in the Bible and replicated in the rituals here below. Theory in this case cannot be social. It is theological. Theological analysis of the Christian myth and ritual has apparently been a very enticing and engaging intellectual project for many centuries, but it has its place in the long and rich traditions of philosophy and theology, not among the disciplines of social studies and the investigations of culture and society.

The theory of myth and ritual to be considered in this book

intends a social and scientific description and explanation. There will be a few terms such as *mythic world* that need to be redescribed lest it continue to suggest the Christian notion of the "cosmos," with its idea of "transcendence." Other terms such as *social interests* will require some stretching of familiar categories in order to consider them. And, in due course, some other familiar terms, such as *social formation, myth, ritual,* and *culture* will need some redefinition. I will try for some conceptual clarity about these terms, for they are all important as components of the theory. Once the theory is recognized as coherent and cogent, however, it should be possible to analyze the current state of the nation and the world with respect to the functions of myths and rituals.

MYTHIC WORLD

We can begin with the observation that people live in a world of *two environments.* There is the natural environment and the social environment. The natural environment is of primary importance for the material resources of life and for the sense of place in the world at large occupied by a particular people. The social environment is important as the arena within which the common practices of living together take place as a common way of life, and as the calendar of their history. It is also important as the arena in which language is constantly in use. Language could be called a third major environment since it is shared by all the people and must be used to refer to the objects of the world around, orient oneself and one's projects within it, and negotiate agreements. And because of language, the objects and events of interest and significance to the daily round of a society automatically take their places as objects and concepts in the other two environments as well. It is language that makes possible the reports of experiences away from the village and the questions and discussions that may arise from them. Language makes possible the conversations and negotiations necessary for the resolutions of various differences of interest and opinion in the ongoing work of daily life. And it is language that makes it possible to refer to the past, to traditions as *histories* in which precedent events and opinions come to mind on occasion and provide patterns and meanings for the structuring and practices of a society and its common way of life. The two more obvious environments (nature, society) are normally taken for granted as the way the world is there and has been there. The language component, however, tells us that the people know the world is there, as well as how they know it and what their knowing adds to its scope and shape. I want to expand these environments in the direction of conceptualizing the way they fuse together to form a single encompassing *world* picture that stretches a people's imagination beyond the present horizons of both the natural and the social orders (space and time). This expansion allows them to locate mythic images, events, and symbols in a realm of memory and semipermanence, making the surrounding world familiar, meaningful, and intellectually challenging (as words and meanings need to be crafted in the processes of naming and reflection).

I have used the term *mythic world* to name this comprehensive environment, thinking that the common uses of the terms *myth* and *world* in popular discourse allow them to cover many arenas of social and intellectual space without immediately suggesting the connotations of the familiar Christian cosmic or transcendent universe. The world I have in mind does extend beyond the material/empirical natural order and the social realm of contemporary practices and projects. It therefore encourages the realization of an order of existence that is larger than the present contemporary world of physical and material reality. But it would not be helpful to think of this linguistic-imaginary extension of expanded horizons as constituting an ontological order of "divine" reality, as Christians do. Rather, it defines the horizons of the collective human imagination. Imagination makes memory and reference to past events possible, as well as allowing for the questions about them that may occur. This world of the imagination serves as the canvas on which the panorama of big pictures is painted. *Mental world* also comes to mind as an appropriate term for this linguistic environment. Without recognizing the way in which the encompassing environment is a world of the imagination that allows a term to refer to the empirical order and also have a location in the imaginary realm for recall (and all words do), we will be unable to describe a social theory for myth and ritual.

Thus the *mythic world* of the encompassing environments becomes a kind of mental map in which a people orient themselves to their histories, their traditions, and themselves. We might imagine the scope of the environment as a huge encompassing sphere of consciousness, except for the fact that it is always taken for granted, hardly ever thought of as a matter of consciousness. This does not mean, however, that it is not known, that the people of a given society are not aware of its scope, contours, and contents. It is lived in and taken for granted with no need to question or confirm its existence. It becomes the environment that structures space and time within which everything takes place. It is the collective mental map in which a people orient themselves to their environment as their *world*.

The social world is not only a dynamic environment, with some folks here and some there engaged in this practice or that project; the awareness of the society at work is made dynamic by means of the decisions that are made daily about dealing with a task or an issue. It is made dynamic as well by means of the un-acknowledged but automatic effect of traditions, that is, folkways and judgments from its history that continue among a people as social habits. These patterns of practices and their precedent moments are there in the traditions as collective memories and shared images, but need not be noticed consciously in order to be influential. Certain events from the past and certain lessons remembered from important figures and events are commonly recalled on some occasions in every society. But even these are seldom mentioned as if they were symbols or rules for the common practices and attitudes they represent. They simply illustrate and signify "the way we do it."

The memories of such a social history are very important for the collective agreements necessary for the practices of a society to become common and habitual. Memories can become fuzzy, of course, and can easily become invitations to embellishment. Then, too, not all of the past can be kept in mind. Selections must be made and, since there is no one in charge of selection, the common memory can change slowly in the course of time with its many occasions for offhand references and the sense of appropriate timing. Some social occasions will tend toward this or that memory feature for precedence. And as a phenomenon of the collective memory, the social history of a people often stretches to precedent events thought of as the first time or origin of a tradition or practice, sometimes said to be "at the beginning." This means that the horizons of both the natural order and the social history are somehow in mind even if not available for contact or direct questioning. The processes of report, representation, memory, selection, experimentation, negotiation, and coming to agreements in a society are enough to establish the importance of a given tradition settled upon for a common practice. No one asks to see and question the mythic agent or event responsible for a tradition. A practice is simply "given," it is the way some hero or ancestor is remembered to have done it, and therefore needs no further documentation of its "reasons" for being the "right way" to proceed.

Thus the two major environments are hardly separate worlds. They are a single, encompassing world of exceptionally rich images and memories, the imagination of which places them in a collective mental space at a distance from the everyday world. If we had such a concept in our social anthropology, it would then be available for study and analysis as an important feature of human culture, social formations, and their mentalities. The description of the imaginary world as the normal mental milieu for a people would make it possible, for instance, to see that common language references, policy conversations, social negotiations, and the many ideologies and self-understandings of major social organizations function in ways similar to the myths and rituals analyzed by anthropologists and historians. It would be important to do this in order to assess the curious confusion that reigns in our time about the significance of society, conflict, and culture, all of which are currently out of hand. In this study we ask which features of our current practices may still be beholden to unexamined sensibilities rooted in Christian myth and culture.

SOCIAL INTERESTS

Ethnography is the field of study most helpful for the concepts of *social formation* and *social interests.* From the beginning of the twentieth century, major work has been done on the myths and rituals of tribal societies that had recently come into view during the period of Western colonial expansion. Scholars such as Franz Boas, Émile Durkheim, Marcel Mauss, Bronislaw Malinowski, Åke Hultkranz, Marshall Sahlins, and Claude Lévi-Strauss have collected data on tribal religions that launched a discipline now called ethnography. Ethnographers discovered that tribal societies are complex yet coherent units of social formation. They have also been able to mark the similarities of interests among many different tribal societies.

These interests include a strong attachment to the land (as place, provider, and territory), the importance of genealogy for their systems of kinship and their social significance (for families, rites of passage, and networks of relationships), the assignment of roles (for productive activity and the maintenance of social practices and activities within the society's whole way of life), ranking of authorities (such as the differences between mothers, fathers, and uncles), training in skills, distribution of goods, organization of working parties, assignment of roles for the special responsibilities of each clan in the interest of the whole pattern of life, astronomical calendars and their importance for seasonal activities (for agriculture, occasions for social gatherings, celebrations, and festivals), and markers of tribal identity (such as clothing, crafts, churingas, perhaps in distinction from other adjacent tribes). These interests are taken for granted as features of a dynamic, working society. They are linked in overlapping networks of responsibilities and practices that structure the society as a working unit. They are the *social interests* of the collective.

To call these features of a society their *social interests* needs some clarification. The term *interest* in common parlance is loaded with connotations of purposive intent and conscious design, motivated by expectations of some return. It is grounded in an individualistic psychology honed to perfection by participation in our capitalistic system. These connotations will have to be set aside in order to grasp the significance of the term *interests* in relation to society as a collective. We do not have an adequate social psychology to understand how a society as a whole can have "interests." And the "interests" in view cannot be attributed to the motivations or designs of a single founder figure. As a matter of fact, we have no language for the way a society thinks, decides, and understands itself. Yet a close reading of ethnographic descriptions shows that, as a collective, a tribal society is invested in its social interests. It is therefore in the use of the term *social* as an adjective in combination with the term *interests* that this shift from the personal to the collective can be underscored. Thus the connotations of agency, inventiveness, creativity, and the self-understanding that attend the interests of individuals need to be reconceptualized as features of collective interests *in* the social that are shared in some way by all members *of* a tribe. The features of a society listed above are, after all, recognizable, acceptable, and important for the construction of the society and for the way in which myths and rituals reflect upon them, focus upon them, and deal with them. That is why we need a special term for them in order to explain the significance of myths and rituals.

But there is more. To see that a tribe or society has "interests," even though we have no social psychology to compare with our psychologies of the individual, is not enough. There is also the fact of *intellection* that must be woven into the picture. This is another term that we have understood solely in terms of an individualistic psychology. Societies do not think or know about their collective interests (so we assume). The changes that may occur in a society's patterns of practices, to say nothing of its political structures, are usually understood as the results of powers and policies in the hands of individuals who do think. But political strategies are not enough to account for the list of social interests characteristic for a society. And to approach the set of social interests characteristic for a society only as practices that are somehow taken for granted and thus agreed to by the people is also not enough. There has to be an underlying agreement, even if inarticulate, that the operations of the society "make sense," are reasonable. We might want to say that there is a logic to a society's operations that all members of the society implicitly understand, a logic that does not need to be surfaced for analysis. The closest we have come to finding a word that catches some sense of the *social intellection* that accompanies the *social interests* of a society is the use of the term *mentality*. But this term, from the French cultural critics of the late eighteenth and nineteenth centuries, though very important for current English literary criticism, has not been translated into its characteristics as an intellectual system. We will have to look at *mentalities* more closely in the course of this essay. But for now, we need to see that our term *social interests* requires some sense of *social intellection* as well.

The concepts of *social interests* and *collective intellection* have not been easy for Western academics to accept. Lévi-Strauss is a major exception, for his work as an ethnographer and theorist has consistently emphasized the intelligence of tribal peoples and the thoughtfulness involved in the construction of their social patterns and practices. Jonathan Z. Smith also has worked out his theories of myth and ritual by noting the social logics of their significance. Both the concept of *social interests* and that of *collective intellection* are important for the theory of myth and ritual (that is, religion) we are exploring. In order to grasp the importance of this assessment of the intelligence and intellectual labor of tribal peoples as fundamental for their systems of knowledge and life together, one needs to recognize the intellectual features involved in the practices that people take for granted in their enterprise of social formation and existence.

MYTHS AND RITUALS

Since we do not have a conception of society as a collective, the term *social interests* may not be enough to prepare us for the significance of myths and rituals and the way in which they manipulate the collective intelligence. But we can start with some observations about the social interests themselves. The features of social interests are more obvious in tribal societies, and that is where ethnologists have discovered that the awareness of social interests is related to the language used to locate them in the overlaps among the several environments. From the many stories and practices of a tribe, all of which indicate social interests, myths and rituals focus upon a select few. These are the practices and traditions of primary significance for the society. As practices of the daily and yearly rounds these traditions do not call for special attention. But relocated in a myth or ritual, the mythic frame of reference suggests another set of connotations. A myth may well recall a familiar ancestor and thus upgrade its significance as tribal symbol. A ritual will focus upon a practice common for the maintenance of the society, but perform it with perfection as if uncommon. The result is that certain primary figures, gestures, and actions are taken from their normal location within the social environment and relocated to the imaginary world where the three large environments overlap. They do not have their place exclusively in any one of the three, but perform the function of working out the relations among them. They do this by focusing on a particular practice or image that has what we might call a basic significance for the society: a practice that itself has roots in all three environments. This is where the usual significations for a figure can be playfully compounded by suggesting references and connotations in all directions to all three environments, thus turning a figure into a complex symbol of the social within its universal world as a whole.

The mechanisms used to do this have been worked out by Jonathan Z. Smith in his *To Take Place*. Briefly, rituals are a special performance of a practice common for the life of the society such as grain harvest or animal husbandry. The special performance marks the practice in such a way as to celebrate its significance for the society and encourage awareness of its place in the operation of the society as a whole. Myths are the way in which the horizons of the three environments of a people can be imagined as an encompassing world within which the people live and have always lived. Myths tell about events of the past in which ancestral agents established precedents for the shape of the society and the reasons for its practices. Rituals focus on basic practices of contemporary society to mark them as events central for the structures of the society. Taken together, tribal myths and rituals place a tribe in the center of the three environments in which it lives, the natural order, the history of its social enterprise, and its symbols (the language of self-understanding). The focus is upon the pattern of practices that marks the social life of the tribe as workable and productive.

The occasions for the recitation of a myth and the performance of a ritual also turn out to be thoughtful manipulations of collective intelligence. The people are gathered. The story is told. The ritual performed. Myth works by calling attention to what happened *then* in a story about ancestral/founder figures. But the story bears some relation to the way things happen *now* in the everyday life of the people. The gap between the *then* and the *now* is the space available for "seeing," reflection, conversation, honing self-understanding, and discussion of the tribe's projects. The comparison can highlight features of the society and its heroes that are not normally noticed and thought about. Rituals take a common practice away from its usual place over *there*, and perform it in a controlled space *here*. The gap between the *there* and the *here* joins the gap between the *then* and the *now* to evoke heightened awareness of the present moment. Thus basic categories of time and space are manipulated in the interest of intellectual activities at a profound level of awareness, criticism, and constructive assent.

Myths are the way in which a people paints a picture of their society and its place in the imagined world at large. The background of this mythic world is frequently a panorama of the two environments, the natural world and the social history of a people. Myths can expand the canvas to the horizons and beyond. This puts the canvas at the limits of a people's imagination, at a distance from the society in which one's daily life is lived. The imaginary world thus created has been called *cosmic* in the sense that it comprehends all of the time and space (history and cosmos) imaginable for a particular tribe. The atmosphere created by this imaginary merger of time and space is curiously constituted and dynamic and, while not in motion itself, except insofar as a narrative of the myth may have a sense of direction, allows the mind to move from one scene to another in contemplation and response to its various moments, events, and images. The yearly round of activities and its calendar of festivals is another mechanism for suggesting comparison and thought. The images bring a kind of suggestive focus on particular mechanisms and practices of significance for the structure and performance of the society. The selection of these images is often quite small when compared with a people's knowledge of its natural and social environments, but the importance of a particular image can be immense, basic for the distinctive character and spirit of a society. Such an image can give rise to symbols of a people's *ethos* and identity. Such symbols can then be used to represent (or "stand for") a society and mark the importance of its culture.

CULTURE

The term *culture* also must be redescribed as a component of the theory we need to conceptualize. The term's current reference to the environment of modernity is not sufficient to suggest the residual effects of the Christian myth in that environment. We need to see that the way myths work is a mechanism that can be applied to the social interests of a society that need not be regarded as religious. Myths are frequently projected onto a worldwide screen as images that depict precedent events of significance for some fundamental practices and mechanisms of the society. A myth can narrate the way an event happened. (It is this narrative form of description with its past tense and first-time connotations that results in the mythic notion of origin.) A myth can also serve as a portrayal of the way things have been and are done in a society, a sort of fictional instance of a recognizable ritual or pattern of practices. The protagonists in such narratives are frequently depicted in roles that outdistance the features of the performers of these practices in the everyday world. That is because their importance as symbols for the role's mythic significance has to gather up myriad characteristics of its people and cover all the time and space depicted on the canvas. And besides, the repeated telling of a story from the dim past, generation after generation, gives the storytellers and their hearers the chance to embellish the details. This mythic function can expand the feature of performance to power, event to agency, authorship to authority. It can also call attention to the narrative functions of preparation and accomplishment, sequence and consequence, problem and solution, cause and effect. The setting of a myth in the *mythic world* of the imagination distinguishes it from the "once upon a time" of other human narratives, and its symbolic aura distinguishes it from other more current fictions or reports of events. It takes on more significance than a generalization of those features depicted. It attracts notions of timelessness and ultimacy. There is a sense in which a cosmic myth can be taken to represent "ultimate reality" and to suggest an ontology. This at least is the way in which the myths of the so-called "world religions" have resonated on their cosmic canvases.

Such features of a myth in narrative mode can be understood by a people as "the way the world works" (or perhaps worked, or is meant to work). This in turn is capable of suggesting those attitudes and practices that are characteristic in the society, or perhaps even the "reasons," or the major metaphors used, for norms, rules, or laws that structure and define the *habitus* of a society. This perception of a mythic narrative's *ethos* is hardly a clear picture of a given society's actual systems (social or legal), nor is it a kind of constitution from which to reason or argue for a society's rules of conduct. It cannot work that way because of the great distance and difference between the two worlds (mythic and social, imaginary and material) and because the function of a myth is reflexive and suggestive, not legislative. But since a myth often has a *narrative grammar* just as all stories do, it means that the events depicted on its cosmic screen manifest the social logic of the world pictured there and signify the importance of the society's patterns of practices.

This logic is given in narrative mode, and that means that the "reasons" for the structure and events of the world can be seen there, inferred, or deduced from the actions of the figures portrayed as if we were reading a novel. These then are the "reasons" a people can think of as justifications for the common attitudes, practices, and mechanisms of their society. It is true that the mechanisms of a society's ordinary patterns of practices are not the result of intentionally trying to keep the rules as pictured in the myth. The relation between the mythic world and the practices of a society is more complex, especially for a culture that works with the categories of cause and effect as ours does. In such a culture the relation can easily slip into the nuances of which comes first, or which came first, that is, considerations of the "origin" of the system or the "causes" of a particular event. But thinking in terms of the origin of a practice and its social justification in a mythic world frustrates the dynamic of the relation between mythic mentality and society. Both the practices and the myth are better understood as the result of the social experiences of the society in evolutionary mode: the myriad experiences of social agreement that have occurred in the processes of learning to live together and construct a society. The systems of agreements take place as patterns of practices. The patterns can then mark certain events for celebration at special times, and the terms of referral can become common linguistic symbols. The many stories from the past can be sorted by repetition in relation to these significant events, thus becoming myths. Yet once the systems are in place, it is the narrative logic of the myths that supports an array of attitudes and sensibilities about the "right way" to do a thing, "the way we do it." Thus there are systems of honor and shame that come to govern the *ethos* of a people whether its rules and rewards have been given second-level legal rationales or not. And of course, the naming of an event, a gesture, or a practice of significance can anchor itself in a discourse and give rise to the knowing use of terminology or other daily observations with raised eyebrows and/or humor.

This theory of myth is idealistic in its picture of "learning to live together" as the basic motivation and rationale for social formations. It emphasizes the "bright" side of a social anthropology. Unfortunately, it does not yet account for other features of human behavior such as conflict and predation. As characteristics of human societies there are also autocracy, slavery, and war. These features will need to be addressed as the subsequent chapters of this book unfold. Nevertheless, the constructive theory can be used to study the origins and history of the Christian myth as a preparation for a discussion of its influence in the twenty-first century. It will be seen that the social formation of Christendom determined a particular set of social interests and a peculiar mentality that the "grand Western tradition" has cultivated. It is this mentality that has influenced the role of the United States in the current confusion of international affairs.

CHANGE

The term *culture* is currently doing much of the work in the description of modern societies, especially among journalists and academicians concerned about postmodernism. They are talking about the breakdown of the grand tradition of Western civilization, and the fragmentation of collective consciousness that has left individuals and small groups without a big picture of their world. They focus on the public discourse available in the media, the motivations and rhetorics that drive advertising and the consumer society, and especially the arts and entertainment. The result as they see it is a shift in Western social and cultural history that has focused upon the construction of the individual. From an identity rooted in belonging to a society and/or community (as in religion), the self-understanding of the individual person now is a "freedom" from traditional social constraints. Thus the entertainment industry makes news by portraying moments in the life of an individual grounded in "me-isms." And the term *culture* is used frequently to refer to this social cultivation without being able to say much about it as a factor in the analysis of our collective well-being (or mal-being, as the case may be). We shall have to parry this use of the term *culture* in Chapter 6 (Cultural Analytics) as an insufficient understanding of our social milieu. For now, we can recognize this social atmosphere as a challenge to our theory and to the Western tradition of Christendom and the Christian myth. In order to prepare for the study to follow we need to recognize the relation of a people's culture both to its social interests and to its mythic world.

We have used the category of *selection* to note the differences among the various practices and social interests that have organized societies and been taken up in a society's myth and ritual. In Chapters 1 and 2 examples have been given of societies centered in hunting, agriculture, domestication of animals, irrigation projects, the building of cities, writing of laws, scribal centers for accounts, counsels for the king, and so forth. The series has run from tribal societies to the kingdoms of the Ancient Near East, and the empires of the Greco-Roman age. In the case of the Christian myth and social formation, however, there was no given society for which the myth-in-the-making centered the social interests of material productions and state interests. The early Christian associations were at work inventing a distinctly subcultural identity as school traditions in the wake of a temple-state that had been overrun by the armies of others. Their mythic ingredients were taken from the ancient cultures surrounding them, also now in disarray, caught in the political uncertainties and mistaken moves of the post-Alexander and Roman armies. So the cultural values with which the early Christians had to work in order to mythologize their fictional Kingdom of God ideas were in many ways quite grandiose. But none of them made much sense in the real world until Constantine used them to expand his own grandiose visions of the Roman Empire. This resulted in the formation of Christendom, a social structure whose myths, rituals, and *social interests* were focused upon the power and sovereignty of god and king (eventually to be located in god, pope, and emperor), necessary in order to control the kingdom and guarantee order.

This means that our theory of myth and social interests, derived from ethnography, has been challenged by the social histories of the Western nation in the post-Christendom age. The theory seemed to work for Christendom as long as the social interests of the church and empire were sufficient to keep the mythic world in place. But the church and its mythic world were not able to contain the social interests of the people that began to surface in the Renaissance, the Age of Discovery, the Reformation, and the Enlightenment. The big picture expanded, but it was no longer to be painted in by saints and angels. Industries, nation-states, technologies, and global expansions have painted the new canvas with their own interests and colors. This will be our challenge as we seek to trace the influence of the Christian myth from the medieval period to the so-called Christian Nation of the twenty-first century. We will notice that the commercial interests of postmodernity have overwhelmed the social structures that once were the keepers of the Christian myth and the values cultivated by the Christian churches. Yet the churches are still there, and the mentality of the Christian myth is still discernable. It will therefore be important to work through the history of the Western tradition and the social interests it has produced in order to understand the social issues of the present and ask whether a new big picture is possible.

3 THE CHRISTIAN MYTH

Our theory of myth and ritual was put to work in the Seminar on Christian Origins (a seminar of the Society of Biblical Literature, 1994–2003) by means of the categories of "mythmaking" and "social formation." It was in this collaborative project with New Testament scholars that the ethnographic theory of myth proved helpful as a way to investigate the significance of the social reasons for the making of the Christian myth during the first three centuries. The seminar worked with the social histories of the many fractured nations of the Hellenistic era, including the Judaic peoples, the Semitic Levant, the Greek remnants of the former Alexandrian conquests, the Greek "schools," the Roman Expansions, and the "associations" of the "Jesus schools" from Syria to Macedonia. The seminar found that the myths created by the Jesus schools about Jesus their founder/teacher, though extravagant in terms of the political importance and divinity implicitly attributed to him as a wisdom teacher of the times, were nevertheless understandable attempts to draw upon the venerable traditions of both Judaic and Greek myth and thought, in order to claim for their schools and associations a place in the large and fragmented Greco-Roman world. The Jesus associations were caught in the middle between Judaic sensibilities and the larger Greco-Roman world, and imagined Jesus as the teacher about a "Kingdom of God," that is, a society that would work better than the erstwhile kingdoms of the recent kings and currently fragmented societies. That, of course, is mythic thinking. But since there was not yet a common movement of the Jesus people as a social formation to mythologize, and since these groups generated many ideas about the popular philosophies of the time, the seminar was not able to determine all of the factors from the writings and histories of the first three centuries that may have been involved in what modern scholars have imagined as the "origins" of "Christianity."

Nevertheless, the theory of myth and social formation derived from ethnographies was enough to tackle the many moments of the early history and analyze the process by which the Gospel stories came into being and how the early Jesus people must have understood them. The question of interest to the seminar was why the stories in the gospels were told in the first place. Eventually the categories of "mythmaking" and "social formation" slipped into place as a way to do the research required. If the social and intellectual reasons for the making of some of the Jesus myths could be discerned, seminar participants thought that it might be possible to understand the reasons for their continued attraction and retelling down through Western history. There are now two volumes of seminar papers available: *Redescribing Christian Origins* and *Redescribing Paul and the Corinthians*, both edited by Ron Cameron and Merrill P. Miller (Society of Biblical Literature). A third and final volume about the Gospel of Mark is forthcoming. The seminar began with a recognition that the familiar model of Christianity's myth and ritual was not yet in place during the first three centuries. The eventual form of the Christian myth as a credo had not been composed, and the Protestant reading of the Bible as epic history was not yet imagined. There was, for instance, no overall Christian church or "community" until the fourth century, and that formation was mainly Constantine's idea. Yet the many links between the various Jesus myths and the social formations of the Jesus schools allowed the seminar to reconstruct this early history to make some sense of the Jesus people before the time of Constantine and so theorize Constantine's reasons for wanting them to constitute the religion of the Roman Empire.

During the late first and early second centuries, the various Jesus schools and groups of intellectuals exploring the ideas of Jesus as a founder figure found themselves forming networks of recognition as if engaged in similar pursuits. The closest analogy to these schools that were interested in the teachings of Jesus was the Greco-Hellenistic philosophical associations. The interests around which these Jesus schools formed were those of diaspora people seeking ethnic-cultural comradeship. In the case of the Jesus groups it must have been a place to talk about the times and explore the teachings as a workable form of collective identity. We might call them discussion groups or schools of thought needing to find or make their place within the larger unsettled world of the times. The unsettledness included what to do about the institutions of Greek culture that Alexander had tarnished by using them for his imperial designs; what to do about the hoary traditions of Near Eastern cultures that had been brought to an end by Alexander; what to think about Alexander's successors (*diadochoi*) in the Levant; and what to do and think about the

Romans and their steady advance toward the eastern Mediterranean. Now that the lands of Judea, Samaria, Israel, and the Galilee had come under Roman control, the problem apparently was how to think about one's "national" identity when the superstructures (temple and priesthood) and homeland had been dismantled. How to think about a "Jewish" identity without a temple, priesthood, or king must have been one of the social issues for discussion. And in the case of the Jesus schools, the question of their identity in terms of relations to traditional cultures and extractions must have presented a most invigorating problem.

One of the more striking mythologies about Jesus started with the thought that, like Socrates, he must have been killed by the authorities as a teacher whose ideas and students were cultivating sedition. There is no indication that such was actually the case in any of the literature of the time, and biblical scholars have found it preposterous, not finding anything about the Romans, Jews, or early Jesus followers to give such an idea credibility. There was, however, lore about the "noble death" of a teacher for political reasons that seems to have been common in the turmoil of the times. A current mythology about the Maccabean martyrs, for instance, was available to imagine the innocence of a teacher and his teachings held to be seditious and killed by authorities. The point of such a mythology at the time was to turn the tables on the authorities who had wrongly taken offense. It was this mythology that Paul found helpful for his constructions upon the Jesus schools as the "congregations" of (Jesus as) the messiah (*christos*). In Paul's mind, imagining such a destiny for Jesus whom, as he said, he had not known, could nevertheless account for the rejection of the christos congregations by the

Romans and others, and at the same time reveal the "truth" of their teachings about him. As an argument for the significance of Jesus as the prophet or teacher appointed by God to tell the Gentiles that they belonged to the "children of Abraham," and so could continue the epic of Israel despite the troubling times, Paul's christos myth was soon received by many Jesus groups as the way to think about themselves as well. In due course the term *Christ* came to be used as a proper name for Jesus and the term *Christians* for those who formed schools and congregations in his name.

Interest in grouping and talking about the social situations at large were apparently energized by the heady notions from the teachings of Jesus, who had appeared in the Galilee in the thirties, forty years before the Romans marched on Jerusalem, but during a period of general ideational distress about the temple, its priesthoods, and their clients in Judea, Samaria, and the Galilee. The teacher Jesus was remembered as a kind of popular philosopher who had encouraged an ethic of independence and talked about a kingdom of god. The kingdom apparently did not need an earthly king, temple, or land. The literature of the late first and second centuries tells us that these Jesus groups (loosely knit "schools" on the Greek model of philosophical schools) were energized by Greek and Jewish systems of philosophy and ethics, not plans for an earthly kingdom. But since the notion of a "kingdom of god" (basileia tou theou) was rooted in the political and philosophic discussions of the Hellenistic age, and since the Jesus schools were struggling to find their own place in the social and ideological systems of the times, and since some of these groups tended to form networks of mutual recognition as school traditions sometimes did, and since the leaders of some of these Jesus/Christ groups had taken it upon themselves to look after the widows, orphans, and the needy in their districts (in keeping with Hebrew traditions), the Roman emperor Constantine took note in the early fourth century and thought these so-called Christ people might be a good influence for the now troubled governance of the Roman Empire, which had lost its own rationale for universal governance. The ease with which the leaders of these Jesus groups assented to Constantine's invitation to accept his largesse and take their place in the Roman Empire as the religious officials of privilege is absolutely astounding. There was nothing in the earlier myths or ideologies of these Jesus people that could have prepared for such a strikingly novel thought about their orientation to the Greco-Roman world. But it worked, taking on features of the ancient Near Eastern temple-state, and eventually resulting in the creation of a religion whose "social interests" could now be focused on the maintenance of the church as an institution and the empire as a kingdom of the Christian's god. Thus there were two intermingled institutions of authority and power that appealed to a single all-powerful deity for legitimation as an empire of universal scope. That is mythmaking with banners.

CHRISTENDOM

Under Constantine in the fourth century the Jesus schools were transformed into a myth-ritual religion and institution somewhat on the model we now have in mind for the subsequent Christian church and religion. That model focused on a martyrological myth of Jesus as the Christ that had developed in the Pauline traditions to which a dramatic event of his crucifixion and resurrection had been attached and storied in the gospels. It was not long before a ritual of memorial turned the Gospel story of the "last supper" into an occasion for meditation and "participation." This ritual took place in the new basilicas that Constantine built for the new religion as their "temples." These basilicas and the rituals taking place within them were presided over by a hierarchy of priests and theologians busy with biblical texts, epic histories, and credos that positioned the church as a religious institution in the center of a universal history and cosmic world. This was a novel social construction in the interest of and to the advantage of the Roman Empire. It was not a normal outworking of the Jesus schools with their teachings of Jesus about how people could live according to God's rules. The Roman Empire–Christ kingdom configuration compressed the erstwhile collection of private Jesus schools into a public state institution in veneration of Jesus as the martyred Christ. This produced a myth-ritual practice that collapsed the myth-history dialectic of the earlier Gospel stories and turned the Gospel events into a timeless, eternally present divine event to be "reenacted" by priests in the service of the believer and devotee. This made it possible for persons to "experience" that founding event of cosmos and history as their contemporary moment of personal religious experience. It was as if the "Christ event" itself transcended history and was available for reenactment in the present time, a most amazing combination of myth and history. None of that was available in the texts and histories of the first two centuries.

If the gospels provided the narrative logic of the Christian myth for Christendom, a mythic worldview provided the picture for seeing the placement and structure of both church and empire in the larger cosmic world. This cosmic world was the normal horizon for the religious imaginations of the peoples of the Ancient Near East and the Greco-Roman worlds. The Christian myth added some features to this cosmic worldview that were not normal for its predecessors. There was now only one god in control of the cosmic forces (such as planets, stars, and angels), and this god was now in charge of creation and history (from the Hebrew epic) as well. The Gospel events from the Christian myth had rearranged the traditional astronomical cosmos into an arena of divine activity that focused on the deity's plan to "send his son" to gather the Christians and rule the nations. Thus the merger of the Jesus/Christ networks with the Roman Empire by Constantine placed the Gospel events into the cosmic structure of creation and history, thus making possible the familiar worldview of Christendom. We know what the shapes and placements of the church and empire looked like from the artifacts of a somewhat later the time. Churches and cathedrals centered the towns and cities. Steeples announced the connection to the heavens. Palaces for dukes and kings called attention to the centers of civil authority. Townhouses and city squares handled the crafts, commerce, and the keeping of records. The town squares provided the places for meetings, markets, parades, and theater. The hierarchies of governance were obvious in the networks for commerce and communication. And both the dioceses and dukedoms presided over districts that had their own proper names by which the indigenous peoples kept their erstwhile tribal identities and customs alive. Everyone who lived within this world certainly knew the landmarks and had some sense of its size and shape. Were the duke to appear, the church to celebrate a holy day, or word to arrive of a visit from centers farther afield, the venues in place would easily be opened to the world events of the time and the narrative worlds of history and cosmos that belonged to the larger picture. These worlds were always available as pictures inscribed on the walls of churches and civic buildings, and they were played out in pageants of the regular rounds of landed rituals and social activities. We can call this familiarity with the mythic world a worldview. If we think of it as the picture of the world taken for granted by the people, the structural shape of mythic and social worlds did not go away in the transition from Medieval to Reformation times.

We need to pause for a moment at this point to notice that, as comprehensive as this mythic world was intended to be, it was not able to envelop or address the *social interests* of the peasants at work in the rural and village worlds beyond the walls of the church and palace. The popes and kings ruled as viceroys of the cosmic realm of power but had little to say to the peasants except for some instructions in piety. The myth and religion of the Constantinian Catholic Church were focused almost solely on the events that manifested the authority and power of the single monarch in heaven. As for the *social interests* of his two viceroys on earth, they were focused almost entirely on the church-palace arrangement itself, not on the well-being of the aristocratic estates and their peasants. When either the priest or the duke took notice of the peasants beyond the walls, it was usually a matter of concern with their forms of obeisance as loyal servants of the church and kingdom. The social interests and rituals of the local, rural, and home-place cultures were left mostly to the peasants themselves and their "pagan" traditions. These, however, were continued without interruption. Sir James George Frazer has collected an immense documentation for the European distribution of such practices (for example, the Maypole dance, Easter Fire, harvest wreaths, and the like) still being performed in the eighteenth and nineteenth centuries (*The Golden Bough*). This is a very clear description of rural folkways and "religious" beliefs and practices right under the noses of the Christian priests and nuns, but barely noticed by them.

The church did succeed in the invention of a most remarkable institution of religion on the model of the aristocratic temple-state and its cosmic myth of the Kingdom of God, and it cultivated this notion of divine sovereignty to structure its own institutional hierarchy as well as to preside over the actual kingdoms within its sphere of influence as their moral conscience. But it was hardly prepared for the Enlightenment or the Protestant Reformation, the demise of feudalism, and the emergence of the nation-state. All of these historical changes in social practice and formation were rooted in interests other than cultivating righteousness or indulging the church's interest in piety.

REFORMATION

One might think that the Protestant Reformation (sixteenth century) should have tempered the attraction of the cosmic picture for Christians, so clearly etched on the portals of the Cathedral of Notre-Dame and elsewhere, and in some respects it did. But the matters calling for reformation were hardly matters of distress about the worldview. They were matters of consternation about the Catholic confessional, ritual, and practice of selling indulgences. In view of the dawning Enlightenment and the Age of Discovery, the conflicts among the petty kings of Europe called for an awareness of the social interests of the several ethnic traditions that surfaced in Europe now that their encompassment by the Holy Roman Empire was dissolving. The emerging interest in the texts and histories of Antiquity, a result of the Renaissance, determined that the pieties of penance were no longer convincing, much less sufficient for understanding the function of the church for the believer. However, the medieval notion of *kingdom* was not dropped when the protest against the confessional gathered strength. It played a major role in the ideological separation of the two forms of Christendom. Martin Luther actually extracted the notion of the kingdom from Catholic Christendom and applied it to the role of the Protestant churches in their various European kingdoms by saying that the Protestant church continued to represent a "kingdom," but that the Christian view of the church in the world was now a matter of having two kingdoms. He coined the phrase the *two kingdoms (divine and secular)*, which turned civil society into an order that was not at all devoid of Christian interests and mores even though thoroughly "secularized." This implicitly claimed a civic authority for the Protestant churches without calling the cosmic myth into question. The cosmic myth was simply left in place while the substitution of the biblical form of the myth for the Catholic ritual focused exegetical attention on the Bible and the early history of Christendom. Protestant scholars wanted to jump over the history of Catholicism to get at the "origin" of Christianity recorded in the New Testament. The study of the Bible would be the way Protestants understood and confirmed their "faith" as a matter of intellectual commitment to a biblical theology. This transformed the liturgy of the Mass into a "service of worship" in which the Bible and preaching were central. Per the famous aphorism from Luther, "Where the sacraments are held and the Word is preached, there is the Church."

The Protestant translation of the biblical myth into personal and intellectual terms calling for "faith" did not erase the erstwhile Catholic cosmos of the divine. The details of the mythic worldview were transformed into the Protestant concepts of sovereignty, authority, power, glory, election, vastness, and superiority by the manipulation of the biblical references into placements in the two kingdoms. Thus the culture of Christendom was transformed into the Protestant culture of the Western traditions. The dialectic did determine an awareness of the conflict between the mystic perception of the transcendent picture and its rational interpretations for civil societies of the modern worlds. And this eventually resulted in the now familiar tussles between theology and philosophy, imagination and concept, experience and reason, feeling and abstraction—all of which have troubled the more recent investigations of the cultural traditions of the arts, literature, criticism, philosophy, psychology, and social ethics. This tussle continues to evoke a full range of sensibilities in the recognition of the "beauty" and "power" of the artist's (author's, architect's, performer's) achievement ("creativity") in matters of form, genre, style, translation, intention, and understanding of the social world at the level of significance or meaning. However, much of that tussle is now passé, erased by the emergence of modernism and postmodernism. We will address this again in Chapter 6.

STATE CHURCHES

If we think of the picture of the world taken for granted by the people during the medieval period of Christendom, the structural shape of this worldview did not go away in the transition from medieval to Reformation times. What did change took place as the casting of new actors to play the traditional roles in slightly revised scripts for the production. The pope's place was now taken by bishops in the countries that had become Protestant. These lands and peoples had become Protestant by means of a decision rendered on the part of their dukes or kings. "As the ruler [decides whether to be Protestant or Catholic], so the people" was the rubric they used. The result was a cluster of "national" Christendoms, structured and governed on the model of what we now would call a "state-church" arrangement, a monarchy with an official religion. The religion was monotheistic. The church as an institution of the monotheistic religion was integral to society and supported by the monarchy. Each was equally a part of the social structure, and each of them had the whole society in its view. Each had final authority in its separate domain, but they understood their separate roles to mesh for the common good. The pattern of this social structure has stayed in place until our time, revealing an amazing toughness as a skeletal structure even as drastic changes were being made as kingdoms became nations, nations became nation-states, and nation-states became democracies. These political changes were taken in stride as activities natural for the pursuits of the kingdoms until the American and French revolutions. It was in the American and French revolutions that radical moves were made to restructure monarchy and reject the authority of the Christian church in civic affairs.

But as William Shirer's history of the Third Republic in France from 1871 to July 1940 makes clear (*The Collapse of the Third Republic*), the Revolution was not able to put either the royalists or the Catholic Church out of the older picture that still informs French mentality. And as for the American Revolution, the need to construct a new nation without a history of monarchy or a single state religion did not mean that the European heritage had been erased as the picture of what a nation-state should look like. It was still recognizable in all its structural parts as a reading of Alexis de Tocqueville makes clear (*Democracy in America*). Tocqueville was in America for a very brief period, 1831–32, and as a member of the French aristocracy he was interested in what "democracy" looked like in America. In France, the revolutions in the interest of democracy had been violent, and the results were still not clear either in the formation of a nation-state as a democracy or in terms of philosophical and political ideologies. But as a Frenchman, fully aware of the European histories subsequent to the Protestant Reformation and the fragmentation of Christendom that had ended feudalism and was just then creating kingdom-states and nation-states, his ability to analyze the social-political structure of America as a democracy fifty years after the American Revolution is astonishing.

So how was this nation-state formed in America if it did not have a history similar to the European nations'? The American history started with emigrants from Europe who first formed colonies, then states, and finally a federal union. As the colonies formed states, the pictures of the European nations were always in mind, of course. Many colonies took the presence of a Christian church for granted as belonging to the social formation, and in some of the colonies, notably in the northeastern areas, a particular denomination was not only accepted but also legally constituted. Nevertheless, the differences among the states in demography and religions prohibited a single denomination from becoming the state church of the federal union. As a matter of fact, the framing of the Constitution for the federal union included the Bill of Rights, in which the First Amendment clearly stated that "Congress shall make no law respecting an establishment of religion, or prohibiting the free exercise thereof." Throughout subsequent history this amendment has been referred to as the principle of the "separation of church and state." This principle did not keep the many denominations of Christian churches, including the several Catholic configurations, from taking advantage of the "freedom" granted religion in the United States. Many have flourished and formed independent institutions with roots in particular locations, such as the Congregationalists in New England and the Baptists in the southern states. But none of them functioned as a legal component of the structure of a state or of the federal union. This means that Christianity as an institution of religion in America was even more fragmented than in Europe. And since the people were so thoroughly engaged in the practical matters of family, farm, and state building, very little thought was given either to cosmos or history. Christianity was reduced mainly to the level of Protestant preachments to the individual, and concerns for the ethical standards of citizenship in the secular society. There was no big picture to imagine the federal union as a *nation*, much less as a *Christian Nation*, and no myth-ritual for the Christian celebration of the *social interests* that soon came pouring in to occupy all of our energies.

In the course of our brief history as a nation-state, the awareness of ourselves as similar to the European roots from which we came has not been emphasized. It has been the sense of difference that has prevailed. Differences have been noticed at various times mostly to mark features of our country that could be celebrated as distinguishing characteristics. Many of these have become definitional concepts or symbols of historical moments from which we learned who we were as a people. This is not the time and place to rehearse that history except to say that some rather common memories have rather powerful images and symbols to their credit: Tea Party, Bill of Rights, Separation of Church and State, Statue of Liberty, the Flag, the Western, Homestead, Land of the Free, Freedom, Independence, Can Do, Gold Rush, and "Over There." Along with this history some decidedly strange attitudes have settled in that make it very difficult to sort out the relations among the various Christian theologies and the social history of the United States. Our history of obsessions with being the "land of the free" (meaning the freedom of individuals to do as they please; freedom from Old World conventions and government control; freedom from taxation; and so forth), our capacity for scientific research, the creation of machines and practical inventions, and our recent sense of destiny as the ruler of the world are the more obvious indicators of our sense of being a nation. We usually think of these as features of our society as a "secular" nation, features on the state side of the church-state accord, leaving religious matters to the churches and the personal experiences of individuals. But at that level, the

Protestant form of the Christian myth did survive. Protestants did not need the medieval worldview of cosmos and history to preach and experience the Christ event. The Bible was all they needed. But the Christian myth in its biblical form did ask the believer to see the breakthroughs of the divine into human history from the creation to the eschaton. And it has been this version of the big picture of Christianity that has settled into the Christian mentality of Americans.

MYTHIC MENTALITY

Internalizing the *ethos* of a people's myth and its narrative grammar results in a mentality. *Mentality* is not a common concept in the United States. The term is not often used to designate the mythic rationale of a society's particular way of thinking. But we do use the term to notice that another person's views on a matter reveal a mind-set different from one's own. This is especially true in the case of encountering a person from another culture. The everyday discourse internal to a society need not be conscious of its mentality. That is because at the popular level of discourse it is not necessary to make reference to the articulated form of the myth. It is possible, however, for references to be made to the narrative symbols of a myth in clichés. In the case of an argument about social issues at large, such discourse can be seriously intended as if the mythic grammar is self-evident. But such discourse is not critical intellectually as if such a reference to attitudes and truism might be questioned and/or countered. It serves only as a knowing observation that the occasion or situation be taken seriously "in light of" the larger world of mythic truisms. Should the mentality involved be questioned by another person, there is the risk of being regarded as overly critical of the culture in place, if not hostile.

In the case of the Christian myth and its mentality as manifest in the political discourse of the parties and administrations from Reagan to the second Bush, the social-cultural situation was much more complex than those political thinkers imagined. It was not merely that the Christian religion no longer had a worldview capable of keeping kings and kingdoms in their places. It was that the social logic of the erstwhile Christian myth had nothing to say to the contemporary world of social interests that had emerged since the Enlightenment and Industrial Revolution. Yet the Christian myth was somehow still in mind for these conservatives as a cultural mentality. This meant that their call to "return" to the Christian Nation we were imagined once to have been was an appeal to a history, myth, and its worldview that are now passé. They were apparently not aware of this history and the significance of its demise for the many movements, industries, nation-states, and ideologies that now filled the social and intellectual vacuums created by its absence.

The theory we are exploring can handle such a blind spot by making a distinction between the myth and its mentality. Myth is articulated, rehearsed, and ritualized (in the Christian religion), thus manifest. Mentalities are sensibilities rooted in truisms that determine the attitudes and practices of the society, thus subliminal. The problem for cultural critics attempting to analyze the conservative mind-set of the second Bush administration, and what its members meant by the term *Christian Nation,* is that the mythic mentality of the conservatives was not able to argue from the myth and say what they meant by *Christian Nation.* Mythic mentalities can remain in place for a time after the pervasive grammar of a culture has lost its myth by means of social changes. Such a mentality, robbed of the effectiveness of its mythic authority for the social institutions of influence in the society, is no longer able to envision the future constructively, debate cogently among political alternatives, or think clearly about the authority of such texts as the Bible and the Constitution or the concept of the common good for their significance in relation to the quality of life in the society. Christianity had lost its big picture of a world that worked for the authority of the church in the interest of the piety of its Christians. It had nothing to say to a world that is embroiled in competing pursuits and violence. It has nothing to offer to a conglomerate of discordant social projects and institutions that are not working together in the interest of a common good society.

CHRISTIAN MENTALITY

One of the truly exceptional features of the big Christian picture of the world is the narrative grammar of its myth. The Bible is a double quest romance with two agents in an irresolvable tryst. The divine agent should be able to have his way, for he is the all-powerful creator of the world. But his need to be recognized, adored, and obeyed as the Father of his children and as the sole sovereign of the universe keeps running into trouble, for humans find themselves distracted by one another in their own quests for advantage and power. These human questings are regarded by the divine monarch as evidence of intransigence, and he responds with threats and promises. The threat is of punishment and final destruction. The promise is of forgiveness if his children repent, or adoption if the ungodly convert. Viewed by Protestant Christians as the divine plan for human history from beginning to end, it is the only history that counts.

There is a social logic to this narrative grammar that is troubling. The logic determines the way in which Christians learn to think about everything in their world, and to make judgments about the right way to classify and define things. It begins with a logic of the singular which says that there is only one god, one law, one credo, one system of values, and one right way to live and please the sovereign. In the Catholic tradition all of that was taken care of in the institutions and rituals of Christendom. But in Protestantism, this logic frustrates the Christian's quest to be sure of one's "election," to know for sure the right way to live in the world, and what to think about political loyalties. It is also the logic behind what we can now call the Christian mentality, the cultural preference for thinking that there is only one correct definition for an object, and that the really important events and decisions are, as we say, "unique," that is, singular and incomparable. The trouble with this logic of the singular is that it cannot handle the real world. And it is compounded by a mythic logic of the dual. The logic of the dual starts with the divine demand for obedience, which recognizes the fact that humans can disobey. The logic of the dual then continues with the distinction between the human and the divine, the cultural division of the human race into Christians and all the others, and finally with the oppositions of "right vs. wrong," "us vs. them," and "good vs. bad." This has made it extremely difficult for Christians to accept and appreciate difference, to compromise with other points of view, and to negotiate with non-Christians and other cultures. Scholars have traced aspects of this cultural mind-set to the Greek philosophies of "being" (versus "becoming"), and the Aristotelian theory of language whereby a single definitional term or name for a thing must be found before "knowledge" of the thing can occur (cf. Saussure's *Course in General Linguistics*). However, Heidegger's analysis of this philosophic tradition in *Sein und Zeit* makes it clear that the Greek culture alone cannot account for the absolutism of the singular in the Western tradition of philosophy. It is true that the fixation on the "singular" definition of an object is a cultivation of the "mono" mind-set of the world of "being" that has been pursued by Westerner philosophers. But this Western tradition of philosophy is a combination of Greek and Christian concepts and worldviews. The Christian myth also works with a mono logic. Thus cultural critics in our time are referring to the *Christian logos* that has been involved in contemporary cultural manifestations. In Chapter 6 we will need to ask what these modern scholars see when referring to the Christian logos as a description of the Western cultural tradition. For now it is important to see that the Western traditions of philosophy and theology (not always seen as forms of the same pursuit) have been grounded in the Christian worldview and the social logic of its myth. This means that a Christian mentality at the core of the Western cultural tradition may be the form of Christianity that underlies the ways in which the people of the United States think about themselves and the world at large irrespective of the type of Christian denomination or theology to which one happens to belong. It is that suspicion, in any case, that I want to explore as this book unfolds.

For the past three hundred years Western "civilization" has produced projects of *social interests* that do not appear to have been initiated by Christian thinking or motivation. As a matter of fact, some of these projects have been attributed to what later has come to be called "humanisms," intended to be taken as an anthropology different from the Christian's fascination with the divine. These developments include the views of the Renaissance, Enlightenment, Industrial Revolution, and more recent projects of the twentieth and twenty-first centuries. Many of these more recent organizations of human energy found the United States to be a society that welcomed experiments not easily imagined in more traditional national structures. So it was here in the United States that certain features of the current global picture have emerged. These include "military empire," "global corporations," exploitations of natural resources around the world in the interest of American capitalism, worldwide networks of financial institutions for banking and investment, the International Monetary Fund, "free-trade" markets, scientific research centers into all aspects of physical realities, electronic communications, surveillance systems, agribusiness, fossil fuel energy, and the "mission" of the United States to spread "democracy" around the world. How all of these organizations of energies and institutions have occurred in the United States is the subject for the next chapter. They paint a dynamic picture so complex that it is all but incomprehensible as a single coherent society.

It was for this reason that the emergence of the term *Christian Nation* in the Reagan and second Bush administrations came as a surprise. They used the Christian myth to justify their political ideologies that called for Christians to take charge of executive power and privilege as those who assumed our superiority in worldwide "leadership" because we were a "Christian Nation."

Since this way of seeing and thinking about the world was taken for granted by these Christian conservatives, and produced the white papers calling for us to gear up for the American century, the surprise turned to consternation when these papers were revealed. Then the 9/11 "attack" on the Pentagon and the New York towers was interpreted as a call to arms, and the "war" against "terror" began. There did not seem to be any way to stop the furor or ask whether the administration and Pentagon understood why the "attack" had happened. I wrote the book on *Myth and the Christian Nation* to clarify the reasons for the unthinking involvement in world affairs that this situation revealed. Now, after seven years of wars and rumors of wars with no solutions to the social issues that underlay and still underlie the posture of the United States, I want to explore the influence of the Christian mentality that seems to be the problem.

There is a chilling picture by John Gast entitled *American Progress* (1872) that David A. Sánchez has reproduced in his book *From Patmos to the Barrio*. It is in a wonderful chapter on the symbols of "manifest destiny" during the middle of the nineteenth century. The picture shows Lady Providence as an ethereal heavenly figure spanning the space between a valley below and the clouds in the heavens above, bent forward with one foot close to the ground, and looking ahead. She is leading the way west for the settlers. In the picture of the valley below are wagons, homesteads, hunters, prospectors, roads, bridges, ships, railroads, telegraph wires, all leading west. Other authorities from the time are cited by Sánchez making the point that manifest destiny was a notion based on our sense of being an exceptional people, and that this notion was clearly understood as the result of being a chosen people. Thus Christian mentality appears to be capable of imagining more of the world as "Christian" than the medieval picture of Christendom or the mythic narrative of the Bible easily reveals. The biblical form of the myth is so anchored in the transcendent world and sweep of divine agency that its ritual recall in the church, and its entertainment for personal meditation, become imaginative experiences of that spiritual world. But the mythic image of a Christian nation, ultimately derived from the social formations of Christendom, is apparently capable of application even to the modern nation-state. It is not yet clear to me whether and how the modern Protestant church carries and projects this picture of itself as the religious center of the Christian Nation, but the recent articulations of conservatives cited by Jeff Sharlet, Erin Runions, and others tell us that the projection is seriously social and political, not merely a matter of being concerned about the morality of individuals. The leaders who have talked about a Christian Nation seem to have focused on the Bible as law and the power of God as the means to realize a promised political destiny for the nation. So that makes our questions about the persistence and reproduction of this mentality quite complicated. It appears that models of power and property (capital) are now part of the mythic entanglements.

It is this society that is now in trouble and needs to be studied in terms of the human interests it fosters, the social interests that it assumes, the unacknowledged mythic rationales it has produced, and whether it is possible still to imagine social formations in which the common good is privileged in place of wealth, power, and sovereignty. I intend in the next chapters of this book to address these issues.

4 SOCIAL INTERESTS

News of the world in this second decade of the twenty-first century does not paint a pretty picture. The conflicts among nations, political parties, ethnicities, ideologies, and between governments and their many institutions and enterprises present us with fluctuating agitations of diverse interests that often eventuate in scenes of blockage or violence. There must be social reasons for these conflicts, reasons that by and large have escaped our media and reporters. Journalists and cultural historians usually stay close to the description of a single contemporary event. But the reach for reasons often takes a backward glance at the configuration of influences that preceded the present. This is helpful, for it frequently spreads a history of an event out to engage features of a larger social history that may impinge upon the stream of events under investigation. If so, it means we need to pay closer attention to these social histories than is customary in the media. It may be that following a particular stream of related events is too narrow for the complexity of the larger picture and so erases aspects of the social interests we need to consider. This is usually the problem with the naming of an event that comes to focus on a single or small set of observations at the popular level of awareness and discussion. The answer must be that we need to see a history of similar events, such as gun violence, intertwined with other social interests and their histories in order to account for a particular conflict.

In order to guide us in our quest for some clarity about the reasons for the apparently irresolvable conflicts and agitations that are currently painting the global pictures of our human enterprises, our theory of myth and social interests can be used to mark those moments of our Western history where interests developed out from under the influence of Christendom, interests that have had a great effect upon the social and cultural formations of what we used to call the Western "tradition." Such are the differing interests involved in the emergence of the Renaissance, the Reformation, the Age of Discovery, the Enlightenment, and the Industrial Revolution. Each of these historic moments of significant changes in the social history and thinking of Western civilization produced social interests that continue to affect the patterns of practices and their rationalizations in the contemporary world. It is the confused configuration of these interests and rationales that we need to acknowledge as we make the attempt to understand the reasons for the conflicts that are now threatening our societies, civilizations, ecologies, and cultures.

I must assume that the reader has a sense of Western history, if not some knowledge of its scope and pertinence for understanding the social and cultural issues of our time. One need not put aside the current fascination with postmodernism and the discourse about the "End of the Western Tradition" in order to have some knowledge of that "tradition" and ask why it began to unravel, or to understand the survey that follows of the diverse social interests that emerged in the so-called historical periods of transformation. But it might be well to say something about the Christian myth and worldview that pertained prior to the breakdown of its encompassing canvas. That is because many of the human enterprises that mark the history of the breakdown still assumed the cosmic worldview of Christendom even while taking up the interests that occasioned its breakdown. Thus the Christian myth and worldview continued to function as the larger cultural frame of reference for understanding and rationalizing interests that were actually inimical to its internal logic. We can use this contrast in logics and worldviews implicit to the several major social interests that have emerged in the past five hundred years to prepare us for an analysis of the social situation of the present time.

The big picture encompassing Western civilization during the medieval period was the cosmic universe of the Christian myth. The earth centered the heavenly spheres that traced the orbs, and the transcendent god authorized the church to preside over the dispensation of divine power and the piety it called for among the nations. As for the kings and holy fathers finding their places in history, it was necessary only to imagine the epic as etched into the archways and arcades of the basilicas and cathedrals. There the historic figures of power and piety were lined up upon the division of time into the "old" and the "new" (with just a touch of "chronological" sequencing) in such a way that the more recent kings and pontiffs could easily be added. There was no other real history of Western peasants or other non-Western peoples that counted. In order for the pious to imagine the epic history that did count, they needed only to attend the ritual and recall the myth. There the central event of epic history was actually "experienced" in the Mass, an event of the transcendent breaking into time. There was no need to think more about the ordinary histories of peoples, societies, and nations. Kings were given their places in the series of prophets, apostles, priests, and kings according to the biblical epic and its extension into the times of the Christian empires. The future as portrayed in the myth-ritual picture of the universe was hardly imagined as a worldly society. Instead it was a "future" imagined mainly for individuals as an ascendance into heaven or a sinking into hell. And as for the present tense and time, the pivotal event of history was not imagined as passé. It was reenacted regularly as an event in the present at the altar with an invitation to the pious to be "present." It was this worldview that began to break down when the Renaissance and Reformation began to investigate other human and social interests.

This chapter intends a survey of the major social interests that have developed in the West since the worldview of Christendom began to lose its control of social and intellectual practices. We need to acknowledge each of these major moments of social and cultural changes in order to assess the underlying reasons for the many conflicts that describe our current situation in the next chapter. It will be sufficient in this chapter to say something about the Renaissance as the "discovery" of the "individual"; the occasions for the emergence of science; the Reformation as that form of Christianity that has most affected the mentality of the United States; capitalism; and the emergence of the nation-state. This will prepare us for a discussion of the social issues confronting our postmodern culture today.

RENAISSANCE

The Renaissance ("rebirth") has usually been described as a two hundred–year period beginning in the fourteenth century characterized by a "rediscovery" of the "classical tradition" of Greek and Roman ideas and literature. This characterization is understandable in view of the fact that Western scholars had not cultivated the Greek literary tradition for an intervening thousand years as had the Islamic intellectuals whose interest in the Greek and ancient Near Eastern cultures and literatures made it possible for their "rediscovery" in the thirteenth and fourteenth centuries by Christian scholars. It is also understandable in light of the effect this feature of the Renaissance had upon the subsequent preoccupation of Western scholars with texts and history (including the Bible). But it overlooks the significance of the shifts in interest that took place from the Christian cosmos to the natural orders, and from a focus upon the god of the transcendent realm above to the human beings on the earth below. The life of Francesco Petrarch (1304–74) can represent the momentous significance of these shifts in interest for the subsequent history of social and cultural pursuits. He was recognized at the time as the major scholar of both the classical and Christian traditions, and consequently as the founder and representative of European Humanism, the quest to combine Christian and classical moral traditions in the light of the conscience of the solitary individual. Two stories have frequently been told to illustrate these features of his quest. Both stem from his *Secretum meum,* a set of three dialogues Petrarch held with Augustine in the presence of the personification of Truth. In one of them Petrarch confesses that he was overwhelmed with the beauty of the natural landscape below as he looked down upon a verdant valley from the perspective of a mountaintop (probably Mont Ventoux, France). He felt guilty to find the earthly realm as lovely as the spiritual realm of the divine above, the realm that the devout should have exclusively in mind. This was his experience of "the fall." The other story is probably from this same experience, when Petrarch takes the *Confessions* from his pocket and opens it to Augustine's mention of men who "go to admire the high mountains and the immensity of the ocean and the course of the heavens . . . and neglect themselves." Thus the "discovery" of the *individual* in the *natural order,* a discovery that was destined to shape the social interests of the subsequent history of human endeavors comes to us as a marvelous inversion of mythic categories in the interest of encouraging human observation of the world: thus anthropology supersedes theology. As the subsequent history of what we now call the humanities unfolded, from "confessions" to "biographies" to novels; from the arts and critical essays to psychologies; from the philosophical essays on "man" to what Lionel Trilling has called "the liberal imagination," the Renaissance interest in the human world has produced an amazing social interest and cultural production that still affects our thinking.

I am not aware of any description of this feature of Western culture as a tradition produced by a class of thinkers, much less as a *social interest* that helps define the collective thinking and motivations underlying our practices. In the case of writers, their literary works are commonly regarded as "literature," not as, say, "philosophy." The literature is studied in terms of aesthetic genre and the author's skills in composition, seldom as cultural criticism. But other persons belong to this class as well as writers, such as artists, playwrights, theater people, essayists, sculptors, and architects. The class may be defined in terms of a set of characteristics shared by most artists and writers. These include a poetic sensibility, an interest in human relations and social moments, a capacity for insight and analysis while observing the human drama, and especially the intellectual labor involved in perfecting their skills in creating images and narrative that describe or reflect upon the world as they see it. These descriptions are set forth in ways that make it possible for others to share the "observation" and penetrate the "reasons" suggested for the way the world seems to work. We will want to look into this tradition of *social interests* in more detail in Chapter 6. The current form of what used to be called the arts is now such a display of "cultural production" that its studied analysis, now called "cultural criticism," has pursued a very impressive tradition of intellectuals, academicians, and journalists focused on the questions of how the arts understand what is making our society tick, and whether the arts themselves may not be that which generates the tick.

SCIENCE

What we call science is another *social interest* and practice of tremendous importance for the way we are thinking about and shaping the world in which we live. We use the term to cover the "scientific method," the history of discoveries about the natural orders, the knowledge obtained from investigation of the physical world, the experiments necessary to manipulate the natural order for practical purposes, and, more recently, to designate the intellectuals and academics who pursue these enterprises as "scientists." Academics classify all of these pursuits as sciences, academic disciplines, or research projects that bring groups of scientists together to form institutes or university departments. These research projects all have names that cover a growing spectrum of natural phenomena such as astronomy, physics, geology, magnetism, chemistry, biology, atomic particles, electronic particles, and so forth. Our period of human history has rightly been called "the scientific age."

The history of Western sciences has customarily been said to start with the astronomies of Copernicus (1473–1534), Galileo (1564–1642), and Newton (1642–1727), noteworthy as the very discipline-to-be that precipitated a scientific view of the universe, one that differed from the Christian cosmos. This was an advance on Petrarch's fascination with the beauty of the natural world. The scientific view of the world made possible by the scientific description of the natural universe was consciously undertaken at the expense of the traditional Christian view of the cosmos. But the human preoccupations with scientific experiments and thinking that astronomy unleashed were hardly motivated by the desire to counter the Christian view, and they did not start there in the sixteenth and seventeenth centuries. The pursuit of knowledge about the physical world belongs to human interest and enterprise from its very beginning. Dick Teresi has traced many of our sciences to very early periods in the histories of other cultures (*Lost Discoveries*). All of them exhibit interest in the study and manipulation of the natural order for practical human purposes: calendars, agriculture, irrigation, fabrics, tools, foods, constructions, metals, stoneworks, numbers, accounts, inscriptions, writing. The scientific investigation of the world must underlie the human enterprise of material accomplishments in the interest of practices of importance for social constructions. It is the combination of "scientific" projects and other interests in the practices of a society that we are calling *social interests*. In the past, when a social interest became recognized as of particular importance for the habits and practices of a society (such as making knives, scrapers, and arrowheads from a particular flint rock), myths and cultural symbols could be imagined to mark and maintain these practices (such as appear to have been the reasons for rock art paintings in a particular location). Myths told of a practice's "first" occurrence, and rituals assured its recognition and repetition.

The older worldview of Christendom was not very good at symbolizing the material practices of the people as *social interests* of importance for the kingdoms over which it ruled. Instead, its own interests produced a set of religious symbols referring to the cosmic and transcendent world that the church represented in the social world. This did produce a rich and sustainable culture for about fourteen hundred years, or as long as the kings and aristocracies were able to maintain their rule of society. The scientific age in which we live has not created this kind of symbol system, nor that of the earlier ethnographic and pre-Christian kingdoms that were normal for the cultivation and celebration of the society. Science has, however, produced a generalized view of the world that combines a sense of indebtedness to science and its knowledge of the natural order, as well as an appreciation for the tools and machines scientists have made possible. It is a "secular" worldview that has been accepted by the people, understood as the result of human energies and investments, and looked to for solutions to the material and social problems and issues that may occur. This has produced a social world that is currently being reshaped by science and industry on a global scale. Science does not claim to be the source for the construction of a culture with social meaning, much less a mode of thinking fundamental for general theories of human self-understanding and identity. But the scope is total, meant to be exhaustive, and so functions as a "big picture" of the world in which we live.

The problem with this worldview is not that it has threatened to erase the traditional Christian worldview, as some Christians have imagined, but that it does not have within it the resources, mechanisms, or motivations for seeing the social as a society that can produce a culture of morals, beauty, and meanings. Thus we do not know what to think about the "values" from past cultural traditions that seem to persist as mere sensibilities. This is a problem not only because of the unexpected effects that scientific pursuits are having in the hands of states and industries upon the physical and social environments (such as global warming, nuclear threats, proliferation of arms and armies, and threats to ecological systems, all of which are currently understood as social issues), but especially because the world of science does not seem to have any internal mechanisms for constraints against dangerous and destructive misuse of its own applications and methods. This is especially true when the scientific accomplishment leaves the hands of research scientists and is put to use in the interest of the military and business corporations. The future is wide open for ever more and greater investigations and inventions, both of the material universe and of human biology. Many of these pursuits are undertaken in the interests of governments, industries, the military, and the financial markets.

The recent turn to the scientific analyses of individual and social behaviors is a most remarkable indication that scientific curiosity has taken note of the human and social arenas of existence as worthy of scientific investigation. But the jump from neurons to neuroses, much less from equations to equity, or from axioms to justice, has not yet occurred. There is little awareness in the mentality of the pursuit of science of a need to explain the logic of human motivations at a fundamental level, or even of the human interests in power, status, honor, art, celebration, or morality as they apply to current social formations. Science has not (yet?) been able to ground the interest in social formation in a fundamental social anthropology. Instead, science is now looking for signs of social behavior in other primates and animals. This means that "nature" is now being used to answer for the full array of human interests, motivations, conflicts, aggressions, predations, and violence. We have accepted these views of the "natural," because they are "scientific," and because the scientific worldview is the environment within which we live. We will need to ask in the next chapter about the effect of science as a "social interest" and its entanglements with some of the "social issues" troubling us today.

RELIGION

Thinking about relations among social interests, worldviews, and cultures brings religion to mind. From ethnographies to the so-called world religions, the religions of societies have identified, celebrated, and given moral support and meaning to the practices of a society. I have theorized that the social interests of traditional societies and cultures are fundamentally constructive in the interest of finding ways to work and live together in the world (*Myth and the Christian Nation*). The religious mechanisms of support and rationalization for a society's sense of morals and well-being have been (1) *myths* that paint the big picture within which a society sees its place in its environments of social and natural histories; (2) *rituals* that display a deliberate performance of a practice of central importance for the life of the society so that the people can watch the practice in slow motion and ponder its place in the larger patterns of practices; and (3) the creation of *symbols,* usually taken from the big picture, used to mark major structural junctures for recognition throughout the society's patterns of activities. Symbols call subtle attention to the relation between the daily round and the worldview. Taken together as features from the painting of the big picture, religion creates a *culture,* and the culture a *mentality* that provides a kind of *narrative grammar* for the acceptable ways of thinking about and responding to the ways of the social world. Lionel Trilling called such a grammar a "set of assumptions" or unconscious attitudes that determine a person's responses to the social world (*The Liberal Imagination*). Pierre Bourdieu called such a grammar a *habitus,* the set of practices common and habitual within which a community lives, and where one's responses are more or less automatic.

In the case of Western civilization the religion of the culture since the fourth century has been Christianity. In the previous chapter I described the process of Christian origins in the first three centuries. The astounding feature of that process was that Constantine turned the Jesus/Christ schools into the religion of the Roman Empire by offering them official status, basilicas, and the largesse of the emperor. No wonder the eventual Christendom painted its big picture on a cosmic canvas of the transcendent world where all the arrangements of power and authority were made. The size and shape of this cosmos were not extraordinary. It was the familiar world of the gods for the Ancient Near East and the Greeks. What is striking about the Constantinian-Christian arrangement was that it linked two social formations under a single deity and claimed for that deity monarchical power over cosmos and history. It is true that the ethical values of obedience and piety were encouraged among the people, and that the church also served as "shepherd" to the peasants in their simpler, more practical rural patterns of life. But the church and its mythology did not have in mind a picture for an ordinary working society that allowed for, much less encouraged, the pursuits of the knowledge and practices customary for the worlds of normal human activity. The "secular" world was now consigned to fend for itself outside of the church and court. The remarkable result of this combination of religion and empire, however, was that the Christian myth and ritual did produce such powerful images and symbols that a comprehensive culture emerged in the shadow of its otherworldly narratives without having to ask about its social or practical meaning. This culture of the church and Christendom actually cultivated itself as the religion and institution of reflection upon the universal cosmic world of transcendence. Thus it had to change slowly by subsuming the many moments of intellectual and artistic developments that surely came to pass in subsequent history. The church did this by making slight adjustments within the familiar cosmic picture, both in terms of additional images that could be placed here and there (as Dante and Hieronymus Bosch did), and in terms of philosophical embellishments capable of expanding erstwhile mythic language in the direction of more "modern" philosophical concepts (as for instance that of the "cosmos," the "globe," the "nations," and "ethnic identity").

The remarkable way the priests, intellectuals, and theologians of the church responded to this subsequent history from the Renaissance to the present needs a story of its own. They had always been in charge of the canvas upon which the Christian worldview was painted, making changes, not always so subtle, to let new "theologies" affect the ambience of the picture, thus finding ways to make places for advancements in science, art, architecture, philosophy, literature, trade, slavery, statecraft, and war, without letting the transcendent order completely atrophy or come apart. They did this for the most part by resignifications of the mythic images of the cosmos without letting its epic logic change. At every point in the history of the Western enterprise, the new shapes of the natural and human orders were translated back into an expanding view of the cosmos without endangering the older biblical-theological picture, and the priesthood saw its own significance enhanced by virtue of its sophisticated representation of the divine world to the social orders in relevant terms. One might think of the ways in which Jesuit theologians cleverly recast the biblical account of creation by renaming the terms of the traditional cosmology to make room for the modern scientific concepts of dust particles, chemicals, and nuclear big bangs. Their point was not to dislodge the creation account from the biblical-cosmic canvas but to pose as the theological mediators between the sacred text and the profane world.

REFORMATION

It was Protestant Christianity that traveled to the United States in the seventeenth and eighteenth centuries, mostly as sectarian formations in the interest of preserving erstwhile ethnic and cultural identities. There does not seem to have been a self-awareness about the historic significance of colonizing a "new land," the venturesome risks taken in the American Revolution, the experimental formation of a "republic," the philosophical grounding and consequences of the Constitution, the brash attempts at an unnamed "social democracy," or the rise to world power status after the Second World War, much less as national events called for by a Christian mandate. There was little guidance from the European experiences in nation building. And as far as the vague memories of European cultural traditions went, there was precious little investment in the education and skills necessary to pick them up as genres capable of informing or analyzing American experience and mentality. Thus the shock of Bible Belt Christians rising up against the progressive trends after the Second World War, and especially after the Vietnam War, by calling us to confess our sins and become a "Christian Nation."

I have discussed that episode of our recent history in other writings sufficiently for this book's purposes (see *Myth and the Christian Nation* and *Christian Mentality*). The important point to make now is that this recent history reveals the lingering strength of the Christian worldview as a mentality that has not been questioned, criticized, or silenced in our public and political discourses from the parish all the way to Washington. As a big picture, the Christian worldview is faded and tarnished now, but it is somehow still there sub rosa as a set of sensibilities that allows a Christian mind-set to flourish in the making of political judgments. It is the only comprehensive big picture painted by the Western tradition, and it is now worn out as a reasonable view of the cosmos and human society's place within it. Its continuing attraction for conservative Christians is a pitiful commentary on the lack of awareness of social and cultural issues among the poorly educated in the United States. Examples quickly come to mind such as the "creation-creationism debate," the conservative coalition's attempts to demolish our welfare state in the name of "Christian values," and legislating the "stand your ground" laws as the "righteous" answer to our gun and violence culture. The European nations have long known that Christianity as an institution was having trouble with its authority in the modern world of nation-states. But as a cultural tradition it is, of course, still influential as a mentality in much of the European countries as well. Mentalities are difficult to discern and address from within a culture because they reside in the social psyche at the level of self-evident assumptions without which one would not know what to think and do. So there is always a lag between actual changes of practice in a society, and the reimagining of its myth and symbol system. But by now the Western world should have become aware that the mentalities of the Western religions, including Judaism and Islam, are wreaking havoc around the world. Thus the present study includes the remnants of the medieval worldview of Christianity as a mentality that impinges upon the several social projects and enterprises driving our social interests in the twenty-first century. None of our social projects has a big picture that works for the coherence of a society as the medieval system once did. The mythic mentality does assume such a coherence at the unconscious cultural level of assumptions. It may actually be one of the impulses oddly still at work even in the progressives' agitations for a common good society. But in the hands of our conservatives, this mentality represents a social *grammar* that confuses any attempt to think about the reasons for our inabilities to control the violence in our world and to chart a sane social path into the future.

CAPITALISM

Capitalism has become a pervasive and totalistic social interest of our society. Its influence reaches around the world. It is time to talk about it as a social enterprise that has its own myth, big picture, and social logic. We in the United States have not wanted even to think about it as a system of motivations. The term *capitalism* has been so closely associated with Karl Marx and our startled anxiety about communism after the Second World War that merely to mention it has always raised red flags. We have preferred to understand our industrial economy as "free enterprise" at the popular level and "free trade" at the international level. We are the land of the free and our task, as the president has frequently underlined for us, is to make it possible for individuals to get ahead by going to school, getting a job, working hard, and having a chance to fulfill their dream of a good life. The problem with this official (and popular) mind-set at this point in our history is that the "chances" to get ahead for the average American have become illusory. And our economy as a whole is showing signs of running out of steam, if not sliding into serious trouble. There has been a steady depletion of wages, well-being, and welfare at the people level despite an extravagant national budget for the military and the continuing accumulation of wealth at the elite level for the CEOs, corporations, and money managers.

The media and the people in their own ways have taken notice of this and have become restless. Neither the government nor our society as a social system appears able to respond to the many inequities and injustices that have gotten out of hand. The internet and print media are full of journal articles and commentaries analyzing the investigations, polls, and agency reports of our economic situation, telling us that this or that feature of the whole has contributed to the problem and needs to be fixed, but without saying how to fix it. The government has given up on regulating big businesses and global corporations. The political scene in Washington has devolved into the throwing of stones at one another. The financial agencies and institutions are suspiciously silent, although supportive economists say "Not to worry," because the banks are too big to fail. The CEOs for international organizations keep their monies offshore. The nations of the rest of the world are not able to control the exploitations of our global corporations in their lands and people. The peoples abroad, taking note of the ways in which American "progressives" respond to particular social and political injustices and issues, have found that they too can demonstrate and shout. But there is no governmental agency or bureaucratic office in our social systems with ability, knowledge, or authority to respond. And to top it all off, our scientists have concluded that our many industries in the pursuit of financial "growth" and empire have overrun the limits of our earth's natural resources but cannot stop digging, drilling, and exploring for more.

Thus our industrial economies have not only produced the

emergence of glamorous cities around the world, a plethora of gadgets and luxuries never before imagined, a seductive marketing system that the peoples of the world cannot resist, and incredible wealth for the rich and the managers of corporate and financial institutions. They have also produced extreme imbalances among the world's nation-states, complex networks of financial and political power for the attempt to control competition among nations, agencies, and industries, and subtle rhetorics to justify the ways in which they use "human resources." Corporations do not contribute to the social well-being of a nation-state, the common good of a society, or the welfare of the average citizen. Their large-scale exploitations of natural and human resources around the world have marred planet earth in ways that scientists say are very serious, so serious that the injuries may not be remedied in the interests of our current civilization's future.

It is therefore time to set aside our fascination with financial greatness, the veneration of the rich, those who manage to become wealthy by manipulating the economy, and the "leadership" position of our nation among the nations of the world in the interest of expanding our economic superiority. It may not be possible to "set aside" such a fascination. But we might be able to recognize our merely fortuitous place in the history of Western civilizations, and ask ourselves what may have gone wrong with our social and economic systems that they have brought us to this moment of political uncertainty and collective perturbation. Some are saying that it is time to talk about capitalism as a pervasive cultural mentality. At the level of popular discourse we have hardly ever recognized that the American way accepts capitalism as its form of economy, thinks in general in terms of the logics of capitalism, and has organized our system of rewards mainly in terms of money. Some of our savants are finally starting to use the term *capitalism* in their descriptions and commentaries of the state of the world, saying that it is time to acknowledge that we are a "capitalistic democracy," and to ask whether our drive for profit and wealth has not gotten out of control. We have resisted this kind of analysis, for it borders on self-criticism, and that is something we have never wanted to do. But if we recognized that capitalism as a social system provides the unexpressed reasons for our thinking and behavior in more ways than required for running a business, making money, or keeping accounts, we would be able to think more clearly about our social concerns. What if capitalism has become our "worldview" or ideology, a way of looking at ourselves in relation to one another and the world, and that it now provides the logic for our social behaviors, our political policies, and private interests? Would it not be well to understand these logics and take them up for analysis and discussion? Many are the commentaries that explore particular factors of our social and financial imbalance, but then, since a remedy cannot be found to assure social and political change, tend to trail off into despair. I want to suggest that, while despair is certainly lurking in the social psyche of our humanitarian intellectuals, we should not yield to it before taking a hard look at the reasons we may have for thinking the situation desperate. Notice, please, that we have not analyzed all of the reasons for the success of the capitalistic system, nor have we asked ourselves where our fleeting outbursts of anger and cynicism may be anchored in some alternative social visions. We should not cave in to cynicism and despair before tackling the questions of capitalism as a social and ideological system by means of a thorough analysis of its logics and an assessment of its effectiveness as a social self-understanding. We have not yet done that.

The strange thing is that it is Karl Marx who can help us with such an analysis. Marx was an avant-garde analyst of the Industrial Revolution and its effect upon the structures of society. We need not think of him as the philosopher-founder of the "communism" we first feared in its Russian form (which he was not) in order to learn from his profound insights into the social changes that were taking place with the emergence of industry during the eighteenth and nineteenth centuries. He focused entirely on following the social changes that the emerging industries made on the patterns of life at his time. What Marx noticed about industrial society was that the machine changed all of the social structures and relationships that had pertained in the erstwhile feudal and monarchical societies. These societies had been sustained by agrarian labors and handcraft. When the machine stepped in to do the work once done by handworkers and craftsmen on the farms, estates, and small guilds of the town, major changes occurred in the ways workers became organized and paid, as well as in the "values" of the workers' work or productions. We can summarize these changes briefly by making four observations.

Number one: *Values*. The machine could turn out more products faster than the handworker. There was now a surplus of commodities available for marketing. Thus the value of a given object changed from its "use value" as before to its "surplus" and "commodity" values for the market. Ouch. The workers lost possession of their handwork and became "wage laborers" for the owner of the machine shop. The owner of the machine shop or factory was now the owner of the surplus products and commodities. And the trick soon learned was that the difference between the costs of production and the market value of the surplus amounted to "profit." Profit could be enhanced by reinvestment in the "growth" of the enterprise by "expansion."

Number two: *Nation-states.* All erstwhile nations, accustomed to the age-old model of being "kingdoms," with royalty at the top and an aristocracy on their estates, now had to think of themselves as governments that needed to accommodate the growth of populations clustered around factories in the cities. It was this social configuration, created by the movement of a rural population to the city, that Charles Dickens found disgraceful at the level of the working class, and that Raymond Williams studied as the social change that forced a literary culture to social critique among forty authors in England from 1780 to 1950 (*Culture and Society*). The ugliness of the industrial city was obvious, of course, but the reasons for it and the problems it created for governance were not. As governments responded to the needs of the city and the growth of its industries, however, changes began to take place in the practices of the society as a whole. Most of these changes were not thought of as attempts to solve the social *issues* of the industrial city. They were simply the next steps thought necessary to keep the social machinery of capitalism working.

It did not take long for governments to realize that their industries were the means for revenue and the "wealth of nations." Thus the nation-state was born, together with taxation, policies for the enhancement of trading, charters for the banking institutions, expenditures for roads and civic buildings, and laws designed to keep the social machinery operating. Eventually this posture of the nation-state was justified by saying that such governmental activity and supervision was necessary "in the national interest." The populace had little time to think about the changes taking place as kingdoms became nations. They had their hands full coping with urban arrangements, doing their jobs, and making ends meet. But they did learn that the strange new concept of being a *nation* now filled the horizon of what a society was understood to be. This new concept actually erased many of the memories from the kingdoms of the past.

Number three: *Capital.* With the changes in practices from rural trading, through factory manufacturing, to wage labor, profiting, and marketing, *money* became the common coin of values and the keeping of accounts. The accumulation of monies became its own value and was called *capital.* The economic system of the nation-state now required a banking system, control of interest rates, and rules for exchange and investment in order to keep its *economy* growing. Financial institutions emerged that actually traded in the money in their accounts as their capital. It was now possible to invest in a company in terms of its promise of future profits and returns. The value of money as capital created an economic market in money. Stocks, bonds, and the value of businesses and their futures could now be traded, sold, and forfeited if unsuccessful. And the strength (importance/value) of an economy became the register for the value/strength/importance of a nation-state and its businesses. The financial institutions were the businesses that counted.

Number four: *Expansion.* Marx was especially clear about expansion as a requirement for a capitalistic business or economy.

It needed an expanding market for the always excessive production of commodities, and the accumulation of capital had to be
reinvested in enlarging the business. A feedback loop between
costs and profits then determined the value of a commodity in
the market. And the surplus mechanism determined that the
market needed to expand in order for a business to continue
to grow. The trick was not difficult for a capitalistic economy to
learn. A shop, business, or factory had to manipulate resources,
machinery, and labor in order to move ahead. The market had to
expand in order to help the factory grow. *Growth* was therefore
the goal if a business or an economy wanted to survive. And
ways were found to make that possible.

One approach has been to create an attractive image for the
product and company by means of advertising. Another on the national level has been to construct monopolies, either by cornering
the market or by buying up competitors. Still another approach
has been to turn businesses into corporations with many levels
of responsibility, many products, several "centers" for production
and marketing, as well as agents abroad, and connections cultivated to governments and financial institutions. This approach
distributes responsibilities throughout the system, making ac-
countability difficult to trace. Such a business system is almost
invulnerable to state or market control. A fourth approach has
been to "outsource" resources, labor costs, and production in the
interest of cutting costs, expanding one's market, and avoiding
taxation. All of this we know because the media have been reporting on Big Oil, Monsanto, Agribusiness, and the exploitation of the natural resources and human labor by corporations in
myriad countries around the world. The problem is that know-

ing about the need for capitalism to grow if it wants to keep its profits is not enough to understand why a culture would find it attractive and allow it to expand beyond a nation's borders, what its value might be for a society as a whole, or what might be done to constrain it or force it to acknowledge the consequences of its operations on other peoples and social interests. The corporate systems of business and finance that have developed globally simply have no brakes, no self-control, no way to curb their extravagancies, no concept of the consequences of their exploitations and predations for a fragile world in danger of sustaining injuries it is not able to heal.

I have made a summary of Marx's description of capitalism and brought it up to date with a few illustrations in order to let the full spectrum of actions, statements, attitudes, and economic events that are now overwhelming our news media register *as a system*. It is capitalism as a system of interlocking social agencies, relations, and practices that marks the genius of Marx's analysis. Starting with the obvious changes that were taking place for the worker when moved from rural life in feudal society to factory labor in the city, Marx was able to trace the changes to social relations that occurred at every new level and social configuration throughout the entire society. That he was able to link these changes as a system of newly fashioned social roles resulted in a picture of the *structure* of the industrial society that reveals the internal logic of capitalism. Eventually, his description of the people coming to terms with their new roles at every level and position of employment and power in the society became a picture of the social spirit of a people that looked like an *ethos*. Marx did not philosophize about such, but as he traced the connections among the social rolls and relations within this structure, the words he found to name and describe elements of the system soon became definitional terms. We are indebted to his diligent labors and genius for the terms we still use in talking about economic systems, concepts such as *value, labor, commodity, surplus, wage, growth, profit, capital, investment,* and so forth. It is that description of the capitalistic system that we should have used to recognize the changes that took place in our society because of our response to the Second World War. It would have helped us understand the reasons for our surprising place of leadership among the nations and the success of our industries and economy in a much more sober and thoughtful way than we did. It would have made it possible to think more clearly about the challenges of the future and prepare for some sound ideological support for the important social programs somehow inaugurated by the Roosevelt administration.

We did not do so for several reasons. One is that, during the Cold War, Marx came to be associated with communism, communism was associated with Russia, and Russia was thought to be our mortal enemy. All of that McCarthyist ranting was largely rooted in our inability to think clearly about the challenges of the postwar situation. We did not have any social/political philosophy at hand with which to handle the hazy awareness of our own rise to global military power, much less the historic significance of the war for Western civilization. We could not even see that the reasons for our newly assumed superiority and leadership among the nations of the world were mainly due to accidents, not matters of great purpose and design. We refused to read Marx because we were frightened about his notions of revolution and communism as the way in which the "allied" nations would falter and end. We innocently included ourselves in that roster of "industrial" nations without ever having thought about ourselves that way. And we set the Marxists aside because they spent most of their time recommending communism and criticizing the more recent forms of industry's inability to share their profits with their laborers. That neither they nor Marx had a clear notion of the society they projected on the other side of "the revolution" did not keep them from their critique of capitalism. Our failure to see the consequences of this ideological issue was a shame, because, for Marx it was not communism as an ideal state that filled his mind and pages. The notion of communism was never spelled out, or intended, as a model society to compare with the industrialist societies he was analyzing, or as a clear vision of a social formation that worked in the interest of the common good. Those who picked up on the vague notion of *communism* and used it as an ideology, thinking to reshape the Western nations in the wake of the war, such as in Russia, could not wrest free from the traditional models of governance and authority they thought they were criticizing, and simply made a mess of their autocratic experiments. We cannot afford to let that recent messy chapter of Western social history keep us from seeing the value of a social vision for the well-being of the collective that might enable us to make a studied critique of the current extravagancies and dangers of our capitalistic system and work to develop another set of social values and interests.

The rise of capitalism in the wake of the Industrial Revolution can be explained without having to start with our current fixations on wealth and power, as if capitalism emerged *because* those were the values that motivated the inventors of the machines and the owners of the industries. These fixations built up slowly in the course of the historical development of capitalism for about two centuries. It is a rich history of activity in the interest of expanding our industries, inventing products, cultivating markets, arranging for employments, applying wages and profits to personal and family interests, struggling with budgets, and, in general, taking for granted what might be called experimentation in the workings of a new economy. It is difficult to find any particular fault at the personal level in this rich history to blame for the way in which it has come to its ending in our time, resulting in the social and environmental disruptions and despoliations that have finally caught our attention. Along the way, however, we can chart the steady development of capitalistic mentality by noting that the "value" of everything was translated into dollars, and that the "costs" that accrued in the processes of living became the frame of reference for thinking about all of one's financial security, plans, projects, and achievements. Our obsessions with wealth and power were caused by falling into the single focus on financial gain for thinking about one's objectives, a mind-set that has come to permeate the fluid atmosphere of our social and cultural systems. It is this single focus of human interests that underlies our unexpected acceptance and understanding of the way the world works, and our accommodation of the capitalistic system. This single focus of human interest is not a matter of being constantly conscious of the motivations driving our economic and social systems, nor of a self-awareness of one's own basic motivations. It is a shared mentality taken for granted that has grown accustomed to the way society has actually been working, a view that now works on the model of a mythic worldview.

I have read Marx and pondered his social theories, his ability to understand the human investments and motivations of the industrial society while, at the same time, describing the society as problematic for the working class and other human relations. It was a remarkable accomplishment. In the background, of course, he seemed to have an alternative social view in mind that he called "communism." But it has become clear in retrospect that he really did not have in mind a clear picture of a communistic society that he intended as an ideal or social vision that would (should) come about after the "revolution." He did have a very consistent sense of the human motivations and reasons driving the emergence of capitalism within the Western traditions, and he argued that their consequences for the workers as a class called for a dramatic change in the structures of a capitalistic society. But he also explained the history of the development of capitalism in ways that described the process as understandable. This dialectic between an understanding and a criticism of capitalism and capitalistic society has produced an amazingly rich and insightful intellectual tradition of cultural critique among Marxists and other intellectuals who are now currently involved in the cultural criticism of "modernism" and "postmodernism" as products of capitalism itself (see David Harvey, *The Condition of Postmodernity*; Fredric Jameson, *Postmodernism; or, The Cultural Logic of Late Capitalism*.) It is not that the picture Marx painted of capitalism in his time still works for the analysis of "late" capitalism required in our time. It is also not that his concept of communism is the place to start with our attempts to imagine an alternative society. Marx is important because he found a way to analyze and describe the effect of the capitalist practices upon the structure and workings of society as a whole, asking about what we might call its effect upon the quality of life in such a society. We are not yet able to follow his lead in this kind of description and critique. It has become too abstract for our single-focus sensibilities, risky for our investments in capitalism, threatening for our resistance to critical thought. We are not interested in any investigation of the motivations involved in social formations at the level of a fundamental social anthropology. But as an example of what a studied effort in social analysis might produce for us, the works of Marx have become very helpful. He studied the effect of the social changes of capitalism upon every human role and relationship: internal family relationships when moved to the city; workers and employers; the skills of labor and the wages offered by the owner; renters and the owners of apartments; the need for social agencies to address homelessness and poverty; the positions taken by the press and the intellectual community; the responses of government and governance; banking and the keeping of accounts for others. His conclusion was that the shift from exchange-trade to commodity capitalism created and then took advantage of the working class. It created a newly shaped world for which peasants were unprepared.

Since then, the machine age has so focused on economic accounts that interests in society as the human community where an entire range of family, social, and cultural values determined the quality of life have been overwhelmed as social concerns in need of attention. Thus the problems we are facing today are complex. Capitalism has won as the major manager of all of our pursuits. Every level of society thinks of the costs and constraints of their projects in its terms. All accounts of social and cultural values are now fully and completely thought about in terms of their beholden-ness and contribution to the capitalistic system of valuation. The success of capitalism is not merely obvious in its matter-of-fact acceptance by the populace as a whole; it is also strongly profiled in the way every major institution in our society is now managed as a private business. Such is the case with social institutions and practices that traditionally were not thought of as businesses at all. Many standard projects and institutions had their own ways of being supported, many by the noncommercial investments of energies on the part of interested persons, some by government funding in the interest, say, of education, others by the donations of loyal supporters who shared interests in the purposes of an institution. This was true of private colleges, state universities, public schools, hospitals, medical institutes, and many scientific research institutes. In the case of civic agencies, such as police departments, fire departments, park services, civic administrations for legislation and governance, the support was understood to be the responsibility of the people as a whole, raised by means of taxation and other methods. All of that has changed. The criticisms that now occur in a constant stream of demonstrations, opinion articles, movements, and incidents of protest are the result of particular grievances about the failure of government and big businesses to address their violations of legal and social issues, such as failures in matters of regulating the economy, constraining the exploitation of natural resources, addressing serious human rights issues, and so forth. Then there are civil rights issues and others having to do with care for the poor, control of military expenditures, arms trading, outsourcing industries, abuse of workers in foreign countries, and so on and on. A study by Paul Hawken has listed the thousands of associations that have arisen around the world as protest movements and agencies for change by citizens trying to correct the state of affairs (*Blessed Unrest: How the Largest Social Movement in History Is Restoring Grace, Justice, and Beauty to the World*). The declarative "is restoring" sounds good. One needs to know, however, that Hawken's study is actually a thorough rehearsal of both the energies invested in protest movements and the intransigence of conservatives in politics and business when confronted by these grassroots movements. Thus, despite his optimistic subtitle, there is no indication of a structural change to the way society is functioning or of a systematic plan for substantive change. There is no clarity about whom or what to blame.

This means that we are caught in a curious conundrum. On the one hand capitalism as a system of practices and thinking has come to define our primary social interest as a nation. On the other we find ourselves upset with the ways in which other social values and interests are no longer working as once they were. We have not been able to analyze our capitalistic system to the point of asking whether its single-focus fixation on wealth and power is enough to motivate the human interests and energies required now in order to address social issues. We cannot imagine how an alternative society might work in the interest of living peacefully together, much less how the extremely productive capitalistic system could be used to achieve and guarantee such a common-good society. And supposing that the single-focus fixation is actually enough to motivate the energies needed to construct a society, what kind of society could it be? Could it provide a vision or picture of a society that guarantees the common good without addressing the extreme imbalances in wages and welfare that capitalism has produced? Or what to do about the loss of erstwhile cultural features such as an orientation to one's history, literature, the arts, religions, and personal and social identities that the postmodernists have identified as having been erased by late capitalism? We need a vision in which a full range of human interests, labors, and creativities is recognized as important for social formation and rewarded as features of a common good society. Only then will the many progressive projects now in place have a chance to cohere as contributions to a new polyculture. Working toward such a vision, the policies required for its execution would give our politics meaning again, and the necessary *constraints* on our current fascinations with power and wealth could come into play as necessary features of our society. To be sure, this would require a marked change in our average mentality, one that would begin to make a difference even (and especially) in the minds of legislators and CEOs. We would need to work at the task of thinking about all of our social interests and daring to project lowercase utopias for discussion. But just think of living among the cultural productions of a polycultural world as a multicultural people in a society organized for the common good.

THE NATION

We now use the term *national interests* as if we all know what that means. It certainly has the connotation of a large comprehensive social unit of government. But as soon as "government" is mentioned, the term that comes to mind is not simply *nation* but *nation-state*. When we look at all the "national interests" that have surfaced since the Second World War, then, it is clear that the concerns circle around the interest of the "nation-state," not the nation as defined by Merriam Webster or Wikipedia. There *nation* refers to a people, with its traditions and cultural history, living together in a place understood to be their land. In the interests of our nation-state, however, the list looks somewhat different. "National interests" include matters of finance, defense, protecting our industries and corporations abroad, intelligence collecting agencies, surveillance, secrecy, the military, and so on. Not much nation-state interest in education, the arts, welfare, poverty, land misuse, health insurance, minimum wages, collective well-being, care for the planet's ecology, tax reform, and exploring the reasons for violent behavior. So we do have a most interesting social interest project on our hands, thinking about the *national interests* of our nation-state.

It is true that, in light of our history, the term *nation-state* may be a misnomer. It was a helpful designation for the European nations that were separated from one another by the dissolutions of the larger medieval kingdoms and empires and so had to find ways to govern themselves more or less independently. Thus they became "states" and spent two or three hundred years working at the task of turning into nation-states without becoming fascist dictatorships or going to war. That challenge is still in progress, even though the remarkable display of success with the European Union should have shown all parties what a difference such a restructuring of governance could make for quality of life together without abusing national and ethnic interests.

It is even the case that most of the European nations, erstwhile kingdoms, have not had to dismantle their royal houses. They have, instead turned them into fairy-tale reminders of their earlier histories and coddled them with celebrity status in an ongoing national drama of courtship and intrigue. The United States was neither a "nation" nor a kingdom from which to morph as a nation-state with a fairy-tale past. We formed a "federal union" out of a disparate collection of colonies on a "new land" where Native Americans "had to be" pushed aside and African Americans were imported to work the lands of the South as slaves. The independence of the states (for we did learn to call the colonies "states") was the major political issue at the time, not only from the king of England but from one another. Their economies were variously grounded and allowed to take care of themselves. Thus there was not much of a big picture to start with. Our leaders and intellectuals did manage to convene a Continental Congress, compose a Constitution, and make it possible for the Bill of Rights to expand as the subsequent experimentations in nation-state building progressed. But it took some time for the vastness of the continent to become "our land" and lay the foundation for a national story to evolve from "The Star-Spangled Banner" (1814) to "America the Beautiful" (1893/1911), where "brotherhood" "crown thy good" "from sea to shining sea."

Had we lingered there with the peoples, materials, achievements, and challenges of the nineteenth century long enough to construct a social democracy for our embryonic nation-state, we might have developed a social vision of which we could be proud. But the twentieth century turned our attention to industry and war. The two world wars called us into assuming our current role as the "world leader." The "leadership" was a matter of largesse and military might. Our infrastructures were not destroyed as those of the European and Eastern nations were. Our amazing capacity to quickly build industries for the wars could be put to use for the postwar era of affluence. And our military, already stationed around the world, could be put to use as our ambassadors of "democracy" and the "American Way of Life." Thus the nineteenth-century elements of nation-state building were not worked through as a project of social formation that would have been seen in retrospect as "historic." Its energies were taken up by the "military-industrial complex" that soon overwhelmed the state, the people, the economy, and the self-understanding of the nation with the noise of guns and gadgetry. The twentieth century did succeed in painting a big picture of the globe waiting for our "leadership." And it had no trouble in expanding our military, corporate industries, political and ideological "missions." A sense of power and righteousness became pervasive, uncanny souvenirs from Christendom. Some flags still fly on the Fourth of July, but "patriotism" has withered as a sign of loyalty to our posture of superiority within this big picture. Instead, *patriotic* has become a term used for conservative single-issue rhetorics that border on the hysterical, as if there are threats to the nation we once were. One does not find many voices cheering the global picture of the world we have painted, or parading for the society in which we now live.

We have used the term *social interests* as a concept of importance for a general theory of a people's social formation and its mythic rationale or culture. It may therefore seem odd to include *national interests* in the list of those social interests that are providing major cognitive and attitudinal features of the current culture of the United States. *National interests* is certainly not used in common parlance as a concept of importance for thinking about our society as a culture, or as a feature of our society that may be questioned in relation to the interests of the people. It is a term closely tied to the political interests of the nation-state, and all of these interests have been revealed as defensive. We the people have grown accustomed to the term as a cipher for legitimate state interests in a time of unexpected conflicts with other nations and peoples, as well as for defense against what we have come to call "terrorists" at home and abroad. Instead of understanding the reasons these other nations and peoples have had for their hostilities against the United States, our nation has taken offense and reacted defensively as if the others are not able to understand and appreciate our interests and interventions. This situation has succeeded in turning our "national interests" into a list of policies that now threaten the erstwhile political and humanitarian values (or "social interests") that we the people thought our nation represented, such as civil rights, *habeas corpus*, justice, freedom, and so forth. Thus the slippage in reference from the *interests* expected of the *nation* in the well-being of the people, to the *national interests* of the nation as a military machine in the interests of our industrial corporations is revealing. We can use this slippage to advantage as we proceed with our analysis.

Among the many instances of social interest swirling around among us and making a difference in our ambience as a society, *national interests* is the only term that fully recognizes one of the institutions involved as having interests in making an effective difference for the collective. *Nation* may be the only term in usage that carries the connotations of the society as a whole, aspects of its structure and governance, the social formation to which we "belong" that is worthy of protection and defense. That the federal rationales for protection and defense are seriously in danger of violating the democratic and humanistic values they claim to be protecting is not a matter for castigation, given the embryonic state of our social democracy and the more or less unintentional mistakes we have made in our global behaviors since the Second World War. But it does give us the opportunity to recognize the reasons for the people's recent discontent with the "government." Many are concerned about the current chaos of violence in the world, the state of our economy at home, the threat that our industries pose to the ecological health of the planet, and the sorry scenes of distress and killings at home and around the world of nations. Many would like to see our current list of *national interests* redirected toward the social issues that these interests have unintentionally occasioned. So yes, the "national interests" of our government need to be included in the roster of "social interests" we are exploring precisely because they have in mind our "big picture," and they are in league with the many other interests that have generated the social issues we want to address. More will have to be said about this in Chapters 5 and 6.

We have not covered all of the histories of all of the *social interests* making an effective difference in our society today. But we have sketched the major traditions involved in the dynamic composition of our society and culture. With the Renaissance two important streams of interest entered the picture, notions of creativity and mentality that are still with us. The one is the shift from the mythic concept of the world as an organic entity to the philosophic orientation on individualism. The other is an increasing fascination of what we now call "the arts." It has been the cultivation of the individual psyche and the arts that has given our culture its social interests in literature, theater, art, and the various forms of aesthetic productions. This is the feature of modernity and postmodernity that has fascinated our current cultural critics in their analysis of the mentality of our society. See Chapter 6.

Science and capitalism are so pervasive and dominant in our society both as practices and as mentalities that reasons for their inclusion in a list of our "social interests" is not a surprise. It is important only as a reminder of the ways in which the mentality of the people takes them for granted and cooperates implicitly with their own interests. In the next chapter their own interests will be engaged in more detail, given the fact that each can be reduced to basic human motivations that need to be acknowledged, and that are now in conflict with one another. We will see that neither of these social interests, organized and working in their present form, is serving the interests of a sustainable common-good society.

Religion has been included as the remnants of a mentality that persists even after the institutional modes of the Western Christian religions have lost their attractiveness for a majority of the people. This presents us with a curious manifestation of a mentality grounded in an obviously dysfunctional "cultural tradition" that has not been relinquished by segments of the population despite its lack of social logic.

The use of the term *national interests* has been included as a clear reference to the social interests of the federal government because it projects the only big picture we still have of our nation as a *society*, and because the big picture it projects includes, or is meant to include, all of the social interests at work within it. It is this comprehensive connotation of the term *nation* that gives the big picture the sense of a totality, even though the several separate national interests describe a political state. That the federal government has not been able to govern many of these separate activities in the interest of a common-good society is a critical issue that will help us understand why the current shape of our social interests and cultural mentality requires an alternative vision of the big picture.

Taken together, the histories of these *social interests* are enough to suggest a picture of our current social situation as an assemblage of projects with separate logics entangled within our practices and purposes as a society. In the next chapter we can move to an analysis of the social issues now being discussed in public as the result of these entanglements. But first a few observations can be made about the selection we have discussed. One is that these social interests are extremely complex matters in which the interests of individuals, groups of individuals, and state and governmental agencies converge. Another is that none of these social interests has produced an articulate myth of its own sufficient to be given a central role in the society as a whole. It is possible, of course, that we are very close to thinking of ourselves as members of a "corporate America," and finding that belonging to such a corporate state might be a sufficient *raison d'être* with which to work and plan for the future. But the vociferous expressions of popular and academic uneasiness with such a thought tell us that we are not there yet. And a third observation is that the awareness of what has come to be called a "social issue" is now pervasive. This awareness includes a number of ideas having to do with the "cause" of the matter, usually to the detriment of those thought to be responsible for the situation. Such ideas are often regarded as the only way of understanding the reasons for a failure of the social system, or for imputing weakness, failure, or even self-serving corruption to the person(s) or agents in charge, as if the reason has to be a matter of morals, ethics, or character. In the next chapter I intend to put forth another set of reasons for the great number of social issues agitating the sense of dismay that has become part of the ambience of our time. These reasons will be found in the overlaps that exist among the various social interests of this chapter, and the conflicts that result in the disparate "logics" involved as they impinge upon one another and upon our interest in making sense of our world. It may well be that the unexpressed (often unconscious) logics of these social systems as organizations impede our attempts to analyze their underlying motivations. Thus it may be time to ask about these underlying motivations that have contributed to the erasure of those patterns of thought and projects we once took for granted. It is this Western tradition as a common culture that has become problematic in our attempts to analyze and understand the many specific interests, activities, and histories now playing out in the world. The thesis of this book is that we are in need of another set of social interests capable of maintaining a multicultural society without the need for power abuse, guns, and violence.

5 SOCIAL ISSUES

The media are currently painting two big pictures about the state of the world. One is the scattershot approach to the news about yet another sensational event without explanation. This picture has no theme or story line to give it any narrative logic. The events just pop up for immediate attention, then fade while others appear. The sensational events do include large numbers of public demonstrations, attempts by the police to control the mobs, violence, and courtroom scenes, thus transforming the scattershot approach into a peppery picture of the world that suggests constant unresolved conflict as a kind of theme coursing through the separate news and advertising events. The other picture of the world painted by the media is a disconnected series of people posing as their own alter egos in a display of their sexual attractiveness, sporting competence, or business sagacity and in some present moment of inviting the viewer to see them taking pleasure in their display of themselves. Most are smiling, constantly smiling, cool and competent, except, of course, when the situation threatens violence. Then the masks change to match the cinema of guns against evil monsters, but never with the look of victimhood, always with the look of superior power. When this fantastic display of virtual reality goes this far, the male with the gun can take on the features of his apelike predecessors or even of the primate monsters now becoming the supermen of the horror show. Neither of these media pictures is much help in understanding why the world produces so much violence and seems to be destroying itself, or whether these pictures are the only ones possible, the media having covered up other activities that belong to the worlds of constructive social activities and interests. What these pictures suggest is that there are no forces in the worldscape capable of constraining titillation and violence, and at the people level there is only oneself and one's fantasy as a means of escape.

As for governments, the age of empires is about to pass, and it was these erstwhile social formations that once were capable of painting big pictures of divine (benign) power and control. But America's short stint of "world leadership," born of incredible naïveté about its accidental role after the Second World War, is over. The election of President Obama was a sign of sanity, and his foreign policies to mollify hostilities abroad and bring our wars to an end were judicious to a degree, but only as attempts to be true to his earlier philosophies in some small way. Now we see that neither the pre-Obama world vision of the American military empire, nor the vision of the world now in view responding to Obama's attempts to disengage, can tell us what role governments might play in repainting that bigger picture. Poor John Kerry, the peacemaker secretary of state, constantly on the move, flying down out of the sky to tell opposition leaders the compromises they need to make with each other (and others) in order to keep the American show on the road. The media only hint at his lack of power except for the money he must have in his attaché. Putin is pictured there in Russia, presiding over the threat of losing yet another chip from the erstwhile Soviet Empire, and looking stern.

So the media do not give us much of a picture of ourselves and the world to work with if we want to explore the reasons for the social issues that *are* mentioned occasionally, such as gun violence, global warming, educational curricula, foreign policy, wars, military spending, and a sense of the future. We can link *social issues* of these kinds to the list of *social interests* discussed in the previous chapter. These organized interests can be analyzed as practices where conflicts among them occur. The thesis of this chapter will be that because each of these large-scale social interests in our history has developed its own big picture and rationale for its pursuits and practices, the overlap with other social interests at a particular site or location can challenge its control of its own field of interests. In this chapter it will be possible to identify a number of these interorganizational interests where conflicts occur. In the next chapter a more detailed analysis of these social issues will be possible in order to ponder ways to address these conflicts in general.

GUN VIOLENCE

Gun violence has become a common occurrence in America. The killings in which a number of people are gunned down in a public place send shock waves throughout the entire nation. The media document the event but find it difficult to uncover the motivations involved. The names of the schools, churches, public festivals, and other places where these shootings take place become symbols of the occurrences. These reminders stack up to tell us that something has gone wrong. The people sense this problem but are not able to grasp the reasons behind it. The first response to the shock at one of these incidents is incredulity, "How could that have happened in this place?" Subsequent discourse begins to surface fear and frustration because the reasons for such incidents are incomprehensible. The second response is that "it must not happen again!" All of us would probably understand this sentiment, but no one knows how to make sure that it would not happen again. Many people think that gun control is the answer, and they are partly right. Gun control makes sense for many reasons and might well help curb the magnitude of this violence. The European nations have practiced gun control for many years as a matter of course without having to justify the concept. But attempts to legislate gun control in America have run into hostile opposition, and the few bills passed have not been successful. So there must be social reasons behind these outbursts of violence that are peculiar to America, as well as for our inability to control them. These reasons must lodge in the history, practices, and attitudes of our society: reasons that we have not acknowledged or been able to address. The present discussion is an attempt to explore some of these reasons. We need to understand the social histories and issues involved before asking what we might do to control them.

We can start with an analysis of the debate about gun control in Congress and the media. We will see that this debate swirls around reasons *for* guns and *against* gun control. There is little argument *for* gun *control* except as a measure to stop the violence. Although this public debate does not get to the heart of the matter, it does touch upon features of our attitudes about guns that point to issues beyond the current situation, issues that can be traced back into our history of having guns and our fascination with them. These are features we will want to explore in some depth. But first we have to be clear about the current use of the term *gun control* as a legal and marketing prescription, for that will tell us why the bills that have been proposed are not enough.

Several proposals for gun control have made their way to the Congress of the United States since Ronald Reagan's Brady Gun Control Bill of 1983. Most of these bills have consisted of four major prescripts. (1) The sale of guns to felons and the mentally ill is not allowed. (2) Felons and the mentally ill are not allowed to have or own guns no matter how procured. (3) Some form of "background check" is required on every person wanting to purchase a gun. The retailer is required to perform this check, normally by calling the police or FBI to determine that the person's history is "clean," that is, not on the FBI's lists of felons and the police's lists of the mentally ill. (There is also some indication that "terrorists" are now understood to be included in these lists of inappropriate gun owners, but I have not been able to determine how the local retailer is supposed to know whether a customer is or is not a "terrorist.") (4) The identity of the person purchasing a gun is required, and must be logged, along with the type of gun purchased, as a record of the transaction. In some cases this seems to serve as a kind of "license," should the police ever question a particular person's possession of a gun.

As one can see, these bills focus on the commercial issues of transaction, ownership, personal identity, and a control of the market in the sale of guns. This has not kept gun sales from booming. In our population of 311 million people there are now roughly 300 million firearms owned by civilians. And these bills have not solved the gun violence problem. Two-thirds of all murders in the United States are committed with firearms. In 2011, the last year for which I have seen the records of the Centers for Disease Control and Prevention, 11,000 Americans died in gun-related killings, and there were 19,766 suicides by firearms. Judging from most of the stories reported to us by the media, the persons involved in these shootings were not considered "felons" or "criminally insane" until *after* the violence. If so, our gun control bills do not even address the social issues generating gun violence, much less curb its incidence.

So it seems that Congress has not been able to enact a bill that can address all features of the phenomenon and stop the violence. As a matter of fact, many of the more thoughtful bills proposed have simply failed to pass in any form. That is because many members of Congress are beholden to the National Rifle Association (NRA) and other gun lobbies, those who do not want gun control in any form and have always sought to tone down, incapacitate, or kill any bill for control. The result has been that guns have not been "kept out of the hands" of people who might use them in murders and suicides. We may not be aware that the picture we have of indiscriminate gun violence is a quite recent phenomenon, sensationalized by the media who tend to focus on the character of the individual person, the kind of weapon used, and suspicions of racial motivations that may have been involved. As a matter of fact, however, we have had a gun-friendly culture for much of our history, a culture that did not associate the gun primarily with violence. It is the use of the gun in the incidents of indiscriminate gun violence that has "called for" gun control. And, as a matter of fact, these incidents are now in danger of turning our troubled society into a culture of violence.

We should be asking ourselves what there is about having guns that we have found so acceptable. We take guns so much for granted that it seems we cannot imagine a society without guns in the hands of the people. But now that the issues of gun violence and gun control are being discussed by our legislators and media, the NRA has taken it upon itself to argue for the right to have guns. The reasons given are intended as arguments against government controls, but they reveal much more about our fascination with guns as a nation, for their arguments touch upon the place of guns in our society from its beginning. The first is that the "right to bear arms" is enshrined in the Constitution. This is actually a contested, self-serving, if not cynical "interpretation" of the Second Amendment. It clearly violates the original intention of the amendment, which was about the right for the new states, not individuals, to have "militias." Since the United States did not have an established army, but had found it necessary to fight the British in the Revolutionary War, it seemed reasonable to state in the Constitution that the states had the "right to bear arms." The NRA's self-serving reading of this amendment might be excused because of the change in social ambience from that time to this, and because of our current focus upon society as a collection of "free individuals," but it cannot be excused when thinking about the constitutional law of our society. Whether this appeal to the Second Amendment in favor of the gun industry is due to intellectual failure or cynical ploy, arguments against it on the part of our legal scholars have not been able to curb its influence in the Congress or the press. That is because the NRA is waving the flag of the "right" to individual freedoms in support of the "right" to own a gun. In this case, however, the NRA is close to implying that those asking for gun control are threatening the constitutional charter of our society. The confusion this creates in the mind of the populace is enough to cover for the real interest of the NRA, namely the protection of the gun industries and international arms trade at $60 billion a year.

There is a second stream of argumentation that is meant to come to terms with the current situation of gun violence run amuck. The cliché has it that "guns don't kill people; people kill people." That gets part of it right, of course, and lets us know that the NRA has taken notice of the use of guns for killing people. But as the people using guns to kill people became the problem that needed to be addressed, and especially after the more recent events of mass killings, the NRA had to shift tactics from rifles for sportsmen to revolvers for civilians. And wouldn't you know, now the "reason" for having a gun was for personal "protection" (that is, from other guns). This is taking the symbol of the use of guns in modern warfare as justification for the use of guns in personal conflict. The notions of "offense" and "defense" in warfare could be applied when thinking of the dangers that "terrorists," enemies, or other persons threatened. In the case of the school shootings, the NRA's proposal was to have an armed guard in every classroom. And in the case of individual incidents the proposal has been for everyone to have a gun "for protection" or to "stand your ground." Jennifer Carlson, in an article in the *Los Angeles Times* about "the NRA's hidden power" (January 3, 2013), states that "the National Rifle Association is the national leader in training those who choose to get . . . a license [to carry a concealed weapon]." She explains that more than 750,000 Americans go through some kind of NRA training every year. Most of the forty state laws for such licensing "implicitly or explicitly require people to get NRA training." And the NRA's basic training in handling a revolver incorporates a philosophy used to justify its use for killing. From the training manual used in Michigan: "If you do defend yourself, it is important in the aftermath to remember: You are a good person. . . . You are a moral person. Your attacker was the one who chose a lifestyle and sequence of events that led to this encounter. You were morally justified in protecting yourself and your family." How is that for linking our Christian mentality concern for personal morality and righteousness with the military atmosphere of "shock and awe" in the interest of "defending" the righteous nation and justifying a moral murderer? And so it is that military encounters abroad have come to determine the way we think about our culture of gun violence at home. I do not need to elaborate the ways in which this culture continues to spiral into ratifying self-protection by "standing your ground" despite the studies that say it does not work, that the "fast draw" is impossible when "attacked" by a gunman, and that owning guns increases fear and violence without providing protection. It appears, then, as if we are left with our culture of guns in hand and do not know how to control it, or even to realize what difference it is making for the ambience of our society.

Part of the reason that the NRA gets by with such impertinence is due to its long-standing representation of our use of the rifle by farmers and hunters for work and sport. We do need to see this as a third reason for the NRA's pro-gun position. It has not been set forth as raucously as the first two argumentations because it rides on a long tradition of familiarity with the use of guns by our hunters, farmers, and cowboys in the "taking" of the West. On the way, hunting and fishing became the practice of "settlers" in search of shelter, food, and then sport. These traditions underlie the NRA's subtle reminders of the rifle as the symbol for hunting as a sport, along with the Forest Service's promotion of hunting as a sport, magazines of the *Field and Stream* type, and the many private agencies that cater to the sportsman. Since every adolescent on the farms and in the rural villages of the continent learned about handling the rifle with caution and skill, a deep attachment to the hunting rifle is the primary reason for the hue and cry not to "take our guns away from us." It is a sentiment about as "American" as "Mother and Apple Pie." You cannot counter such an attachment by means of rational argumentation. But now that the issue is not hunting, but gun violence, this long tradition of fondness for the rifle cannot be used as an argument against gun control either.

There is, however, another familiar use of the rifle on our way West that is not so innocent. The various stages of our "taking" of the West have been studied by Henry Nash Smith in *Virgin Land*. From Thomas Jefferson to Frederick Jackson Turner, Smith collects the letters and essays of politicians, the poems and orations of public figures, and the novels of authors about the legendary "heroes" of the West. He traces the changes in the conceptions of the West and discusses the social histories that gave them birth, as well as their significance for the various self-understandings of the United States as an emerging nation having to justify the possession of an entire continent. These conceptions or "myths" include the West as Wilderness (west of the Allegheny Mountains), as Garden (Paradise, in keeping with the biblical Eden), as Passage (to the Pacific, in keeping with the post-Columbus idea of circling the globe to India, clearly articulated by Jefferson), as Fee Simple Lands (to link the Homestead Act to the economic advantage of farming), as Economic Safety Valve (the Midwest as continuing stimulus for an agrarian nation in competition with European industrial economies), as Mountain Man Country (the Far West as lands yet to be exploited for mining and ranching), and Manifest Destiny (a constant theme since the 1840s). There is frequent mention of the "fight with Indians," but Smith does not emphasize it as an encounter that ends with killing. That, however, is a standard conclusion to conflict with Native Americans in both the earlier myths of the West and the later Western cowboy novel. Apparently Smith was not comfortable with this feature of the Western story, choosing rather to emphasize the various myths that determined the policies of our governments with regard to the Western lands during the period from about 1830 to 1890. But the features of the Western novel are not difficult to trace through this literature discussed by Smith because it gathers up the characterizations of the heroes such as Boone and Leatherstocking who learned to live apart from "civilization." These heroes find that the Indians who were already there in the "Wilderness" can get in the way as "civilization" begins to advance. These heroes create the mystique of the single individual who does not need (or want) the support of the "civilization" left behind, but will have to protect it should the "savages" threaten it. The early heroes are not yet cast as "cowboys," for the cowboys appear only later, when the prairie turns to range land for cattle and sheep herding. But the plots of the early hero tales do prepare for the later mystique of the lone cowboy with only his pony and gun to defend the weak and threatened settlements of the West from the Indians and Outlaws. Thus the appearance of *The Virginian*, a story set in the West, written by Owen Wister in 1902, and assigned as classroom reading in our public schools for many subsequent decades, set the pace for the Western at the very beginning of the twentieth century. The Western cinemas (from the 1930s), and radio series such as *The Lone Ranger* etch the shoot-out scenes and the barroom brawls into our minds as the standard climax of the Western plot. These are scenes in which the "bad guys" force the Western hero to fight. That the hero wins with a fast draw and a silver bullet marks the Western as the American narrative of individualism, the single person who succeeds on his own, and killing as the solution to his conflicts with the "bad guys" who stand in the way.

Will Wright has analyzed the basic structure of the Western and four of its variants in *Sixguns and Society*. He shows us that changes in the characterization of the heroes in the Western followed the social changes during the previous century without changing the structure of the plot. The characterization of the hero and his social contexts evolves beginning with the idealization of individualism early in the century, through the rise of the city as the center of our economic livelihoods, and the emergence of capitalism, to the "corporation man." In every story, the "cowboy" emerges from the edges of "civilization" in trouble, and although he is not the one who threatens the civilization, he encounters the hostility of the "bad guys" who do threaten it, and he has to kill them before moving on. Reading the summaries as a set, one is overwhelmed by the simplicity of the "climactic event": it is always a fast draw and a kill. These events happen matter-of-factly and are easily described as the fitting climax to conflict. They reveal, in fact, the model of our imagined solution to social hindrances and conflicts. The solution is to get rid of the problem by gunning it down. We have become inured to the scenes of shooting to kill in the Western novel, because this novel draws upon themes from the very beginning of American literature about the West, and it romanticizes the cowboy-Indian encounters as part of the story of our manifest destiny.

But now that the Western has given us the basic plot for the entertainment media, as Wright has demonstrated, one can no longer avoid the films, videos, and programs in which an encounter with some monster provides the plot, and the "thrill" of gun violence takes care of it. One cinema critic at the *Los Angeles Times* has even written, in a feature criticized by some thoughtful and sensitive readers, that the cinema of violence should not be thought harmful to our society because it is only reflecting that society; she finds the violence "thrilling" herself, and enjoys watching it. So that is where we are: the media's cultivation of a social-psychological mentality wherein monsters, exterminations, and killings constitute thrilling entertainment.

Repeated instances of gun violence and growing awareness of our gun culture have prompted advocates for gun control to ask for legislation. They are, however, finding it difficult to make their case. The reason is quite complex. It has to do with the current state of our society in light of the recent history of the Western nations and our culture's lack of a collective agreement about guns and many other matters. I have touched upon some of these matters already, but others quickly come to mind. When investigating the circumstances involved in these events, we notice factors of cultural and racial interaction, demographic changes, economic inequality, unemployment, the withering of welfare, posttraumatic stress syndrome, anger, vengeance, and the need by the perpetrators of violence to make "statements" to the "world" about why the violence was called for. Cross-cultural ideological conflicts have also been identified as possible motivations. It has become clear that our nation is confronting a challenging national and international environment without a social vision to guide us. We have lost our big picture of a stable society that supports human values as a matter of course. Our psychologists and culture analysts are close to identifying such social ills as criminality, insanity, terrorism, and mental illness of many kinds as features of a dysfunctional society. So it may be that our inability to imagine gun control is due to our inability to imagine a healthy society.

That means that two questions need to be asked. One is whether a social democracy needs to have guns in everyone's hands. The second is whether a society that does not need or allow guns in everyone's hands is still possible in America. At the end of my books and articles that seek to engage just such social issues against the backdrop of what I have come to call (a dysfunctional) Christian mentality, I have frequently asked the reader to think with me briefly about such questions. I have found that it is difficult for the reader to think about another picture of society that looks something like our experiment in "social democracy" but does not have the social problems we are encountering. I have not been able to spell out more than a sketch of such a society, and certainly not an agenda for ways to reshape our present structure. But in this case, the issue of whether gun control is thinkable, I need to suggest that this is one of the more obvious differences between the United States and the social democracies of central and northern Europe. Having lived there for a few years while pursuing my education in religion and culture studies, I can attest that Europeans do not feel the need to own guns in order to see themselves as protected and safe. The governments may be indebted to the harsh lessons learned from the wars of the twentieth century, of course, and they have not had to parry histories similar to that of our American "taking" of the West and our resultant fondness for rifles. But whatever the combination of histories and thinking about firearms, it is simply the case that the European nations have developed various forms of social democracy in which the people do not need guns in order to feel or be safe. And in the United Kingdom, where even the bobbies do not have guns, civil liberties and safety have not been diminished by their many Assizes of Arms and Firearms Acts since 1181. All European nations allow guns for hunters and "shooting clubs," but prohibit them for other purposes. Why is it that we have not studied the sanity of their achievements in this regard? Why is it that we have not noticed the insanity of our American fascination with the gun and our wholesale manufacturing of weapons for international arms trade? Do we really think either are doing any good in the world, that we need to be engaged in such business? Is it not time for some gun control in America and the regulation of our arms trade? We would need an alert, strong, and sensible Congress, of course, something we do not currently have. But were it possible, such legislation could actually be the start of the conversation we need to have in general about "regulation" and "social democracy" in the interest of "well-being" and what we might call the "common good." The issue of gun control should not be a matter of special interests. It should be a matter of social interests, and that would require the Congress of the United States to legislate its regulation.

PLANET EARTH

Planet Earth has been talking back to the industrial civilization of the West. America has been having trouble hearing what the planet is saying to us. That is because Western civilization has not been attuned to its effects upon the earth's ecology and climate. It apparently did not need to consider the possible damage to the planet's balance of natural forces before the Industrial Revolution. Prior civilizations responded to extinctions by moving on to find other resources to exploit. It seems there was always enough animals, grasses, arable lands, trees, fish, and minerals to satisfy the needs of smaller tribes and simpler societies. It was the Industrial Revolution that introduced huge changes in the social systems and patterns of life of the West, changes that have had marked effects as well upon the ecologies of the natural order around the globe. The Euro-American peoples have been dealing with these changes in our social structures and patterns of human life for the past two centuries at the political, social, and industrial levels. And from these collective efforts an array of social institutions has developed to translate the older feudal, aristocratic, and monarchial kingdoms into nation-states. Grappling with these changes in the modes of industry, production, commerce, and governance has occupied most of our energies and ingenuities, leaving little time for attention to the changes that have been taking place in the natural world. We now know, however, that these changes in the life systems of planet earth are direct results of our industrial civilization and its exploitation of the natural resources of the planet. And our scientists are telling us that if we allow our commercial drives to continue at the present pace and in the current ways, the changes they are making to earth will make it impossible for the planet to sustain our civilization.

I have been looking for some analysis of this situation that explains why we do not alter course, and how it can be that we cannot find the words even to introduce a discussion of the issue at the political level. What I have found instead is a burgeoning number of essays, opinion articles, and books of the crisis and urgency genres, using the first person plural imperatives of the "We must" and "We should" variety without a recognition that the collective "we" they address is not listening intently to what they are saying. Many of these are studied books and essays, however, such as Jeremy Rifkin's *Entropy*; Joseph Tainter's *The Collapse of Complex Societies*; Clive Hamilton's *Requiem for a Species*; Chris Hedges's "The Myth of Human Progress" (*Truthdig*, January 10, 2013); and Bill McKibben's "Time Is Not on Our Side" (*TomDispatch*, January 6, 2013). The data are documented in the reports of the National Climate Assessment and Development Advisory Committee. The list of threatening consequences to our exploitations is sobering: storms and the inundation of coastal cities; droughts and the shrinking of arable lands; air and water quality pollution; global toxification; and a sharp reduction in population due to poverty, hunger, and disease. The industries in view have long since been identified: fossil and other fuel industries, chemical agribusinesses, and land-use developments of the deforestation variety, to say nothing of the threats to our planet by nuclear power plants, or to our civilizations by arms manufacturing. But this discourse could not answer my question about why we cannot stop our exploitations.

Then I came across an essay by Paul and Anne Ehrlich, professors and research scientists of biology at Stanford University and its Center for Conservation Biology, called "Can a Collapse of Global Civilization Be Avoided?" (*Proceedings of the Royal Society,* January 8, 2013). I found it a beginning for an analytic approach to the question of our inability to deal with climate change. That is because the Ehrlichs do not use the image of "collapse" to develop an essay in the genre of crisis and urgency, but stay within the deliberative mode of scientific discourse to explain "the array of environmental problems" that threaten our global civilization. The list is long, and for the most part comprises already familiar material, but the striking feature of the list is that it has been compiled and discussed by scientists who have ventured beyond their own fields of specialization to review the entire scope of environmental concerns and the social issues that threaten our "global civilization." They do not succeed in answering their own question as to whether "a collapse of global civilization [can] be avoided." But in course they make some poignant observations on particular features of our civilization as a complex social system, including industry, science, technology, the "technology-dependent global food system," business practices and ethics (which we might call capitalism, though they do not use the term), education, law, and "a rapidly growing movement towards religious orthodoxies that reject enlightenment values," which they call "endarken-ment." It is that sketching of the big picture in cool rationalistic mode which is unusual. They do it because they see that the envi-ronmental issues "are not separate problems; rather they interact in two gigantic complex adaptive systems: the biosphere system and the human socio-economic system." It is this big picture of our world that has been lacking in our recent political-religious discourse about our nation-state that I have found helpful about their essay. Their summary and conclusion to the essay is found in the abstract at its beginning, where they use the term *cultural change:*

> Environmental problems have contributed to numerous col-lapses of civilizations in the past. Now, for the first time, a global collapse appears likely. Overpopulation, overconsumption by the rich, and poor choices of technologies are major drivers; dramatic cultural change provides the main hope of averting calamity.

Readers of this book know by now of my own academic in-terests in culture and its relation to religion, especially in the way in which religious myths provide a culture with a big picture of a people's world within which their pursuits of "social interests" can be acknowledged and thought about. I found it striking that the Ehrlichs as scientists mentioned the pervasive "endarkenment" by conservative Christians as a factor of importance in frustrat-ing thinking about our social situation. The Christian's mythic worldview, pervasive as a mentality throughout our political and social systems, has frustrated critical thinking for two reasons. One is that the world that centers its interests is a transcendent order of divine power and sovereignty; the social world of human activities is important only as an arena of personal ethical struggle in light of the transcendent world. The other is that the attempt to turn the United States into a "Christian Nation" has produced sermons instead of arguments, thus the vindictive tones instead of visions for the change of culture the Ehrlichs call for. Thus the conservatives' picture of the Christian Nation neither fits the industrial society we have become in the past two hundred years nor suggests any vision of a multicultural world working toward the common good, much less a society taking care of the natural orders for the well-being of the human species. The current political ideology from Reagan to the Bushes and beyond, generated by the conservative religious "endarkenment," has only served the interests of the powerful elite on the aristocracy model. It blocks critical thinking about creating a multicultural society for the common good.

The Ehrlichs may not have struggled enough with this problem of a big picture for our "global civilization," whether one that pictures the reasons for the problematic state of affairs of our current world or one that attempts to project an alternative picture to help us envision the "cultural change" they see required. But they do discuss many of the individual problems they see in separate units of our American society, and they note that several segments of our society need to engage in critical thinking about their role in the larger picture of our social and natural worlds. For instance, they discuss the problems of mechanized food production, "unnecessarily environmentally damaging technologies," and the self-serving reasons a particular social institution claims for a resistance to understanding the threat of a collapse. Their overall message is that "a global collapse is perhaps *the* foremost challenge confronting humanity." They see that science has been involved in making possible both the industrial and the agrarian revolutions. And they call for natural scientists to collaborate with social scientists to explore the reasons for our inabilities to address the challenges that both revolutions have created. They mention the "cultural addiction to continued economic growth among the already well-off," and call upon our educational systems to confront the problem of educating the public about the facts of climate change, and of "finding frames and narratives to convince the public of the need to make changes."

I want now to take this analysis to another level. It is clear that the Ehrlichs work with rational logics both to describe the reasons for our threat to climate balance and to work toward a change in our culture. I would like to bring their observation about the complexity of our society into conversation with their underlying assumption that critical thinking is both possible and necessary. In my studies I too have worked with what I have called an intellectual anthropology in order to understand the ways in which myths (big pictures) rationalize practices basic for a society. Myths, however, work at a distance from practical reality by creating a big picture of an imaginary world that differs from everyday experience. This creates a gap or space between the two spheres of orientation and exists to call for and enable thinking about the social world. Since (1) the major myth for Western civilization has rationalized the interests of the Christian church and its erstwhile kingdoms on the medieval model, and since (2) the big picture painted by that myth is still somehow in mind as a cultural mentality for Americans even though the church no longer dominates society as a medieval kingdom, and since (3) that is the very picture that has caused our "endark-enment" by continuing to use its mythic logic to challenge the ethics (or lack of ethics, as the conservatives would have it) of our society, we find ourselves having to parry an archaic and worn-out picture of the world that no longer works. We do not have a clear picture of our world that comprehends the many social interests driving our busy pursuits. Some historians and political scientists are saying that we are living in a postmod-ern age in which the worldview and logic of the grand old nar-rative of Christian civilization no longer reflects the world we have constructed, and that that is the reason we are having trou-ble comprehending our society as a whole, much less our place in the geologic history of planet earth. We no longer think we even have a "society" with a common "culture." We are on our own under the flag of American "freedom," a freedom from all that has gone before and all the constraints that governments put upon a people, a freedom without content or direction except as the individual decides what she or he likes.

If so, the "endarkenment" caused by the remnants of Chris-tian mentality would be one reason why an awareness of global warming has not become a serious topic in policy discussions. A focus on the "creation" as divine spectacle, human history as divine drama, and the end of history as divine judgment leaves little room for thinking about social interests or the geological history of the planet. And the many segments of our capitalistic society that have been created since the Industrial Revolution tend to be focused on their own interests. These are the interests of our industries, businesses, and corporations, as well as those of our schools, hospitals, civic agencies, workplaces, and so forth.

Our society is a complex network of these projects, linked together to form the organic whole, yet each operating individually as a distinct unit of social organization and activity. Thus we have the scientific "community" that shares research projects wherever located in disparate labs and institutions; schools that share lists of common educational goals no matter where they may be located; the legal and judiciary institutions serving both the market and the state; the academy organized to facilitate and control the quality of our intellectual projects; religious institutions that protect cultural traditions and cultivate personal pieties; big industries and corporations that move our markets forward; political parties organized for deliberation and legislation; states in charge of their superstructures; the military organized for defense and war; and, of course, the Nation itself to comprehend and govern all of these projects as a single organism in its own interests. They all work together as segments of the social system, but organize themselves internally as self-sustained units with officers, rules, procedures, goals, and ways of keeping track of their progress. To labor in any one of these social segments organized for a distinct project, the horizon of "social and ecological interests" cannot be large. Interests within a social segment come to focus on the maintenance and health of the institution's own "business."

The significance of this observation is not only the self-referential sensibility that pervades the framework for thinking, conversation, and policy decisions in a subsocial segment of practice. It is that every segment generates its own interest in its project by means of a self-understanding that serves as a framework for its own self-justification, rules of procedure, and shorthand directives. Thus each segment has its own "logic" that provides the individuals working within it grammars appropriate for relating to one another and the business. Individuals will have other persons outside their workplace as family, friends, and acquaintances, of course. But a regular experience in a given social segment often determines that conversations with others outside of its sphere of influence take place on the margins between two or more social segments. When the logics of those segments are far apart, as for instance has been the case between the church and the public school, clarity of thinking becomes a major problem. I suspect that it has been the fragmentation of our interests and logics in our "businesses" that keeps us, the people, from hearing what planet earth is saying to us as a civilization. We simply do not have a picture of our world that comprehends both of our environments, the social order and its history, and the planet earth and its history. Both of these environments are "big," as far back and as far out as the human mind can manage. We have toyed with comprehending the scope of both environments, but we have not yet brought them together as a frame of reference for the social interests and logics necessary in order to hear nature's voice or entertain its challenge. We have had too many of our own social and political interests and issues to think about without adding the issues of climate change and the future of our global civilization. What this means for the debate about global warming in Washington is not clear. Neither is it clear whether we have any sense of the future that can allow for an imagination of the cultural change required to see global collapse as the "foremost challenge confronting humanity," as the Ehrlichs see it, much less the means to actually address the challenge our civilization has become.

But we know that we are capable of many interests in the natural environment that do not need the motivations and mindset of the capitalistic systems to cultivate an appreciation of planet earth. From the poets of the romantic tradition to the communes of the Walden Pond variety, the diaries and activities of John Muir's Sierra Club, the works of those supporting our state and federal parks, and many of the recent activist groups listed in Paul Hawken's *Blessed Unrest,* there is a strong tradition of popular anthropology that wants to define us as exceptional creatures, not because we were created by God to adore him, but because, as products of a wondrous and incredible evolutionary history, we have somehow developed the mental capacity to explore and enjoy our natural environment. Thus we know full well why we cannot imagine stopping our global corporations from their business. It is that the logics of business (capitalism) have permeated our collective mentality. That shared mentality makes it difficult to think critically about the process by which we outfoxed ourselves, the process by which our industrial civilization got us into trouble, or what it might take for "a dramatic cultural change" to occur. Only a few journalists have dared look into a future in which our industries do not stop until they are stopped by the collapse itself. So we are dealing with the powers of at least two mentalities, that of the Christian myth, and that of the capitalist myth. Both are "reasons" for our inability to stop global warming. Both are reasons why we need to structure a nation-state that is capable of regulating our industries and corporations, not only for the benefit of a sane economy and a common-good society, but also for the sustenance of the ecosystems.

And so, because the devastation caused by hurricane Sandy

in 2012 focused our attention on the challenge of restructuring our shorelines as a defense against future storms, it might be helpful to conclude with a final observation. It is that there are other examples of Western nations dealing with the global warming that threatens our civilization. Some of our historians and culture critics have been trying to call our attention to them as a comparison that could be helpful to our own analyses. I'd like to cite Mark Hertsgaard's letter to the *New Yorker* on "Adapting to Change" (February 4, 2013):

> The Dutch lead the world in climate-change adaptation largely because their history and geography move them to elevate the common good over individual interests; to regard government—and the taxes that fund it—as a reliable tool rather than as a hapless oppressor; and to respect science, even when it clashes with ideological or economic preferences. The best adaptation plans in the world won't much help New York City—or any other place—if the United States cannot leave climate denial behind, mobilize the government to implement strategies, and, above all, halt global warming before adapting to it becomes impossible.

So the questions we should be discussing in policy circles may be about what kind of *change in thinking* it will take for us to "halt global warming."

THE MILITARY

An article by Jill Lepore in the *New Yorker* has asked the question, "How Much Military Is Enough?" ("The Force," January 28, 2013). She describes the patchy history of military spending in the United States from the establishment of the War Department in 1789. She notes that the United States did not have a "standing army" until the Second World War and that, despite strong resistance from those who did not think the American people wanted "to rule the world," the Armed Services Committee was formed in 1946. Lepore then brings that history to focus on the recent debates about the military budget in Congress under Howard P. McKeon, chairman of the committee. She reminds us of the issue in the following summary:

> The United States spends more on defense than all the other nations of the world combined. Between 1998 and 2011, military spending doubled, reaching more than seven hundred billion dollars a year—more, in adjusted dollars, than at any time since the Allies were fighting the Axis. The 2011 Budget Control Act, which raised the debt ceiling and created both the fiscal cliff and a Joint Select Committee on Deficit Reduction, which was supposed to find a way to steer clear of it, required four hundred and eighty-seven billion dollars in cuts to military spending, spread over the next ten years. The cliff-fall mandates an additional defense-budget reduction of fifty-five billion dollars annually. None of these cuts have gone into effect. McKeon has been maneuvering to hold the line.

She ends with a description of the hearings of the House Armed Services Committee under McKeon on "The Future of National Defense and the United States Military Ten Years After 9/11." At the October 13, 2011, hearing, testimony was heard from Leon Panetta, secretary of defense, and General Martin Dempsey, chairman of the Joint Chiefs of Staff. Under aggressive questioning, both Panetta and Dempsey seemed hard pressed to defend defense spending on particular items in support of recent wars in the Near East. But they were adamant in their support of our military presence around the world in the interest of keeping the peace. Dempsey declared:

> I didn't become the chairman of the Joint Chiefs to oversee the decline of the Armed Forces of the United States, and an end state that would not be a global power. That is not who we are as a nation.

This statement by General Dempsey is worth taking some time to analyze. It reveals a concept of the United States and its military that runs deeper than the usual arguments about "national interests." As a matter of fact, the usual arguments about national interests had been worn out in responses to the questions of the committee and guests in that two-hour-plus hearing. There was a high level of critical awareness, questioning, and subtle protest about our military involvements around the world that Dempsey finally had to address. I want to analyze his statement, noting the terminology of "decline," "end state," "global power," and "who we are as a nation." It is obvious that a relationship between "armed forces" and "who we are as a nation" underlay the argument for our being "a global power" that should not "decline" and come to an "end state." His statement is the articulation of a mentality in the mind of a general who thinks of our nation as a global power that needs our armed forces at their current strength (at minimum) to be stationed around the world. The armed forces dare not be "reduced" without threatening our position of global power and dominance.

This is a shocking revelation of a mentality that apparently pervades the top brass of the Pentagon. It is shocking because it defines the United States in terms of military power, and because it reveals a view of a world destined for control by our armed forces. There is not a sense of history to say why this needs to be, or a picture of what it is about our nation that is worthy of such a role. Since it does not call upon any history to explain itself, or project any purpose for the use of our armed forces in the world except to maintain our position of global power, questions must be raised about this mentality. How can it be that such notions about the United States and its role in the world of nations are thinkable at all, much less that they should be the convictions of persons in authority? I want to explore some answers to this question in a combination of our recent history and its cultural changes. I will sketch some of the reasons that can be given for the emergence of this mentality by means of a brief review of our history. It will then be possible to offer a critical assessment of the mentality itself.

The sketch of our history can begin with the Second World War. We did not become involved in the war because we wanted to be a world power. Quite the contrary. But because we managed to produce a military machine that was victorious in both the European and the Pacific "theaters," and because the other nations, "allies" and "enemies" alike, were unable to recover immediately, the United States found itself a participant in postwar diplomatic endeavors. We were involved in creating the Marshall Plan, the United Nations, and other agencies and operations of cooperation without thinking of ourselves as a (or the) world leader. As a matter of fact, our diplomatic efforts during this early period were all in the interest of making sure such a war would not happen again. But our military units were not immediately disbanded, and they found themselves in the various theaters of the war to function now as our agents of control and security. This was our first period of military "presence" in lands beyond our border. It was not driven by the need to be a global power.

It was the so-called Cold War with Russia that forced us to think of having another "enemy" out there in the world. The Allies had divided Germany and the adjacent nations Germany had "annexed" into protectorate districts for the purpose of post-war governance and security. Russia and the United States had trouble with their separate objectives for the reconstruction of Germany and the new Europe and thus became engaged in a period of conflict. The "enemy" for this Cold War was the combination of another nation (Russia) and an idea ("communism"). We were never quite clear about what "communism" was, or what was wrong with it. That made it difficult to "combat." We certainly were not able to comprehend its philosophy or why we thought it a threat. We learned that there was a political and ideological conflict between Russia and the United States, of course, but since we had never worked out our own philosophy of democracy or free enterprise, it was not clear why that conflict in Europe was so threatening to our thinking or way of life in America. Yet "communism" was soon thought to be a threatening force in the world of nations, as well as a threatening idea that might infiltrate the thinking of some in the United States. The sorry history of the House Un-American Activities Committee and the "loyalty" investigations by Senator Joseph McCarthy played on our ignorance and paranoia without bringing any enlightenment about this "conflict." The best we could do abroad was to counter the moves Russia made on the playing field of European politics. When some of those encounters required our military, such as for the "Berlin airlift," we started to find "reasons" to think of our military as a representative and defender of "the American Way" away from home. This added a rather profound, if vague, sense of importance to the presence of our military around the world.

It was this notion that kept our military busy and expanding throughout the rest of the century, and that got us into trouble with the unwinnable Korean and Vietnam wars, the attempts to force "democracy" on the emerging "socialist" nations of Central and South America, and the sorry intrusions into the nations of the Near East. We usually pick up on this chapter of our history with the Iran "hostage exchange" under Reagan, then jump to the wars against Iraq and Afghanistan. But a complicating factor began to run through this history from at least the sixties that changed and deepened the rationale for having a military presence in the world. That complicating factor had little to do with the purposes of a military for defending the nation and going to war against threatening "enemies," but slowly came to determine our military's primary purpose in the eyes of the government and big business. That factor is the "security" of what we have come to call "national interests." These are the interests of American businesses and corporations that were driving the expanding markets of the nation's postwar wealth and financial strength. Wherever these corporations thought to expand throughout other lands in the quest for natural resources and markets, the military could be called upon to protect their interests and activities. The prime example has been big oil, but many other industries also have the protection of the military in their exploitation of natural resources abroad and the production of their commodities for the global market. It is this history and meaning of our "global power," a rather recent development of our self-understanding as a nation, that lies behind General Dempsey's view of the importance of the armed forces for the United States as a nation.

Then there was the 9/11 "attack" on the World Trade Center towers and the Pentagon that traumatized all of us Americans. It was immediately interpreted as an act of "war," this time by Near Eastern Muslim "terrorists" who had managed to destroy a key portion of the city of New York as a statement of their anger. In our trauma we were not able to understand that statement, or even to reflect deeply upon the reasons these "attackers" may have had for wanting to fly four of our commercial planes into the major centers of our financial and military empires, the very powers that were in the process of turning the attitudes of large portions of the Near East against our intrusions into their territories and nations. Nor were we able to notice that yet another kind of "war" was being added to the reasons building up for turning our armed forces into a global power. This was an "act of war," we said, a "declaration of war" on the part of a religious-political Near Eastern movement, and the religion was Islam! That triggered our "war on terrorism," which, coupled with the sorry histories of our own wars against Iraq and Afghanistan, is still spilling over into military threats (and involvements) in Pakistan, in Iran, and throughout the Near East and Northern Africa. With that recent history and its continuing developments in mind, it is understandable that General Dempsey refused to yield on the question of "reducing" the budget for the armed forces. Our military presence in the Near East had not yet "won" its wars as had been expected, and the debris from these wars, such as the "captives" still at Guantánamo, the legal battles about our use of torture and rendition, and the relation between drones and illegal assassinations, was creating unresolved questions.

The problem was that the history of our military operations in the world abroad since the Second World War had layered reasons upon reasons for thinking that we were meant to be a global military power, but now that we had military bases around the world we were still not dominant enough to set the world straight. So something is missing from Dempsey's view of "who we are as a nation," as well as from my explanation of Dempsey's statement in terms of our postwar military history. The layered reasons from history for the reconceptions of the military as a "global power" are not enough to account for the argument about "who we are as a nation." Dempsey took it for granted that the nation had to be a global (military) power in order to be "who we are." This equation cannot be derived from a history of thinking only about the military and its wars. That history has largely been recent and accidental in the sense that, as I have tried to show, the various stages of encounter with other nations were not part of some grand design of our own making in the interest of becoming a "global power."

"Who we are" as a people is rooted in another kind of history, a history of struggles with the grand tradition of Western civilization as a cultural heritage and resource appropriate for the grand American experiment of nation building. We have not always been clear and creative in these trysts with our past and destiny, or even conscious of the moves we have made that have worked their magic in our favor or to our regrets. But one of the fundamental ingredients of that Western tradition that has not gone away in the tumbles we have taken as a combination of a native and immigrant peoples in quest of social well-being and a common-good nation-state, is a subtle acceptance of Christianity as the religion that belongs to the cultural tradition. As with any cultural tradition, the embedded religion creates a mentality that views the world in terms of its myth and thinks about it by using its system of symbols. For most of our history we were hardly aware of having a Christian mentality. And we certainly did not think of our being Christians automatically. We were busy with other more practical projects, problems, and ways of thinking. But wouldn't you know? Talk about being a "Christian Nation" surfaced in the cultural conflicts from Reagan through the Bush administrations and into the formidable political rhetorics against the Obama administration. I have studied this discourse and concluded that it revealed a deeply embedded mentality or way of thinking that can be traced to the narrative logic of the Christian myth. I have called this a "Christian Mentality" in three recent books that explore the influence of the biblical myth in our collective fascinations with sovereignty, power, innocence, violence, and fear (*The Christian Myth, Myth and the Christian Nation, Christian Mentality*).

This is not the place to rehearse these studies, except to remind the reader that we find ourselves at the end of a Western civilization whose culture has obviously been "Christian," and whose mythic view of the world strangely correlates with the way we still think about ourselves and other peoples in the world who are not Christians. The biblical mythic grammar also correlates with a large number of concepts and self-understandings at the levels of politics, corporations, and the military. The evidence for this mentality in the history of the United States should be obvious if we recall the importance of various symbols and concepts that have played important roles in thinking about "who we are." There are the references to the "city set on a hill," "manifest destiny," "mission to the world," "one nation under God," the frequent mention of our being the superior nation among the nations of the world, and the recent ruckus over "morals" and biblical injunctions on the part of the Christian Coalition and the Tea Party as basic to their concerns about the nation. All of that and more can be studied as manifestations of a pervasive mentality that defines "who we are" as a nation in terms of "superiority" and "righteousness," and "who we are" as a people in terms of our innocence, and those with a mandate to take democracy (the "gospel") to the nations.

If so, Dempsey's concern about reducing the military budget cannot be accounted for simply as a general's desire to keep his war machine strong. It is infused with a mythic concept of the nation that is supposed to be a global military power for the promotion and guarantee of the "American Way" as the "right" way for the rest of the world. That is the scary part. It reveals a mentality that understands the military as integral to the purpose (or "mission") of the nation so that, linked together in mythic mode, the United States has a (divine) right to rule the world. The problem is that the Christian myth and mentality that lie behind this concept of what some have called the "Christian Nation" do not encourage thinking in terms of a polycultural social democracy at home, or a multicultural global world abroad. And since the "democracy" we have in mind for other nations cannot be "forced" on a non-Western, non-Christian, people who resist our military power, the social orders our global enterprise seeks to create in other nations cannot be imagined as the "democracies" we often say we would like to encourage. That means we are sadly mistaken about what our "global power" can achieve.

It is time for realizing that the "global power" of America has created not a world at peace but one that is at war. Our "national interest" in the military has spawned our biggest business of all, namely arms manufacturing. We have automatically supplied our "friends" around the world with weapons to guard our interests and solve their problems, as if weapons are the only way to solve conflicts. At present, the beginning of the twenty-first century, the use of military weapons to counter one's opponents around the world has produced an unending chain of killings that do not solve conflicts and do not make for peace. Thus the thinking that lies behind Dempsey's defense of our nation's "global power" is faulty. We need another vision of "who we are" or "who we might be." The thinking that is called for might start with some big picture of peoples and societies finding it rewarding to live together on planet earth without recourse to (American) military power. Such a global picture, though seemingly implausible at this juncture of American "presence" in the world of nations, would be something worth thinking about and achieving.

FOREIGN POLICY

It is not clear to culture critics that the United States has a rationalized foreign policy, if "foreign policy" still has the connotations of the kind of relations to other nations that require skilled representatives and statesmen able to understand and negotiate the histories and interests of both states. The term *leadership* seems to be preferred as a description of our position among the nations of the world, as if all of our interests in that arena assume our superior knowledge of international relations and our ability to instruct others in the governance of their own nations. Nevertheless, whether as a "policy" or an "assumption," the history of our relations to other nations does exhibit a clear profile of attitudes and practices that can be analyzed as a fairly consistent mode of response to global issues in which we somehow become involved.

This history starts with a sense of caution about becoming involved with foreign nations and their wars that we have called isolationism. As an awareness of a popular stance, isolationism was quite strong at the end of the nineteenth century and was a factor in our resistance to involvement in both the First and the Second World Wars. The surprising success of the war machine we finally managed to put together in a short amount of time, and of our victories in both the European and Pacific "theaters" after the Second World War did not cancel out our isolationist sensibilities, but it did leave us with the circumstance of having dealt with other nations in the serious business of war, and with having military bases around the world as the major form of our global presence in what at first were devastated nations. It was during the second half of the twentieth century that our "leadership" began to look like a "policy." One distinctive feature of our involvements might be called a curious sense of responsibility to provide "humanitarian aid" to nations, peoples, and troubled situations. We did not ask ourselves where that sense of "responsibility" came from. There was the Marshall Plan for the European nations, the Berlin airlift for the Germans, NATO to form the European nations into a union, and many gestures of political and financial aid to Japan. This burst of aid to other nations after the war turned into a role that the United States continued to see as its responsibility for points of distress in Central America, Yugoslavia, Africa, Southeast Asia, East Asia, and the Near East. Our media were easily exercised by tribal hostilities, health and food deprivations, ethnic cleansings, and, as the twenty-first century unfolded, the native disruptions of our own industrial interests in other lands that looked at first like problems that a "developing nation" was having while learning how to engage the modern world. This sense of being responsible for humanitarian aid has produced such agencies as Doctors without Borders, the Gates agencies at work in health care for the underprivileged in Africa, Habitat for Humanity, various women's rights organizations with missions to Near Eastern nations, and bill after bill in Congress to provide funds for nations and peoples in distress.

But a second feature of our foreign policy is the ease with which the notion of *mission* was used to explain this or that political involvement in other nations. Although the term is still used for our address to humanitarian crises, its major use has become a designation and justification for more aggressive intrusions into the troubled situations of other nations. *Mission* is now used to describe our attempts to protect our industrial interests in other countries and to defend regime changes in the name of "democracy." It can also be used to protect governments "friendly" to our own interests against their own opponents. It is not too far an extension of these notions, then, to use the term to justify military aid and intrusions in the interest of combating ideologies felt to be threatening. This has been a remarkable shift in thinking about foreign policy. We have apparently come to take it for granted that the United States should be out there in the rest of the world fighting for "democracy" and against the ideologies of other nations and groups that conflict with our interests. That is a very strange foreign policy for the United States, given the fact that we had never thought it important to consciously construct an articulate philosophy or political ideology of our own. The recent sense of mission to spread "democracy" probably started with our "Cold War" consternation about Russia, as if the issue were the threat of communism "taking over" the world we thought should be "democratic," and as if we alone knew what it took to be a democracy. This strange ideological conflict has played a role in the Korean, Vietnamese, Cuban, Croatian, and other wars we have fought in the name of democracy the past sixty years. It is now a factor in our stance toward the Crimea-Ukraine struggle that serves as a kind of proxy for a Russian conflict with the United States and Europe. But as has become clear, none of these missions (wars) has resulted in the building of a democracy in another nation.

It has been in the Near East, however, where our naïveté not only has failed; it has created havoc. In the Near East the terms of the conflicts calling for military missions have shifted many times since the Reagan administration's tussle with Iran. They have swirled around our "national interests" (in protecting our oil corporations) throughout the Near East and Africa. But the tribal and national conflicts that our military incursions have generated have brought our "foreign policy" to the single focus of military force. And our response to the resulting tribal conflicts has been the distribution of arms to the "friendly" governments fighting their own battles against "armed sectarians," "terrorists," "insurgents," "rebels," and the like. We need not rehearse this history involving Iran, Iraq, Saudi Arabia, Libya, Egypt, Pakistan, Lebanon, Syria, and Israel. In mid-2016, in northern Iraq, Kurdistan, and Syria, three armed ethnic groups with conflicting ideologies are killing one another with weapons supplied by the United States. And the United States has entered the fray with bombings in the support of one or two groups against the other two or three.

Since the Reagan administration our military incursions have been justified for a number of differing "reasons," none of them naming our primary interests in the exploitation of foreign oil, and none of them having achieved their goals. The resulting scenes of arms shipments, tribal warfare, massacres, and anti-American militias and regime changes have advanced only our arms industry, not our interests in world "leadership," "democracy," state building, or oil control. One might think that this history would have provided our administrations with some insight into the failures of our "foreign policy" and some lessons for needing to analyze our global "national interests" in relation to social interests at home. Not so. Our Congress is apparently unable to think beyond the lowest level of party politics. Our political representatives seem completely unaware of the reasons for the amazing success of the Fordism that underlay our twentieth-century economies. They are apparently incapable of realizing that the era of Fordism is at its end (David Harvey, *The*

Condition of Postmodernism). They chastise one another for proposals and bills that address current social issues without making
sure that our military strength and "world leadership" continue
at the high level to which they have become accustomed. They
have no alternative vision of what the United States might imagine as a vibrant and healthy role for itself at home or how it
might take its place among the nations of the world. There is
no vision of society that is not market driven. Thus there is no
foreign policy in the United States that has a society for the common good in view for itself or others.

We might want to investigate the reasons for this troubled
history of "foreign policies" that has come to rest on a real situation of "social issue" because of our presence in the Near East.
Briefly, there has been a combination of Christian myth mentality
("manifest destiny," "mission"), the accidental thrust of the nation
into world "leadership" after the Second World War, the burgeoning financial strength of our corporations and their need for natural "resources" from "foreign" nations, and the heady visions of
the "New American Century" swirling secretly in the conservative think-tank behind-the-scenes plotters of the Reagan to second Bush administrations. This combination of ideologies and
mentalities has produced a sense of American superiority that
has deep roots in all of the traditional "social interests" we have
discussed in Chapter 4.

What I have been reticent to discuss is the collection of papers on the "New American Century" (and other similar titles;
see Wikipedia) written by such conservative figures as Paul Wolfowitz and eventuating in what Vice President Cheney referred
to as the Bush Doctrine. It was this chapter of political thinking

that led the United States into our current military involvement in the Near East. But it cannot be discussed without parrying a list of ideological issues that would take us far afield from our focus on myth and mentality. The questions it would raise have to do with the influence of the German philosophers Leo Strauss and Carl Schmitt on what appears to have been the American intellectuals involved in the formation of "a supranational sovereignty of an intellectual elite and bankers" (citing David Rockefeller in 1991), the notion of the "moral and natural right of these bankers and politicians to govern nations," the "plan" to inaugurate the "New American Century," the secrecy of its documents about the plan, a suspicion of a 9/11 conspiracy in the interest of justifying the American invasion of Iraq, and the subsequent sorry history of the "reasons" for our wars in the Near East. The hesitation has also been occasioned by the ways in which our wars in the Near East have surfaced cultural biases and the question of "religious wars." There are overt expressions on both sides to the effect that both our incursions and the hostilities of the Islamic tribes and nations are driven by religious beliefs and cultural mentalities. I personally think that that is partially correct. But a thorough investigation of the influences of both Islamic and Israeli religious motivations in their current wars in the Near East would be needed to adequately address such matters.

And so we must end our review of American "foreign policy" by admitting that we do not have one, if we mean a policy that recognizes the rights and cultures of other peoples and nations as matters to be negotiated in the interest of living together in a common-good world. We have never learned to stand at the borders with hat in hand to ask for permission to enter another's homeland. We have never said, "Oh, you do have a nice hat. May I come in and see it? I would like to show you mine, too." What a shame that we have been so stuck on our own sense of cultural supremacy that we cannot appreciate what it would take to participate in creating a multicultural world of nations.

A SENSE OF THE FUTURE

The American mental atmosphere is no longer conducive for thinking about the future. Once upon a time, not too long ago, there were several pictures from which to choose, each anchored in an epic of sorts that allowed segments of the population to pursue their interests and traditions with some kind of goal in view. There was the Christian myth, with its endings in apocalypse and/or heaven. There was the *Ascent of Man* myth drawing upon the sciences and evolution made famous by J. Bronowski. There was the myth of science as the secret agent for gratifying all of our desires and solving all of our problems. There was the philosopher's club, busily building concepts of real being into a cosmic scheme of time and space that would have a happy *telos* (end, completion). There was the myth of capitalism's limitless growth, creating wealth, and aiming at globalization. There was the myth of communism, calling for social revolution and promising social transformation. There was the myth of Christian missions anticipating the triumph of monotheism over the rest of the polycultural world. And there were others about America's innocence, righteousness, and manifest destiny used to justify our fantasies of empire, military might, commercial supremacy, and leadership among the nations. All of these are coming to their end in the current troubling chapter of Western history. We cannot reawaken any of them in order to reset our course for the future. The fatal flaws of every projection have become obvious to us. Thus our sense of the future is murky and frightening. It is too soon to announce the end of human history, as some are saying, or the final destruction of the earth's ecosystems, as others are thinking, or the collapse of Western civilization itself. But we have lost our sense of confidence about fixing things social. And that is where the root of the problem resides that leads us to conjure up the images of exterminations, destructions, and horrifying endings. We no longer have a clear vision of the future as a social goal to give us a sense of direction and meaning.

The Christian myth lost its noble magnanimity in the human costs of colonialism, the disastrous wars of the Johnson administration in Vietnam and the Bush administration in the Middle East, and the more recent impossible policies of the "Christian Nation" Republicans and their Tea Party politicians. It is true that some portions of the populace still think of Christianity as the hope for the future. But the only hope for the future still offered by Christianity has been reduced to the "salvation" of individuals. That is not a solution for the troubled view of the state of the world. The Christian myth has no social logic for a polycultural world. It cannot help America understand the current social state of affairs it has helped to create, or provide a vision for the future of a livable, sustainable society for the common good of a multicultural population.

As for Bronowski's glorification of science and the *Ascent of Man* (1973), he was quite aware that science alone was no guarantee of *social* and *cultural* ascent. He was deeply troubled by the ease with which the scientific discovery of nuclear fission shifted imperceptibly to the production of the bombs that we dropped on Hiroshima and Nagasaki. For Bronowski the discovery of nuclear fission was a recent most remarkable addition to his long list of scientific "discoveries," all of which were the result of the intellectual curiosity and thinking capacity of *Homo sapiens.* That he persisted in his view that science, the scientific method, and the rationality of humans could still give us a sense of the future that was hopeful is a mark of his greatness as a scientist and a human being. The reader might need to know, however, that Bronowski had lost several members of his family to the Holocaust, and that he was deeply involved in the politics of the postwar scientific community. This means that his determination to project a better world through science was not the result of naïveté. Unfortunately for his "ascent of man," the forty-plus years since have shown us that our science and technology have been used for the destructive exploitation of natural resources, the development of sophisticated weapons for warfare, and the production of guns and military vehicles as one of the most lucrative industries of our nation. Our current "negotiations" about which nation can or cannot be allowed to have nuclear weapons does not project a positive "sense" for our future on the basis of our scientific capacities. No hopeful sense of the future there. (*A Sense of the Future,* the title of an essay by Bronowski in 1948, became the title of a posthumous selection of his essays in 1977.)

The *telos* that philosophers, theologians, and intellectuals have imagined over the long history of Western civilization came undone when the monoculture of the West was shaken to pieces by the recognition that the world had multiple cultures with other languages, logics, and philosophies that were not going to accede to Western dominance. The end of the colonial era and the slow emergence of postmodernism have left us pondering the end of the grand old narrative of the West itself. Without it, of course, there is no way to justify our current conquests. We can still imagine "endings," but all of them are frightening eventualities.

Capitalism has taken the place of our erstwhile "missions" to the nations of the world. The term now used to glorify the expansion of capitalism throughout the world is *globalization*. Despite the emergence of glamorous cities around the world, capitalism has not produced a picture of a world at peace with itself. As a matter of fact, the opposite is closer to the mark. It has opened the way for massive predations, fraudulent exploitations, mismanagement of financial accumulations, and the use of those accumulations to force the emerging nations to borrow "capital" and join the West's world of "free trade." The result has been the indebtedness of the emerging nation and the enslavement of its working classes and poor. Global corporations think only about their own financial interests, not about the well-being of the nations in which they operate. The huge disconnect between the accumulation of wealth at the management level and the poverty of the poor at the people level reveals the structural defect in the operation of capitalism that cautions against thinking that it guarantees a hopeful future for the world. And the signs of our own ideological and financial bankruptcies are beginning to show in the inability of the Congress of the United States to respond to the social issues now rampant. The Congress is apparently incapable of grasping the reasons for these social issues, much less their consequences for the well-being of our society.

As for America's "manifest destiny," it can no longer be used to explain our accidental rise to leadership among the nations of the world after the Second World War. And it dare not be used to let us justify our conquest of the land and its Native Americans from the beginning. Thus it can no longer be used to let us exult as the world's foremost financial and military nation. The rest of the world is now in the process of underscoring that point both for us and against us.

So our erstwhile "senses" of the future are in disarray. We can, of course, analyze some of the reasons for the breakdown by rehearsing our histories and noting particular conflicts among streams of tradition that did not get resolved. Our academics and intellectuals have been busy at this task for about a generation, and their analyses are now available in strikingly cogent articles and books. We know now about the limits of imperialism, the misjudgments of capitalism, the politics of self-centered ideologies, the reasons for our failure to provide adequate public education, the bankruptcy of our foreign diplomacy, and the stage show of our attempts to "spread democracy" by means of military intrusions. One reads these studies with deep appreciation and a sense of relief. The relief stems from the recognition that there are scholars and thinkers who see the social issues of our time with clarity, and who dare to engage in what might be called a first-level social and cultural critique. That bodes well. This level looks at such overlapping issues as overuse of fossil fuels, demographic growth outpacing sustenance resources, questionable plant modifications for increasing food and fuel production, ecological problems due to the human exploitation of natural resources, climate warming, wars, drone warfare, financial imbalances at home and abroad, famines, poverty, and so on, and so on. Many of these issues have been taken up by our politicians, of course, but they have been "debated" at the popular levels of special interests. What we need are leaders who are capable of engaging our social issues at the level of the social and cultural critique called for by the focused studies of our academics and intellectuals. We know now that our social practices have created problems that need to be fixed. What we do not seem to know is what must be done to fix them.

There is another level of cultural criticism that seems to be called for by our intellectual infirmity, a criticism we have not yet dared to engage. It has to do with an analysis of the Christian mentality that has given Western culture its categories for thinking about the worlds in which we exist. Christian mentality has resisted thinking about societies except in terms of the authorization of supremacy and the morals of individuals. The analysis called for in this time of intellectual uncertainty would be about the social logic of the myth that underlies Christian mentality. It might be called a second-level or fundamental cultural critique. Since Christian mentality and culture is so taken for granted as not to be noticed, it would be necessary to find some way to see it and analyze it from some "objective" perspective. One answer could be to use what we have learned about other societies through ethnographic and historical studies in order to set up comparative analyses. This would mean working toward some general social theory by analyzing the interests and motivations that have energized the human enterprise of social formations from the beginnings of human history. It would then have to use these "social interests" to analyze the motivations of our current social practices and render an assessment of the human coefficients or values that pertain. The human project of social formation is a fundamental collective labor in the interest of living together on planet earth. We do not have such a general social theory to work with. And we do not have a sense of where we are in relation to the history of societies and civilizations. However, cultural anthropologists have intuited the importance of such research projects and now have a large data set from more than one hundred years of ethnographic studies. During this same period, paleoanthropologists have started working with the differences between humans and other primates to determine what may be distinctive about the collective interest of humans in constructing societies. Together, these studies have noted the importance of language, symbols, kinship systems, tuitions, technologies, institutions, and other practices that have made possible the social formations of *Homo sapiens.* Many of these studies are truly enlightening as descriptions of social interests and practices that indicate constructive collective sensibilities. However, we are not yet sure what to make of these findings as theoretical frames of reference for a critical analysis of the more "advanced" contours of the Western tradition.

As a strategy for approaching the cultural critique called for by our troubled times, however, the list of constructive "social interests" derived from ethnographic studies does not seem to be sufficient. That is because there are some troubling practices and features of human history that we conveniently overlook, regarding them as "natural" because they seem to be rooted in our evolution as apelike hominoids. We have frequently accounted for these features by calling them incidents of "savagery," as if they were practices from a past chapter of the human history of "progress," thus forgivable. The list is not long, but it includes such incidents as warring, raiding, raping, massacring, or performing human sacrifice, all purportedly having to do with the treatment of "enemy" (or "other") tribes or neighbors. It is not difficult to see that incidents such as these have not been left behind. They are, in fact, staring us in the face as common to our more recent histories, histories which we are having difficulty acknowledging, much less understanding. Thinking of them as "natural" does provide a kind of justification for our wars, killings, and incidents of international violence without our having to provide reasons for them or see them as the result of social system maladjustments. Now, however, even within the borders of a given society, violence by individuals, gangs, and "terrorists" has created a social pattern and situation that can no longer be overlooked. And in the middle, between the constructive features of human social behavior and the violence we once regarded as "natural," there is what we now call *predation*, a preying upon the weaker by the stronger for the benefit of the stronger. Predation is another feature of the "natural" behavior of humans when focusing upon their prey in hunting societies. The term has recently come to be used, however, to describe a wide range of practices in modern societies, dealing not only with the exploitation of the natural order but with the spread of real estate "developments," industries, technologies, and financial networks. In every case the "snatch and grab" logic of opportunism seems to be the stronger's self-evident justification for taking advantage of the weaker. It is, in fact, a structural strategy and mechanism of the economic system of capitalism. That it is taken for granted as "natural," as a modus for the human enterprise as a whole, is a large part of the problem we are having trying to control our large corporations, which think only of taking advantage of "resources" and "opportunities" for their business enterprises without having to count the consequences and costs that must be paid for by the people and their society.

Thus there is much less clarity about what we might do to constrain the forces we think responsible for the current state of affairs, or to reconfigure our social systems to enhance well-being instead of breakdown. One of the reasons for this circumstance is that none of the societies assumed in our erstwhile "senses of the future" provided a picture or model of a fully orbed society truly worth hoping for or waiting for, much less working for. All pictures were partial to serve special interests as ideologies. So we do not have a vision of the society we should like to become. And now our political process is overwhelmed by special interests fighting over minor matters of budgets and disputes about details of constitutional law. There is no larger picture of the social. All of the terms used to name a social concept, practice, or collective unit have become shibboleths or fighting words for party ideologies. One has to put quotation marks around all of the terms that were once thought of in positive terms: *America, freedom, right, Christian, fair, democratic, free trade, social, socialism, civil rights, patriotic, common good,* and so on. None is a concept that we are able to define, debate, or argue about in order to clarify our thinking about the social logic and human values we once thought were lodged in our erstwhile mythologies, much less the society we need to imagine for the future.

This means that we do not have a future vision to counter the ominous atmosphere of the times. We have no social vision to call upon in order to say what we think is "wrong" with the ominous atmosphere or what we should be doing about it. We are depressed by the massacres, wars, drones, guns, and violence filling the media every day, but we are not able to say why we are depressed or what it is about killings that we think is "wrong." We do not even know how to say it is "wrong" for the NRA to lobby for the gun industry, or for the government to protect the gun industry as a successful American business. And coming closer to the issues about which we need to make decisions, suppose we wanted to look the Tea Party in the face and ask it why it did not want everyone to have health care. It could not handle that question because its partisans' view of the social has been reduced to the single issues of wanting a "Christian Nation" and balancing the national budget. That is not a sufficient view or policy from which to think about society as a whole, or to actually argue for denying health care to those who cannot afford it. Neither could we, the questioners, handle such an exchange, because our "reasons" for asking such a question are grounded in a sensibility, not in a shared rational model for a common-good society structured in such a way as to reward well-being and moral values. The list of moral, ethical, and "progressive" concerns among us goes on and on, of course, but all of them are products of sensibilities felt to have been violated by the troublesome state of affairs. We do not know exactly why these issues of concern are significant, and why we are distressed. As an example, the thought of losing our privacy to universal surveillance agencies is now creating consternation. But as Scott McNealy, cofounder of Sun Microsystems, said, "You have zero privacy anyway. Get over it." So it looks as if we may be stuck with the social uncertainties and ominous atmosphere of our postmodern world.

Some seem to be saying, "Well, if there is nothing we can do to fix the ways the world is working, let's live it up as long as it lasts." That is what the producers of our new "social media" tell us to do. And it has worked like a charm, or perhaps a virus, to project a smiley-face culture into the vacuum created by the loss of traditional values. Our traditional societies kept us in touch with one another at the workplace, on the streets, and at home to talk about our projects in conversation with other people in the context of real time and space. This is the way we found our places and ourselves as individuals in our societies. That is the way we learned about responsibility, achievements, honors, and celebrations. Our collectivity provided us with meaning and motivation sufficient to engage the challenges of living together in the world. In its place, however, we now have a "social media" world of fictional connectivity and virtual reality in which the focus on the "me" cancels out the empirical world, and the constant cultivation of the "now" overwhelms any interest in social history (past or future). The constant bombardment of stimulating images provided by this and other media is designed to keep the "me" and the "now" busy with the titillations and fantasies of sensational fictional experiences. There is no longer any time for reflection, thinking, and discussing projects together. A telling review article by Evgeny Morozov about this feature of our new culture can be found in the *New Yorker* ("Only Disconnect: Boredom Reconsidered," October 23, 2013). For Morozov, after reviewing a number of books on the way in which the new marketing media and internet of connectivity program us by the constant flow of disconnected images in the interest of getting our attention and encouraging us to respond to their fictions of the real, the advice is to stop, disconnect, and rediscover the value of "boredom" and distance in order to ponder and think about the real world in which we live. I was impressed with this list of studies about the effect of our "social media" and "marketing media" on what researchers called the erasure of "reflection" and "thinking" about the social world beyond the "me" and the "now." It is that awareness of the larger social arena that we seem to have lost in the swirl of events that has canceled our erstwhile "senses" of the future. And I found it impressive to see that others had narrowed the criticism down to the erasure of time to think and ponder. But if "stopping" and "disconnecting" is the only way to escape the world of virtual reality, the new age wins. That is because the institutional systems in place and their mentalities still have free rein. Big oil cannot afford to shut down its operations. Global corporations handle grievances only as a public relations issue, not as an opportunity to make changes in their practices. Science will still be busy on pharmaceutical and genome research. And technology will still be making progress on the new robotic human and trips to distant galaxies. The culture of *now*, like the circuses of old, has not lost its attractions. And the population around the world will continue to grow larger and find the *now* buttons fascinating. So who are the "we" I have been assuming? Those upset with the lack of a vision for a social world we might hope for or work toward? I have assumed that others also are wondering how it can be that we now make of violence a déjà vu, sensationalize common citizens as celebrities, thrill to disaster as if it were theater, and keep on smiling through the news as if that's the only way the world can work.

I called this social issue a "sense of the future." Now we see that the problems we are having with our current American culture are not only about the future. They are about the depressing political atmosphere in which we are living, features of our popular culture that stimulate fantasies and create stress, and suspicions about our cultural mentality that has allowed us to think of ourselves as superheroes while devastating other lands and peoples. Of course, our current culture of social media can't provide us with a social atmosphere or political polity fit for working toward a common-good society. We have not even allowed ourselves to imagine what a "common-good" society might look like. So suppose we realize that this picture of the world we have on our hands is the very world that we have created. Suppose we consider that the way it looks to others around the world is due to the offensiveness of America's missions. Suppose we see that the extravagance and hectic pace of the electronic media have frustrated thinking clearly about life in America. Suppose we wonder what it can be about the history of our nation that has produced such a chapter of sensationalist media and failed politics. Suppose we recognize that our popular and political discourse is incoherent and incapable of supporting debate about social issues. Suppose we find ourselves asking whether we have not already lost our position of leadership among the nations of the world. What then?

Why, then it might be time to start a conversation on the chances for a new social vision. We need a vision that will not erase the wondrous accomplishments of our Western civilizations. But we cannot afford to memorialize our customary glorifications. The remnants of our once grand myths and social systems need to be looked at very closely. We dare not continue to fawn upon our failed myths or continue to promote our outworn ideologies. But we do need to celebrate the human interests and energies that have poured into the collective enterprise of living together in the world. We can save the memories of those who have shaped our societies in keeping with the ideals for the common good without sensationalizing them as celebrities. And we dare not continue to thrill to violence or account for "progress" by means of wars. We need to imagine what it would be like to shift our social histories and values from winning at wars and commerce to rewarding those who work for the well-being of the common good. And we might well ask a few of our friends and neighbors to help us gain some perspective. Having lived for a time in postwar Europe, I know that the central European nations and their northern neighbors have been watching us closely through our adolescence as a nation. And now that the adolescence of our popular culture, as well as of our current politicians and politics, has become embarrassing to us and obvious to them, we might want to ask them to join in our conversation about a social vision for the future. They have learned some lessons during the past century about how to work a social democracy for the common good. Such a model of society is just what we need. We too have been working on that model in practical terms since the Second World War. If we could imagine the model in theoretic terms, we could all join in a conversation about how to make such a model work for the future. That would be some conversation! Such a conversation could give us a sense of the future worthy of investing in the creation of new myths, rituals, arts, and culture. We might even call it a project in *Culture and Society!*

6 CULTURAL ANALYTICS

A sense of well-being among the people of a society, as well as a sense of discontent, is a matter of the health of a society's infrastructure and culture. We have been exploring a range of *social interests* and *social issues* creating a sense of dis-ease in the United States. This exploration has focused on large-scale projects and productions that have emerged and taken place since the Industrial Revolution. All of these projects had their beginnings in experiments by creative individuals in the interest of exploring common curiosities that produced social interests. In the course of history, however, social interest projects have produced organizations, institutions, and corporations. These institutions now constitute the superstructure of the society and influence the state's control of the way the society works. If we want to analyze the sense of dis-ease experienced by the people, we need to ask about the way these projects work in relation to the experiences and expectations of the people. They are taken for granted by the people, of course, as the features of the society that are simply "there," the machinery that makes the society work. This means that the sense of dis-ease in general is probably not a grievance directed at any given structure of the society per se. It is directed at the way the society is working in this or that instance where some personal or private interest has been frustrated.

Cultural analysts, however, look at the bigger picture of the society and its social structures, asking about the relations among all its social projects. They can notice such things as the conflicts that can occur between and among corporations, conflicts which the average citizen may not even notice. Then there are the consequences of a corporation's practices upon other aspects of the workings of the society. These consequences may be noticed by the people involved, but are frequently seen as issues about which nothing can be done. At the state level, conflicts among major social interests can become issues that require legislation to control social practices and company policies. This range of issues occurs mainly at the level of the superstructure. In our study thus far, the social issues have been noticed mainly at this level. That is because we have been concerned about the state and workings of the society as a whole.

In the background we have also been thinking about the Christian myth and asking what happened to its big picture, the medieval Christian worldview. It was the correlation of the medieval social structure and the Christian worldview that produced a sense of coherence and stability for the society. Looking back, we think we can also detect a sense of well-being for the people. They seem at least not to have been restive and aggressive for large-scale social changes. The myth theory with which we have been working did introduce the concept of *social interests* as a way to bring the empirical practices of a society into relation with its mythic environment and narrative logics. But we have not discovered much interest in or necessity for such a correlation in the rural and feudal conditions of society for the medieval period. The Christian worldview seems to have been a sufficient environment for the peasant even without marking and celebrating its common, material interests. In the case of the more recent history of the United States, however, the major social interests and the narrative logic of the Christian myth no longer seem to be working in relation to one another. In the previous chapter we discussed several major social interests that have developed in fairly recent history and that seem to have their own logics. All of them are having problems with social issues, both at the superstructural and at the infrastructural levels of society. So we need to do some more work on these social interests and their logics before asking our cultural analysts to tell us what they see as having happened to the "grand Western tradition," where our concept of culture was formed and cultivated, and why the current social situation is causing such distress.

First, it might be helpful to see that the practices of the dominant social interests discussed in Chapter 4 (Social Interests) do bear some relation to the set of tribal social interests discussed in Chapter 2 (Theory). The sets are different, however, because of the changes in social structures and interests that have taken place in history. The social constructions of aristocratic kingdoms, empires, and nation-states are much more complex than the tribal societies consulted for the myth theory. But both sets of interests (tribal/Western) swirl around what might be called fundamental interests around which societies have structured themselves. Tribal societies reveal social interests in the land, the family, learning skills, how roles are assigned in the workings of the tribe, the responsibilities of their authorities, trading and exchange practices, marking the seasons, distributing foods, and holding festivals. All human societies have developed sets of these features of social existence (practices rooted in social interests and collective intellection). Sets have been formed in the long evolutionary processes of learning how to live together in social formations.

And there is a basic anthropology that can be discerned on the basis of archaeological data and cultural histories when asking about both the individual and social interests of social practices. Social practices and habits could develop because of what we have come to regard as our collective interests in belonging to and living in social formations (family, tribe, society) on the one hand, and what might be called our interests in practices and practical matters on the other. Humans notice things in their environments, make and share observations, delight in surprises, are curious about the reasons for the ticks in nature, and fuss with what they might make of the natural order of things. They also became good at mapping, making tools, crafts, cuisines, huts, and tepees. As they learned to live together, they found ways to report on experiences, relate memories, tell stories, and agree on the best ways to do a particular task. These agreements led to habits and skills that turned them into social codes, relational habits aware of the social consequences of doing a performance the right (or wrong) way. And watching one another perform, flub, pretend, or accomplish a task, they responded with laughter, smiles, repartee, and/or honors. These are social mechanisms, the primary data for constructing a social anthropology, for distinguishing the human species as a self-aware collective determined by social interests.

Listing these mechanisms as I have done is not much more than a playful attempt at parsing the bits and pieces of our long and complicated evolutionary history, but it might be enough to suggest the intellectualist and motivational features of our collective social patterns of behavior, and thus the significance of the structural features of a human society. It can also help as a frame of reference for asking about what might be called the "basic anthropology" involved in the recent development of major social interests in the Western tradition. We can already see that this modern set of social interests differs from the pictures of the tribal society, the ancient Near Eastern kingdoms, and the erstwhile Christendom of our Western traditions. The suspicion might be that a novel social psychology is currently in the making, or that the general sense of dis-ease is due to problems created by the set of social interests themselves, and that the set needs to be addressed.

One observation is that the ethnographic model for these major social interests was not complicated by the structures of the modern nation-state. Tribal societies did not have corporations, and even though our corporations started as modest experiments of individuals and groups that were not at first incorporated, it did not take long for a successful practice to develop functions and institutions that squeezed into the gap between the people level and the top level to create the modern model of infra- and superstructure levels. Thus the modern nation-state is structured by intertwined movements, organizations, and agencies. Each of these organizations of human energy tends to develop its own infrastructure with hierarchies of executive power and rules or habits of procedure. The assignment is to keep the machinery working and pursue the goals of the organization. But each is also hopelessly entangled with the other organizations, all of which interact in the operations of the society as a whole. These interactions form subsystems of rules, agreements, and supervision that support the separate units as parts of the whole. Such rules can also serve as constraints upon temptations to capitalize on prerogatives and to seek dominion over other substructures of the system. This means that the special interests of each may well conflict with the particular interests of other agencies and organizations. In many cases the conflict can be resolved by means of compromises worked out between the competitors. In others, where a conflict of values is at stake, it may not be resolved if those contesting do not have the power or influence to call for change. Such is now the conflict between environmental agencies and global corporations destroying the rain forests of South America. In yet other cases, the conflict may have to be resolved in courts of law, such as the recent issue of the navy's use of sonar in marine environments where whales are at danger.

When questioned, all of these agencies find ways to argue for their operations in terms of some general conception of legitimate interests, or in terms of some set of rules thought to explain national and social interests. It is usually the case that references to such interests are not spelled out, not analyzed or argued in relation to a commonly agreed-upon concept of the common good. We do not spend much time thinking about the human enterprise of social formation as a whole, debating political philosophies, or engaging in academic discussions comparing various ways humans have found to live together in a given time and place. A brief review of the social interests and issues discussed in Chapters 4 and 5 can help sketch some of the motivations and interests that are driving these social interests at the present time, and thus prepare us for the studies of our current social situation by our cultural critics. I want to make a list of these "interests" as "motivations" that look suspicious as reasons that might be contributing to the pervasive sense of dis-ease in America at the time.

SUSPICIONS

1. We have noted that the *Renaissance* and the subsequent production of the psychology of the individual (Chapter 4) can easily be seen as the result of a mythic and intellectualist invention while working away from the traditional anthropology of the medieval world. We normally do not think of the Renaissance as a current social interest or influence, but it is. The terms that come to mind as the basic anthropological interests of the Renaissance tradition have to do with the value of the *individual* person as an independent entity, the value of learning and knowledge for the formation and self-understanding of the individual, the value of introspection for the works of self-formation and the winning of independence from traditional social constraints, and the sharing of such knowledge by means of writings, discourses, and arts (cultural production). We will see all of these features at work among us in the section below on *cultural analytics*. The question will be whether this interest in the individual can be understood as helpful for the painting of a sustainable society concerned about the common good.

2. As for the world of *science*, it now reaches beyond the hori-

zons, packing the picture of the universe with details from its origins, chemical compositions, geological histories, and the evolution of life forms. The human race belongs to this world both physically and intellectually, and humans find themselves in awe of its mysteries and curious about the way it works. It has taken the place of the transcendent realm of the divine in the worldview of Christendom. And it is a massive extension of the *natural environment* in our theory of myth and society. In this case, however, it has not yet merged with the imagination of the *social environment* to produce an imaginary worldview (or mythic scope) in the interest of the social enterprise. Since the astronomy of the ancients, the making of tools, the explorations of new lands, and the mastery of botanical manipulations and animal domestications, scientific technology has been involved in the creation of societies and the pursuit of constructive projects. The methods for thinking scientifically and doing scientific research have been fundamental for knowledge about the natural world in the West since before late Antiquity, and in the Enlightenment since Galileo and Bacon. Now we have colleges of arts and sciences, graduate schools in specific disciplines, primary research programs, research institutes both at the university, national, and corporation levels, and publications for dissemination of the results of scientific investigations. If we add the amazing advancement of electronic technology that makes information available to all people by means of their cell phones and iPads, the thought world in which we are living could be called "scientific."

A scientific anthropology features the intellectual pursuits that start with observations of the natural world and lead to modes of curiosity, methods of experimentation, the honing of skills required to form useful objects, and the ways in which the knowledge of a science feeds back into the social world. The chief interest that drives this tradition of science is gaining *knowledge* of the natural world and experimenting with ways to make it useful. Science is a means for achieving that knowledge. It is more than a method. It is actually a quest for the *control* such knowledge makes possible. Scientific knowledge has usually had some utilitarian aim to advance the work and production of a society. But scientific knowledge has not been enough to cultivate and enhance a social world in which human relations are significant and celebrated. There is, as a matter of fact, a most curious mentality gap in large portions of the American people about the scientific method and worldview.

Michael Specter does not phrase the question quite this way in his book *Denialism*, but as a staff writer for the *New Yorker* in the field of science, he found himself in consternation that large numbers of the American population mistrust science, deny many of its conclusions, and reject some of its achievements even when the facts are clear. Such, for instance, is the record of eradication of certain diseases by vaccination and the adamant refusal of some Americans to have their children vaccinated. And denialism is not only an odd attitude at the level of the people. At the levels of leadership in government and industry the range of strange ideas and attitudes about critical issues is large, including political judgments about nuclear power, rejection of global warming, bottom-line intransigence of agribusinesses, furor over genome research, denial of evolution, snide disparagements of ecological concerns, and the dismissal of population controls. Specter continues with chapters on Vioxx vaccines, racial anatomy, and so forth. The findings of science have been rejected in every case by sizable portions of the population. Specter and the medical profession trace this irrationality to fear, superstition, and the low level of education in America. If, however, we put both the practice of science and its mistrust by the people into the big picture of life in the United States, the problem of mistrust is exacerbated when we see that science is but one of several ways to think about the world. Science takes its place as an academic-industrial practice among other collective practices, each with its own logic, rationale, and method of explanation. These frequently work at cross purposes, canceling one another out in certain cases, as for instance in the "creation-creationism" debate, neither side of which accepts the science of evolution. If so, there can be no surprise that our big picture has no coherence at the level of common agreements and logics. It is that incoherence that frustrates thinking clearly about the whole, and that therefore lets special interests and inadequate logics take the brush and paint over the worldview canvas with their own colors. For this study the questions will be about the possibility that a Christian mentality has contributed to the denialism of scientific knowledge.

3. Now that it is necessary to ask about the interests of *Christianity* in a society that is pulling away from its erstwhile social values and manifestations, we have a different kind of problem on our hands. That is because the Christian religion as an institution never found it necessary to have great interest in the society outside except in making sure that the people supported their rulers. And the Christians' loyalty to Christianity was a matter more of accepting the mentality of its world than of loyalty to

the church as a discrete institution. In our current situation the falling away of church membership is the worrisome problem from the church's point of view, and from the people's point of view it seems to be the irrelevance in modern times of the church's traditional concerns for living. Thus our question about Christianity's contribution to the current sense of dis-ease cannot be answered as easily as those about science and capitalism, social interests that are regularly in the news. The social effect of Christianity has, in fact, not been noticed or questioned until very recently with the emergence of the "Christian Coalition." But our question is not about the unrest caused by the Christian Coalition and its politics. It is rather about the pervasive influence of Christian mentality in the society at large, and whether that mentality can be a factor in the general sense of uneasiness among us. Attitudes and self-understandings of Christians are not as conscious and obvious as are those about science. We do know that Christians are still interested in their churches, but we have seen that Christianity, especially in its institutional formations, is having a difficult time with the independence of persons in the social world. The focus on the individual person and its "spirituality," thought to be the basic form of religion in our time, has not left much room for social interests. That means that we need to consider the continuing influence of Christian *mentality*.

The myth is clear about fixations on *power* as the way to govern, Christian *mission* as the natural stance toward "others," and "mono-thinking" as the way to create and understand order. We have looked at the correlations of this myth with features of the history of the United States. And we have mentioned several times that there was a vague notion of America as a special nation, and that the problems we were having had something to do with the curious sense of our posture as a leading nation-state among the nations while our promises to construct a common-good society at home were not working. It is the Christian myth that continues to inform our sense of manifest destiny and our notions of what a decent society should be, as well as providing us with an unconscious grammar for thinking about the world and our special place within it. It is the narrative logic of that myth, so deeply embedded in the history of Western Christian culture, that seems to be part of our trouble.

4. *Capitalism* is the driving force in our modern world of industry and finance, the force that has created both the attraction and the ugliness of the picture of America in the world today. Since the concept of capitalism and its manifestations in society are obvious, we usually think of it as a separate tradition of practices in parallel to Christian culture and its myth. Capitalism emerged as a system of financial calculation and investment after the Industrial Revolution. The social interests that evolved had little to do with the psychologies and interests that had been cultivated by feudalism and Christendom. And the persons involved with the creation of the practical and scientific achievements of the industries did not at first imagine or invent those features of capitalism that now drive the collective and corporate machines of the postmodern age. It was the success of industrial production that resulted in an excess accumulation of goods (and then capital) that created our world of private enterprise. However, this enterprise has created a global system of industry and finance that is independent of the state and unrelated to the institutions of religion or the cultural traditions of the West.

The interests that drive it are private, not social, corporate, not national. They are in the process of producing a new social psychology to support the motivations required for thinking of oneself as a competitor in a system in which all of the choices and decisions are already made at the corporate level. The corporate economy has created a set of concepts to serve as symbols for the values at stake in their gaming, such as profit, growth, accumulation, *wealth*, and incorporation. These are secular interests about which the Christian myth has little to say.

But in terms of myth theory, these interests have become the *social interests* of the United States as a society and thus have produced a culture and mentality. Unfortunately, cultural anthropologists have not accounted for capitalism as a culture with its own myths, rituals, logics, arts, and social interests. And of course no one seems to be interested in delving into the social consequences of such interests, certainly not in quest of a cultural anthropology to make intraspecific competition, exploitation, and predation seem "natural." We have rendered a criticism of capitalistic behavior only at the level of personal motivation. But that may be enough to get started with our question about the current sense of uneasiness. Thinking about motivation in the United States invariably has a personal, individualistic psychology in mind. When it appeared that the managers of some of our financial institutions had taken advantage of the system to line their own pockets with funds not their own, there were legislative attempts to control such practices. But the main assessment of the cause of the problem was the widespread rhetoric of greed. This charge had the CEOs in mind, of course, not the system. Yet from the people's point of view, such knowledge about the way the system works is bound somehow to exacer-bate negative personal attitudes toward the system and living within its bailiwick.

But now that Christian mentality shares the arena with cap-italism, and might well have learned to be involved by providing sanctions for some of these pursuits, the issues of understanding what kinds of interests, motivations, rewards, and thinking have brought us to this moment in social history take on a very heavy layer of concern. If capitalism can be seen as the *social interest* of the Western nations, our social theory of religion and myth could handle it at the level of abstract model. That is because myth and ritual are the ways in which a collective notices and pays attention to its social interests, thinks about them, and sets them in place as fundamental agreements for the structure and practices of a society. But if that is so, in the case of capitalism our seeming inability to render an analysis of its value for social formation, much less a criticism, may be serious indeed. That is because such a critique would have to ask about the two myths, that of Christianity and that of capitalism, in relation both to each other and to the social formations of our society, including global corporations. And such an analysis could not stay at the facile levels of rationalization now in place but would have to ask about the basic anthropology shared by both. What, in fact, are the fundamental human motivations and social logics taken for granted by each mythic grammar? Can the Christian myth be justified anthropologically by means of the "natural" human instincts for wealth, power, and violence? Can capitalism be jus-tified by means of the "natural" human instinct for predation? And if so, where does that leave us? Would such an analysis of the two myths give any guidance for the construction of a society that did not need autocratic power, violence, and predation? And could the populace actually entertain the social and academic reasons for such analyses, much less alternative pictures and proposals?

5. The discussion of the *nation*, treated now as a social interest, would lead to questions in general about the social interests in authority, power, and dominance, as well as the history of borders, wars, and violence. I remind the reader that although we are aware of these forces at work in our societies, we have no basic anthropology to tell us why we take them for granted as necessary for social formation. These interests just came along with the several major social changes from empire to kingdom and nation-state, making the transitions from one to the other with hardly any friction. It was a familiarity with the model of a kingdom that made it possible in the United States to form a federal republic by means of gaining control of all the colonies on the issues of authority and power. When it came to the dominion thought necessary to form the federal union, armies automatically were marshaled and went to war. However, it was that these "interests" came along automatically with the formation of the federal union, they have certainly never been questioned as necessary ingredients for the nation-state.

THE STATE OF THE UNION

This set of major social interests, including the industrial corporations, is now more powerful and extensive globally than the medieval kingdom-church world ever was. These social interests compete with and overrule the power in the hands of nation-states, unaccustomed as they are to using their govern-ments to monitor corporations and cultivate cultures. And all of the major traditions of social interests are energized for their own growth, expansion, and self-interests. None of these major social interests has an internal mechanism for self-criticism to account for the consequences of its activities for the society as a whole. And none has a braking device to check its speed. This means that the big picture we are painting is chock full of interests that have not been taken up for analysis as the energies driving our activities. And insofar as these interests and activities are creat-ing changes in the thinking and practices of the society, we are confronted with myriad motivations that are extremely difficult to rank, parse, or control.

From the list of major social interests already discussed (our superstructure) the short list of motivations includes *power, profit, accumulation, wealth, invention, scientific knowledge, control, authority, dominance,* and *superiority.* These are the major organizations of energies driving our current social interests. We might well hope that they are not the basic interests of a general anthropology manifest belatedly in the transformations now underway in the social anthropology of our Western civilization. But they do sug-gest the social interests now taken for granted and at work in our society without much attention to myths of the past or pro-jections into the future. They are not the product of the devious designs of individual persons creating such a world for their own purposes and gratification. They may have gotten out of hand in several respects, thus taking their places in the curious congeries of social freedoms and constraints that is creating the general sense of dis-ease in our time. But it makes no sense to charge any one of them with the dis-ease itself as if it were the single cause of the recent state of the world and should be corrected accordingly.

The problems we are having with various combinations of these interests are to be found in the fact that the several major "advancements" in human "creativity" and "production" that have emerged in the past several hundred years have become the "social interests" of our societies, taken for granted as the way the world works. And they are frequently in conflict with one another, none with an internal mechanism for self-control. As each pursues its own interests, it frequently occurs that two or more organizations of interests converge on some issue or event and come into conflict, especially when an ideological tradition or a social institution encounters another with a different set of purposes. These can be understood as overlaps among the several interests where a marked difference in logics and values occurs. This is where persons with intellectual and moral sensitivities often find it difficult to compromise with or accede to the interests of the stronger as if the stronger should always win. This conjunction of diverse social interests can become a new location for exploring a new kind of conflict that cannot be negotiated without understanding the logics behind the different interests involved. If the logics of the stronger interest have settled into an acceptance by the cultural mind-set, the interests of a minority voice of protest will not prevail unless a third party with power intervenes. An illustration of this situation would be the futile "debate" about "evolution" (science) and "creationism" (religion) that has not been resolved by discussions between the two factions, leaving it in need of adjudication by public legislation and school board policies. Thus the many issues of overlap conflicting in our time tell us that dealing with conflict in general, in the interest of the well-being of the society as a whole, is the major challenge of individuals and society when thinking about the big picture. And since conflicting social interests are both the cause (even if not "intentionally") and the hope (because of the energies and resources they represent) of our challenging social situation, there should be something we could do about it. The analysis proffered in this chapter is intended to take a first step by asking whether a collective understanding of our situation along these lines is possible and helpful. It does seem that, for an individual caught in the middle between two conflicting social interests, understanding and analyzing the conflict at the level of their logics should be the way in which negotiation could begin.

This review of our major social interests has suggested that such an understanding will probably not be forthcoming from traditional disciplines in the study of government, society, and history, or from the leaderships of the major social interests themselves. However, there is a large number of publications in our time generating a public discourse that rides under the rubric of *cultural criticism.* This is hardly limited to a department or discipline in the academy, although many of those who pursue this kind of social analysis have their roots largely in the departments of English literature and literary criticism. As a group of intellectuals and authors, they represent traditions of thought and research about *culture,* or the meanings of what we might call the manifestations of social interests in the arts and public discourse. These traditions can be viewed as a social phenomenon of political and cultural importance that can be traced back to the beginning of Western civilization. Chapters 4 and 5 were intended to remind us of these traditions.

CULTURAL ANALYTICS

We can now return to the concept of *culture* as the way in which a mythic environment is symbolized and made recognizable. Since symbols of a mythic environment work in the space created by the distance of the mythic world from the daily round of practices, they allow for a kind of unfocused but knowing acceptance of the society's mythic rationale that we call a mentality. A culture manifest in a set of symbols is more obvious, objective, and at hand than a mentality that resides at the level of a social psychology. Thus a culture's markers (symbols) are more easily recognized as a way to acknowledge and refer to the meanings of a society's mythic investments. We have not rendered a profile of the symbols customary for the major institutions of social interests, but it has been assumed that the reader will have recognized such in their descriptions. The nation's flag and the Christian's cross are examples of symbols created by two of our major organizations of social interests, the use of each in practice constrained by taboos and codes. There have been investments in these symbols on the part of the people that can erupt in shouts and violent behavior. There are other symbols now at work in our society that do not work that way. An example would be the portrait of a CEO on the front cover of the glossy business magazine (a symbol of the power in the hands of the chief, and his desire to be seen as successful). And what about the seductive smile on the advertisements of the capitalistic/consumer society? There are many others, such as the epaulets on the generals, and the logos of the business establishments that let us know what they want us to think about them.

A society's own mentality cannot be noticed and mentioned overtly without raising questions about its mythic anchorage and rationale. Such an observation about the signs of a mentality is often resisted by the populace as if stemming from a subtle criticism of its culture and myth, or its own sense of identity. Nevertheless, in every society of the Western series of kingdoms and nations since its memorialized beginnings in the Ancient Near East, there have been persons doing social analyses whose observations on the underlying mentality of the culture were recognized not as cultural criticisms but as cultural productions. That is because their cultural productions took the form of what we now call myths, rituals, histories, literature, architecture, and the arts. The societies recognized their works as reminders or amplifications, perhaps even as celebrations, of the society's self-understanding, not as social or cultural critique. But upon closer analysis, many of these works reveal that the authors or artists had thought deeply about the practices of their society and had pondered the mythic logic underlying a people's mentality. We cannot refer to them as a "class," or to their productions as a cultural "tradition" as we have learned to imagine such in the modernity of Western history. They were, rather, individuals who found ways to exercise their intellectual curiosities and capacities in whatever social position they might happen to have. Yet there is evidence that authors read one another's works and recognized one another's projects as explorations of their common social and cultural worlds. Archaeologists and historians have found the results of these projects in shrines, temples, palaces, libraries, theaters, and schools where learned intellectuals must have labored. Thus we can now imagine them as writers, artists, performers, philosophers, and advisers of several kinds to those in power. They produced what we have come to call the early Western "traditions" of history, literature, and culture. They, of course, did not call it that for themselves. They were all taking advantage of the skills ("arts") of their persons and professions to think about the functions taken for granted in their own societies as social entities and explore the gaps between what was said about a practice, and what its consequences may have been. I want to sketch a review of this history of intellectuals as an exercise in parsing the levels of interest and logic that occur in cultural critique. The review may also prepare for a discussion of the burgeoning number of cultural critics analyzing our current social and intellectual scenes. These later intellectuals are much more self-conscious about themselves as belonging to a class or tradition and have even learned to name the subcultures they analyze. In course they have conceptualized, named, and defined several currents of modern mentality by identifying features of our collective thinking and practices that are causing conflicts and uneasiness. These include several political ideologies (for example, communism, Marxism, socialism, and so on) and mentality concepts (such as liberalism, modernism, structuralism, and postmodernism), as well as aesthetic descriptions for various cultural productions such as novels, architecture, cinema, theater, television, advertising, and the video world. Much of their mutual discourse is about how an analyst sees his social scene in relation to earlier forms of cultural production and the understanding of society. They are those among us whose analytic abilities have been stimulated by the intellectual conundrums among the many practices and policies now current in our society. Since that is the case, they may be the analysts who should be able to tell us what happened to our big picture, the Christian worldview that Western civilization once took for granted.

The series can begin with the scribes of the Ancient Near East, those who noticed the extravagant sense of personal power assumed by the monarch and the strange way in which the people accepted the notion of the king and his powers. They were those who wrote the myths of creation (*enuma elish*) by a family of viciously warring deities. No sane person would want to be part of that. They also wrote some laws for the king (Hammurabi) who, in his right royal mind, would never have written them, but who allowed the scribes to publish them under his name. In fact, the scribes even introduced the laws by a first-person glorification to the effect that "[Before the creation] Anum and Enil named me to promote the welfare of the people, me, Hammurabi, the devout, god-fearing prince, to cause justice to prevail in the land" (*Hammurabi's Code*). We now think that Hammurabi must have accepted the scribes' honorific and codes of law, and must not have minded being thought of as a "preexistent." The scribes also wrote a series of fantastic novels about the first king, Gilgamesh, who went on his quests and conquests because he wanted to be immortal, but who failed to reach the world of the gods and was told to return to his city Uruk, write his epic of failures on the stela at its gate, and celebrate the building of a city as the sufficient reward for a mortal's endeavors. Then there were the writers of the Hebrew epics who explored the reasons for their national tragedies without giving up on the notion of a social ethic to make possible the life and history of their people. The Greeks, always worried about the family tragedies of their kings, wondered whether they needed to have any kings at all. They produced philosophers, artists, and tragedians to explore their own social anthropology and mentality. The family intrigues in the world of the gods were brought down to earth for the people to contemplate at the theater. Suddenly there was Aphrodite perched on the edge of the proscenium saying, "Look here. I am Aphrodite, the goddess in charge of such intrigues. Pay attention to me," as if playing a part in a family tragedy could possibly be the answer to the social dynamics in need of resolution. Then there was Caesar at the height of his illustrious career, about to be assassinated in front of the senate, turning to Brutus and saying, "Et tu?" And Virgil's *Aeneid*, now considered by many scholars as the most important epic from the Hellenistic-Roman period to influence the mentality of the Roman-Christian empires.

As for the early Christian authors, they took themselves much too seriously for ironic humor and cultural critique. They painted the pagans as debauched, read and debated the biblical texts as if they were true history, and wrote theological treatises. But even with such an obsession on figuring out the transcendent designs of the divine author and ultimate authority, there eventually could be an Augustine who dared a new genre by writing his *Confessions*. He wrote in the first person about his failure to achieve a settled sense of salvation. It sometimes seemed a tryst, sometimes a quarrel with his god. And after Christendom began to come unraveled, Christianity's special effect on the subjectivity of the individual could create another new genre of literature in the essays of a Michel de Montaigne (1533–92).

His first-person account was not an anguished confession as was Augustine's, nor was he troubled about the beauty of the earth that was forbidden to enjoy, as was Petrarch. In the case of Montaigne's essays the author was at home in the ambience of Bordeaux, a city in which he himself played responsible roles in all of its activities and in its governance. As an Enlightenment intellectual, Montaigne's interest was in the way cities were working as discrete societies *within* the kingdoms of the time. He traveled widely throughout France, Germany, Austria, Switzerland, and Italy.

The genius of William Shakespeare (1564–1616), on the other hand, was to use his skill as a scriptwriter to imagine the theater as a reflection of the social, and the social as the theater of the drama of human intrigues. If "All the world's a stage, And all the men and women merely players," as Jaques says in *As You Like It*, we might want to meditate on the "merely" for a while, then bewonder Shakespeare's notion of the theater as the way in which our social theatrics can be mimicked and analyzed. That he tells us how this works by having a lord, who wishes he were a fool, speak the famous lines on behalf of Orlando's friend, an "old poor man . . . oppress'd with two weak evils, age and hunger," lets us see how important it might be to know how we are doing with our parts. Shakespeare is an amazingly clear example of an artist working with the reflexive relationships between society and mentality without allowing philosophic abstractions to intrude.

It was Raymond Williams who saw that the relationship between culture and society could be a topic to focus an entire history of intellectual production. In 1958 he published *Culture and Society,* a remarkably consistent analytic study of forty intellectuals (novelists, cultural historians, and journalists) from 1780 to 1950 concerned about the social changes brought about by the Industrial Revolution. It was this intellectual tradition that introduced the term *culture* to name the values, practices, and mores fundamental for the traditional English system of civil society, an ethos these intellectuals saw threatened by the industrial society. They had found the newly emergent industrial city ugly and the state of its workers and inhabitants deplorable. This assessment of the changes taking place was extremely troubling to them. They saw these changes as threats to their traditional *culture* and its values. As a collection of intellectual elites working on the analysis of their culture and society, seeking a remedy for social inequities, exploitations, and the ugliness that had occurred, Williams's study is most impressive. It joins the works of Marx, Althusser, Giddens, Bourdieu, Harrington, Sahlins, and others to register the profound learning available to anyone interested in thinking critically about the problem of capitalism and the need for experimentation to be invested in the construction of a social democracy. Twenty years after publishing *Culture and Society,* Williams published *Keywords: A Vocabulary of Culture and Society* (1978). In a fascinating introduction to this study of the changing meanings of the vocabulary that did the work for thinking about culture and society (110 words in the 1978 edition; 131 words in the second edition, 1983), Williams makes the point that the social changes and vocabulary changes were linked in such a way that it was difficult to tell which change came first. This intriguing observation, suggesting the possible role of intellectual discourse within changes taking place in social formation, does seem to fit with the way in which the authors in this intellectual tradition read one another and argued about art, culture, education, industry, and society. I was impressed with the fact that this discourse was available to the public in print. It was Williams who noticed the significance of the terms *art* and *culture* as they entered and weaved their way through this discourse about social issues and what he called the "whole pattern of life." One does notice that this intellectual tradition of social critique did not focus upon the social logic of the Anglican myth or the British tradition. It would be helpful to know the effect of these intellectual and social transformations on the way in which the Christian myth is now understood in England. But of course we already know that the Christian ritual had been translated long since into theater, and that the rehearsal of the Anglican creed (the "very God of very God") had become a mental gymnastic for learning to live with myth as metaphor. This difference from the Protestants in America underlines our challenge. But is also indicates that the British intellectuals had not yet realized that their culture was grounded in the Christian myth, and that the social logic of this Christian myth also needed to be surfaced and analyzed.

CURRENT CRITIQUE

In the colleges and universities of the United States the departments of English literature continued to draw upon the English traditions of literary culture studied by Raymond Williams. And in some sense the European intellectual and literary tradition continued to be the standard texts for the study of literature and history in the United States. But the social situation in the United States became unclear between the two world wars, and especially after the Second World War. It was not yet clear to academics that our responses to the wars positioned us in naïve postures as the "leader" of nations in the entire world, and that this naïveté called for some critical thinking on the part of our intellectuals and advisers to the government. There were, however, important figures who sensed the social changes and the change in cultural mood that was underway. The figures in the fields of English and history at first sought to explain and defend the importance of the grand English tradition of literary culture, aware of the fact that the United States did not have the kind of anchor in the "grand Western Tradition" similar to their colleagues in Europe, and that their students seemed to be less interested in cultivating that tradition. The many essays by Lionel Trilling can be used as an example of this effort to analyze what he called *The Liberal Imagination* and to deal with the relation of the literary tradition to politics, society, philosophy, and culture in the United States. He was concerned about the changes taking place in the period that subsequently came to be called modernism, and his works were read in college departments of English as standard statements on the analysis of literary genres and their social and cultural functions. As he said:

Now the novel as I have described it has never really established itself in America. Not that we have not had very great novels but that the novel in America diverges from its classic intention, which, as I have said, is the investigation of the problem of reality beginning in the social field. The fact is that American writers of genius have not turned their minds to society. (*The Liberal Imagination*)

That was about to change. One of the problems creating this tension between "classic intention" and "the problem of reality" was that the Americas were multicultural, and some excellent novels, stories, and essays written by authors of other ethnicities had begun to appear that caught the attention of the people. Examples are found in the work of James Baldwin, Jorge Luis Borges, and Toni Morrison. These and many others had a difficult time at first finding a place in the academy where the grand Western literary tradition was ensconced. Then there was the Vietnam War, and students throughout the United States began to talk about "some mistaken turn" in the past that created our inability as a nation to address issues of social inequality and foreign policy abuses based on military might. They began to ask for courses that were more relevant to the society we were becoming and the world in which we were living. It was from about this time that the familiar roster of "new" courses began to appear: black studies, Spanish (Latino) literature, "modern" languages (including those spoken by Native Americans and immigrants), cross-culture issues, women's studies, and so forth.

Academics were not prepared for the critical energies and questions of their students. The students wanted to know what the standard curriculum had to teach them about living in their own time, struggling with social issues in a global context. The faculties in colleges and universities found themselves trying to appease their students while holding on to the traditions and methods of their disciplines. After all, they were those who knew what a field of study was and at what cost their own learning of their disciplines had taken place. Harvard University became the center for the academic discussion of this issue. In 1978 the Faculty of Arts and Sciences adopted a "core curriculum" intended to list the standard courses that belonged to the Western tradition of the university and the learning it represented, archived, protected, and worked on in order to pass it on to the next generation of students and teachers. All hell broke loose in the colleges and universities across the nation. The Harvard faculty and its president, Charles Eliot, found themselves in the middle of an intellectual storm, but they could not relinquish their sense of obligation to the accumulation of knowledge they represented. Their proposal of a core curriculum launched the troubling eighties, during which faculties everywhere had to justify their curricula in relation to the social situation, ask anew about the purposes of higher education, and/or join a general discussion about the relationship of college to the constituency and welfare of the society. It was in the midst of this academic and intellectual palaistra that the term *cultural critique* took to the high wire and balancing act. What a marvelous turn to the subject of society and culture on the part of American academics and literary critics. A journal called *Cultural Critique* was founded at the Department of English at the University of Minnesota and immediately drew a large number of authors to its pages. This journal is still published and consistently presents the critical reader with the thinking of the best minds in the field. The first article in the first issue of *Cultural Critique* was by William V. Spanos (SUNY Binghamton) and entitled "The Apollonian Investment of Modern Humanist Education: The Examples of Matthew Arnold, Irving Babbitt, and I. A. Richards, Part 1." It is a thoroughly deconstructive analysis of the works of these authors in their efforts to define the cultural and social values of the Western intellectual and literary tradition on the one hand, while addressing the questions being raised about these values, and especially about the values of literary production and criticism for the education of the people in general. It had appeared that the level of sophisticated learning in America was slowly eroding, and that the self-confidence of the literary academics as the protectors of "the" cultural tradition was also in trouble. Starting with Matthew Arnold, considered to be the founder of the humanities, then analyzing Babbitt and Richards, Spanos revealed two fundamental features in common, features that were telling because they actually described the intellectual ambience of literary criticism as an academic discipline from its beginnings in the middle of the nineteenth century to its awakening as a (the?) vehicle of cultural criticism in the last quarter of the twentieth century. One was that all three, as representatives of the much larger set of authors and critics, thought of the value and function of literature in terms of the "classical" tradition (Greek philosophy, history, and literature). For them, literature was "good" when it could be shown that the author had written in the classical tradition, exemplifying its ethos and ethics as contemporary values.

The second mark of commonality was a set of assumptions about the "good" society, and the ways in which the classical tradition guaranteed its structure and operation. Spanos uses the image and metaphor of Bentham's panopticon, taken up by Foucault in his stunning research into the logics and psychologics of the mental hospital and prison, to describe the shape and function of the social and cultural world at stake for this modernist/academic view of the world. The "Apollonian investment" turns out to be more than a defense of reason or rationality (understood as a legacy from the Greeks); it is actually an unexamined acceptance of the fundamental logic of the Western tradition as a cultural mind-set. Spanos occasionally calls this the *logos* of the Western Christian tradition. The shape of the world in this tradition is that of a sphere. The sphere has a center, from which information, injunction, and supervision radiate. If the center inculcates the classical tradition—that is, educates society in its culture—the result is that the ideal society is ordered and controlled from the center, and that the ideal population is subservient and content, thus guaranteeing peace. It is not too difficult to discern the features of Christendom in this description of Western culture, the culture that provides the mental and social logics for these literary critics, as Spanos reveals.

I have taken advantage of Spanos's brilliant analysis of the mentality of modernism on its way to the fragmentation and thrashing about of the intellectual scenes of our own time, confronted as they are with the troubling state of the world. Spanos's essay is worthy of several seminars and can be used to bring critical focus on many current social issues in need of analysis. It was, however, the clarity with which he was able to isolate the effects of innumerable assumptions unrecognized, unacknowledged, and so unexamined among these giants of our intellection tradition that I found startling. Because his description of the *logos* at the base of "modern humanist education" was so close to my notion of the mythic logic at the core of Christian mentality, I could use it to mark the threshold of the cultural breakdown in our time that has threatened more than the self-assured self-identities of our social institutions of the "classical/Christian" tradition. It is the pervasive mythic mentality of that grand Western tradition that is still at work among us, frustrating other ways of thinking about ourselves and the world.

It was not long before the classical humanist tradition and the core curricula for the university gave way to the avant-garde topics of modernism and postmodernism. John McGowan became interested in this discourse among intellectuals and cultural critics. In 1991 he published *Postmodernism and Its Critics,* a detailed study of the philosophic traditions in Europe during the past three centuries, those that had emptied into the very postmodernists of the twentieth century that have been read in America in the fields of literary and biblical criticism. McGowan was a brilliant postmodernist literary critic and historian of the philosophic traditions within which postmodernists emerged, and he was deeply concerned about philosophy, culture, and society. He was extremely helpful on the academic front. He was able to describe the historical-social reasons for the intellectual shifts that took place away from the traditional, monistic worldviews of both philosophy and theology, through the period of modernism where (1) the foundational principles of religion, imperialism, and patriarchy were set aside, (2) the concept of autonomy governed both the sense of the social world as a human creation and the individual as a singular and independent being, and (3) the "romantic" visions of spiritual, ethical, and intellectual worlds were constructed to substitute for the loss of the traditional monism and to counter the emergent world of capitalism. As a result he was able finally to explore the tenor of the period of postmodernism. McGowan's penetrating study of the postmodernists' quests for freedom from the monolith of an all-encompassing society caught my attention. It was this quest that became the common theme for the postmodernists, and for the anxiety common to intellectuals who could not finally recommend an alternative vision of the social, much less one that could be based on an autonomous individualism. Each of the thinkers McGowan studied had picked up some major feature of the traditional monolithic picture to deconstruct the whole, escape its domination, and argue for autonomy. There were Kant (Reason), Hegel (Spirit), Marx (Property), Nietzsche (Power), Jameson (Language), Derrida (Logos), Foucault (History), Freud (Psyche), and Bourdieu (Practice), among others. In every case the problem was the inability to dispense with a "holism" of some kind without destroying the significance of a totally free autonomy that had escaped the monism, existed outside its limits, and was now excluded from a social context and meaning. Thus the variety of intellectuals, positioning themselves outside the academy's intellectual traditions and the societies within which they labored were found to be cultivating a general anxiety about not being heard. McGowan calls this mode of autonomy "negative freedom."

The picture he paints of our intellectual disciplines at the ending of the grand narrative tradition of Western culture intends a thorough sweep of the academy, and it is quite impressive. At this level of society there is little left of a monolithic system that is seen to structure and explain the totality of a culture. The vigorous academic disciplines have become specializations in research on the pieces of the puzzle, the fragments of the erstwhile confidence in knowing (or wanting to know) how the worlds of social being worked and for what reasons. McGowan's study accounts for this history of philosophic fractures in relation to the momentous shifts in social formations and their consequences for practice and identity caused by the Industrial Revolution and the dissolution of erstwhile kingdoms and empires. His work explains the current effects of postmodernism at the level of the humanities and social sciences: resistance to theory, focus on practice and behavior, grounding in material culture, and modulations in Marxism to account for corporate capitalism. No wonder the Christian myth is having trouble in America, and the big-picture culture of Christian history continues to reside, if at all, only at the level of an unacknowledged, unconscious mentality.

About the same time, David Harvey published *The Condition of Postmodernism* (1990). Most of the book is actually about modernism in the early twentieth century and the transformation to postmodernism in the late twentieth century. What a delightful surprise to find that his detailed analysis of what he calls the social categories of perception is not only a stunning debate with the wild and woolly discourse of his time, when deconstruction and the newly coined concept of *postmodernism* were ringing the changes in the world of intellectuals, but also a most provocative and prescient description of the world of the twenty-first century, with its obvious increase in the "condition of postmodernism," as he calls it. Two subthemes are of importance. One is the change in architectural design as a way to chart the changes that take place in the experience of space and time. The other is the change from Fordism to "flexible accumulation" as a description of "late" twentieth-century capitalism.

In citing the many well-known philosophers and culture critics whose studies and views still define the content and arena for the quest to understand our social situation, Harvey lets the reader know that he too has taken his place among the analysts of culture. But the surprise comes when one realizes that Harvey's own scientific discipline is *geography!* It is this field of knowledge that has given him a sense of the importance of *place* for human societies, and made possible his distinction between *place* and *space*. *Space* is the term currently being used by cultural critics for the "location" of individuals and practices in a world that no longer have clearly defined "places" for social belonging and meaningful projects. Harvey's position is that the loss of "place" is part of the reason for the unsettledness and uncertainty characteristic for our personal and social worlds. He sees that the loss of place is related to the loss of the categories of history and "meta-narrative" (as postmodernists describe our "condition"), and sets out to investigate the "Origins of [this] Cultural Change."

Now for the second surprise. Harvey has reviewed the history of capitalism from at least the time of the financial-feudal crisis of 1850 and Marx's writing of *The Communist Manifesto*. He traces the structural changes of society and the financial crises of the capitalistic system through Fordism (starting in the early 1900s), the First World War (the result of an international competition confused about lands and borders), the depression of 1929–32, the Second World War (when the singularity or purity of the land-ethnicity-nation combination got out of hand), the rise of industry and what Harvey calls the transition from Fordism to "flexible accumulation" in the postwar period, and the stock market crash of 1987, to the dominance of corporations and the financial industry during and after the Reagan administration and their practice of what he calls "flexible accumulation." There is a pattern to the financial crises at every turn. It is that the capitalistic system produces a greater accumulation of commodities and services than a contemporary market can use, and so needs to expand its markets, retool its plants, move to new locations and sources of labor, lay plans for the future, find ways to devalue its excess accumulation, and place its assets in such "financial containers" as banks, credits, loans, futures, and the like. All of this we read about every day in the major newspapers. The question is how all of that has affected the "culture of postmodernity."

Harvey turns to the market and the speed with which the advertisements in magazines and TV, the click of images throughout the electronic media world, and the cinema of disconnected fantasies project a world in which time and space are compressed into a flurry of moments in the present with a focus on the invention of new styles and attractive commodities for the creation and titillation of an individual's desires. This is a description of our media world that should be obvious. What is not so obvious, and this is the third surprise, is that Harvey is able to link this culture of fleeting images to the practice of capitalism's global conquests. The expansions of industries, markets, and corporations leading to the conquest of other lands and peoples, the breakdown of national borders by corporations and international financial institutions, the creation of new monies and fictitious capital, the development of products for mass consumption, and the invention of services as commodities have created a world that is too large, too fast moving, and too complicated for any individual to comprehend. The traditional combination of lands, nations, histories, and futures in the worldview of a people, a big picture that gave them their sense of place in the world and gave meaning to their projects, is no longer working in the age of late capitalism. Traditional sensibilities cannot keep up with the speed of disconnected images and repetitive radical changes created by global capitalism. The moves that corporations make in their ceaseless quest for new resources, territories, and markets are always one step ahead of the people and their government. It is therefore not surprising, according to Harvey, that the culture "historians" of our time, looking for "culture" as if there must be one more or less like the ones we always assumed with the use of that term, have had to call our time "postmodernism." He finds this term terribly inadequate, riding high over the previous period of modernism as its critique and correction, but without investigating either of these "modernisms" in relation to the history of capitalism. It would be better to see postmodernism as the latest stage in the evolution of capitalism and the effect it has had upon the markets and mentalities of the people, including the artists and creators of "culture." It is the accelerating indebtedness, asset inflation, the creation of fictitious capital, and the ease with which capitalism has turned all human projects into businesses for profit that has forced the experience of space and time into the chaotic speed with which decisions now need to be made, decisions that do not have time for analyzing the pictures of context, or for thinking about future consequences. The result has been that the traditional language available for representing culture is anachronistic. The new experience of compressed space and time has empowered aesthetics over ethos as a way to respond. This has made it difficult for the renewal of historical materialism that Harvey thinks is needed in order to construct a social world to replace the loss of place and history. He concludes his chapter "Theorizing the Transition" (from Fordism to flexible accumulation, or from modernism to postmodernism) with the assertion "that capitalism is a constantly revolutionary force in world history, a force that perpetually re-shapes the world into new and often quite unexpected configurations. Flexible accumulation appears, at least, to be a new configuration and, as such, it requires that we scrutinize its manifestations with the requisite care and seriousness, using, nevertheless, the theoretical tools that Marx devised." With that we may be ready for Jameson.

Fredric Jameson is America's leading social and cultural critic, having produced stunning volumes on Marxism, discourse and language, architectural style, political ideology, science fiction, utopian desire, and literary criticism, all with critical insights into innumerable material practices and productions of postmodernity. His book *Postmodernism; or, The Cultural Logic of Late Capitalism* can be used to conclude this chapter on "cultural analytics," because it brings together most of the social and cultural streams of thought and practice with which we have been dealing. For Jameson, cultural critique can no longer be limited to literary production and analysis. That was what the modernists of the previous century assumed. And that was what the Harvard faculties who proposed the core curriculum thought. Modernism was the period of intellectual engagement with the concept of Western culture as the "grand narrative" that could reveal and explain the values of the past, address the social uncertainties of the late nineteenth and early twentieth centuries, and suggest a "return" and "application" by means of formal education. From at least the beginning of the last quarter of the twentieth century, Jameson realized that this notion was mistaken and could not work, that not only were our social practices and thinking breaking away from the constraints of the "Western tradition," but our sense of the autonomy of the individual (as well as society) had begun to produce practices, attitudes, and artistic productions concerned with the new "freedoms" driving our social self-understandings. He saw that our discourse and writings were still beholden to the meanings of the words, syntax, and logics of the past (*The Prison House of Language*). He understood that Marxism was hardly to be updated by finding new ways to address ever more complicated political entanglements with calls for revolution (*Marxism and Form*). He addressed the historical turning point of our popular attitudes toward government in "Periodizing the 60s." He tackled the function of "narrative as a socially symbolic act" in *The Political Unconscious*. And he offered a cultural critical assessment of science fiction and what he saw as a form of utopian desire in *Archeology of the Future*. These studies have amounted to a relocation of culture from the realm of literature and ideas to the material productions of artists and thinkers who are intentionally addressing the social system by reflecting on the effect of its postmodern fragmentation upon the new individualism. An example would be Jameson's fascination with and use of recent architectural styles to emphasize space and openness instead of the more traditional features of functionality.

It is late capitalism that takes the place of erstwhile patterns and values of culture for Jameson. Whereas the media of modernism once evoked the larger contexts of history and society with their patterns and practices, the thoroughly capitalistic worlds of the current media and advertisement now fill the screen of the social world with moments of virtual encounter that are merely attention getting interruptions. One need not read Jameson to know what he is talking about. Reading the daily newspaper is more than enough to realize that what counts as "news" is no longer a selection of public events with social significance reported in a deliberate style aimed at the "reasons" for them and whether the political system has taken or can take them up for consideration. No. The *Los Angeles Times*, for example, now trades in photos and advertisements for striking moments in the recent sports event, the dramatic stance of a super new model automobile, the facial fronts of the next horror movie, and the decision of some celebrity to put her mansion by the sea up for sale—all on page one! Jameson traces this transformation of popular culture from the literary production of the modernist period, through the increase of the media of radio, television, cinema, and videos of the postmodern period, to the ways in which "social media," "texting," and "selfies" are now the sources of communication around and about the world. This knowledge is mainly a matter of a flurry of ad hoc moments in which a tweak catches one's attention. And since the moments have no social or historical context, they accumulate like dots that have no connections except within the illusion of one's personal titillations.

The result, according to Jameson, is that popular media have erased the erstwhile sense of history, place, event, meaning, and society. Instead, the speed with which things happen and the photos are clicked indicates that time as a moment is all we have left for being in the world. With the social psychology created by this media world it is not possible for an individual even to imagine a society as a "totality." One hardly belongs to more than one's "group" as the society within which one knows one's identity. So my large mythic world of the three major environments (nature, society, and language) may not be working any more in America.

What is at work, according to Jameson, is the "production" (his term) of the artist, where "artist" refers to all those creative persons who are finding the unsettled social situation both troubling and invigorating in some way, and are devoting their energies and skills to address one of the fragments of the fractured culture to encourage thinking about the quality of life and the future. Working within the breaks between space and place, individual and collective, time and history, photo and narrative, virtual reality and the empirical, artists are painting pictures, writing poems and novels, constructing buildings, designing monuments, building machines, proposing programs, forming movements, exploring psychologies, and experimenting with politics in the attempt to rearrange the erstwhile categories of social existence in a humanizing way. Jameson used the famous house that Frank Gehry built in Los Angeles as an example of such artistry. It was a "remodeling" of an older house that opened it up to the trees outside with a huge skylight for a "roof" and a "kitchen" outdoors, plus many other additions that made places for traditional behavior in spaces that were neither inside (normal) nor outside (unusual) but visionary. At the end of a lengthy chapter describing this structure and relating an interview with Gehry, Jameson allows himself some meditations on "the strange new feeling of an absence of inside and outside, the bewilderment and loss of special orientation, . . . the messiness of an environment in which things and people no longer find their 'place.' . . . [The house] offer[s] useful symptomatic approaches to the nature of postmodern hyperspace, without giving us any model or explanation of the thing itself. . . . Frank Gehry's house is to be considered the attempt to think a material thought" (*Postmodernism*). Elsewhere, Jameson lets us see that he considers postmodernism a response to capitalistic modernism in which the individual experienced the loss of his possession of his own "production" and its product. This in turn led to depression, powerlessness, and meaninglessness in life. The alternative was "consumption" as an escape, the addiction to the "pleasures" of things one has not had any credit for in the process of their production.

MURKY MYTHS

Jameson does not find any "big pictures" for personal or social orientation in the cultures of postmodernity. Late capitalism has created a culture of consumption in which the image stands for reality, the moment for history, and aestheticism covers for knowledge. That is not quite fair, however, because Jameson's cultural criticism is thoroughly grounded in a deeply intellectualist anthropology. He looks for the ways in which the style of another's "production" is a thoughtful response to a circumstance and social situation. He calls the culture of late capitalism a "logic," and he treats the artist's aesthetic sensibility as a mode of thinking about the world in which one lives. In a sense the entire tradition of literary production and cultural criticism reviewed in this chapter represents the Western mode of critical thinking about society and culture. This intellectual tradition runs parallel to the much more familiar intellectual traditions of philosophy, theology, and the sciences. And its value for the self-understanding of societies throughout cannot be questioned.

But its aesthetic mode of thinking and argumentation has not been analyzed in terms similar to the grammars of philosophy and theology. In these intellectual traditions points are made by definitions, declarative sentences, and syllogisms, all according to the rules of syntactical lines of reasoning. The closest I have been able to come to the aestheticism uncovered by Jameson is my theory of mythic mentality. But in the case of Christian mentality there is a narrative logic in the space between the patterns of a social system and the Christian myth as an articulated story. In the use of the arts for thinking about society there is no narrative myth. The assessments must be made by aesthetic judgments, and the cultural criticism Jameson sees stays at the level of aesthetic sensibility, in this case doing a kind of "comparison" between the sensibility of the social experience and the sensibility of the artistic production. To use the term *comparison* clearly stretches the kind of reasoning involved, but it does indicate the critique suggested by the artist's production and its suggestion that there is another way of looking at a situation or phenomenon. To make possible "another way of looking at" a social situation is a profoundly intellectualist argument in favor of critical thinking, both at the point of making an assessment, and in terms of the more elongated response called for by an art object. So Jameson's aesthetic criticism at the "end" of the long tradition of Western culture does not need our Aristotelian systems of philosophy and thinking in order to say what it is about the social system that needs analysis. The aesthetic mode of "reasoning" is more in the Hebrew tradition of wisdom, in which the making of slightly different but "parallel" images created a space between them in which the "wisdom" intended could be found.

With Jameson's aestheticism, however, it is less a wisdom, more a critique, and the critique is thoroughly aimed at the social system without any suggestion of or call for declarative statements or abstract reasoning. This is new, and the way in which Jameson understands his aestheticism model to work as a cultural criticism marks a major advance in a society that has not been able to think at all about its culture and society. What a timely contribution to the need for analyzing our social situation in the United States.

Unfortunately, the components of Jameson's cultural analysis do not include the energies driving the social interests we have been reviewing. The scope of the social has been reduced to the mentality of aestheticism and the effect of late capitalism upon the sensibility of individuals. This is an extremely important contribution to the analysis of our society, to be sure. But it overlooks the larger pictures and the social issues about which we have been concerned. These social issues have increased in intensity during the period in which late capitalism has produced its culture of virtual reality. The issues have even outpaced the earlier sense of discomfort we have noted as the symptom of the popular response to the social issues in question. Recent reports about the costly failures of the Pentagon's plans for intercontinental missiles; the sobering news items about permanent nuclear fuel pollutions; conflicts among nations about controlling nuclear weapons; the government's inability to control arms manufacturing and the arming of third-world militias; governmental inability to address global warming and climate change due to commercial interests; America's inability to address the growing gap between the rich and the poor; the persistence of the conservative (Christian) political party (now calling itself the Tea

Party); the massacres, militias, and warring in the Near East after ten years of America's presence and "leadership"; and the political deadlock in Washington standing in the way of open deliberation about social and global issues: all these issues are encountered on the other side of Jameson's culture of late capitalism. Late capitalism may have created the culture of virtual reality to keep the populace smiling, but if its aestheticism has taken the place of noticing the social issues of the world and caring about the health of the nation, hope for the future that depends upon the energies and agreements of the people is hardly possible. As a matter of fact, the tone of the public comments and essays about the state of the nation and the world is truly frightening.

Jameson may be right about the demise of traditional Western culture. He is not alone in this assessment of our current malaise. And if he is right, such a historic shifting of cultural values might well help account for the fact that Christianity as the religious institution of the United States has found itself in trouble with its people and their secular culture. In my recent books (*Myth and the Christian Nation* and *Christian Mentality*) I distinguished between the medieval worldview of Catholic Christianity, the narrative logic of the Christian myth in the Bible as Protestants understand it, and the (secular) Christian mentality pervasive within the Western cultural tradition that continues to influence attitudes and thinking among the people at a subliminal level without any reference or appeal to the church and its myth. The point is that even if the church and the myth are losing their erstwhile places of prominence in Western societies, a Christian mentality can still survive. This mentality can be discerned in the political system and legislative debates in the United

States, and it is this mentality that the rest of the world sees (or in-tuits) lurking behind our "missions" to the world of other nations. Apparently the demise of the Western literary culture has not af-fected the sensibility of those in charge of our superstructures. It is between the "base" and the "superstructure" that the grammars, logics, and sensibilities of a residual culture continue to operate in the generation of ideologies. The sense of being right(eous), the constant appeal to the "values" of the (Christian) nation, the crit-icism of "progressive" policies as violating individual freedoms to do business as one wishes without governmental constraints, the adamant call for the military to intervene in foreign affairs where "national interests" are threatened, and the strut of the self-assured attitude of superiority and leadership all indicate an unexamined acceptance of the Christian concept of being the chosen people, having divine privilege, and being charged with a mission to lead the world. Talk about the mythic grammar that lay behind such articulations and the self-importance of the Bush administration's "Christian Nation," and "American Century" un-derstandings!

There is enough resistance to this stance both at home and throughout the world to tell us that the social interests we have naïvely engendered are out of control and serve only the self-interests of the corporate elite, not the well-being of the peo-ple or the nation. This means that neither the current culture of aestheticism nor the erstwhile culture of the Christian religion is enough to paint the global picture that needs to be painted. Thus the thought occurs that it might be well to expand the canvas and make some attempt to put the United States in its place as a na-tion among the nations of the world.

7 THREE MONO MYTHS

The United States has left broad and messy brushstrokes across the entire globe. We have spent many pages analyzing the social issues within the United States only to find that the organized social interests there have taken on global scope. And the media are now painting a blemished picture of the social and political situations around the world similar to the picture we have found within the American scene. It seems most audacious to suggest that our interest in analyzing the relation of the Christian myth to Western culture and the United States should now be extended to the effect it has had in the global world of nations, especially since we have not been able to satisfy our questions about solutions to the social problems that have arisen at home. And it is also odd, if not ironic, to suggest that we follow the "mission" of the United States to the world of nations when we suspect that the very sense of mission on the part of the United States is a Christian cultural legacy. Nevertheless, it just may be that a review of the relationships America has had with other nations can help us refine our quest for the influence of Christianity both within the United States and in today's world.

We will not be able to trace the Christian missions of the churches. We already know enough about these missions as legacies of the colonial era. And it will not be any express mention or interest in Christianity as religion that we seek to document. We have pared down "Christianity" to its "myth" and then to its "mythic grammar" and finally to its cultural mentality. It will be the unacknowledged cultural mentality of the Western tradition in its American formation that we will want to trace as the underlying cultural logic that allows our representatives to rationalize our "missions" abroad. We know how to rationalize our "national interests," of course. But we have no notion of how to deal with the myths and ideologies of other cultures. It is at this level of encounter with other nations that the posture of America has failed to achieve its goals. It has not been able to assess the interest others may have in our "leadership" except at the obvious level of financial and military aid. And America's posture has not encouraged any critical evaluation of our interests in other nations, choosing rather to cover them up with a constant rhetoric of "nation building" and instruction in "democracy." Such a posture has been in place since the Reagan administration. It has been clear enough for diplomats, generals, and agencies wanting to address social ills in other countries to forge ahead with their programs of "relief." Only in the case of obstruction to our industrial incursions, such as the exploitation of another country's oil, does the rhetoric of "national interests" occur as an argument for America's presence and use of military force. The strange thing about this obviously disingenuous foreign policy is that it doesn't register as a problem in the minds of most Americans. It is doubly curious because those in other nations see it clearly and castigate us for it at the highest levels of authority. The clearest case of the chaos we have generated in other countries by means of this leadership posture is, of course, the situation in the Near East. We need not do more than briefly review this situation in order to see what happens to our quest for a big picture of our cultures when we expand the canvas.

THE WARS

The history of militant Islam from the fall of the shah of Iran (1979) to the twin attacks of 9/11 (2001) is available in Robin Wright's *Sacred Rage.* Since that time the media have documented war after war in the Near East, some of an intertribal nature, but all intended to be demonstrations against the years of dominance and oppression by the Western nations and the United States. Our military has been there in obvious numbers since the invasion of Iraq in 2003, and the list of our attempts to quell terrorist attacks since then includes all of the Islamic nations from Libya to Pakistan, with current threats and incursions from Bahrain through Iraq, Iran, and Syria, to Lebanon and Palestine. This has become a crisis situation of unbelievable global proportions, having grown worse than Robin Wright's assessment in 2001. Still, her conclusion at that time is worth citing:

> Unfortunately, despite the evidence of Islam's current appeal and strong future potential, no Republican or Democratic administration has developed a tangible strategy to deal with the use of Islam in politics. Since Ayatollah Khomeini forced the shah from the Peacock Throne in 1979, policy has been piecemeal, often based on access to oil rather than the princi-

ples connoted in Operation Enduring Freedom. At best, it has been inconsistent: encouraging it in Afghanistan and condemning it in Lebanon.

I do wish she had not used the phrase "use of Islam in politics," as if religion and politics could be thought of in separate compartments. That construction upon the situation is similar to the problem Americans have had coming to terms with religion and society. We have thought to "use" other cultures, not negotiate with them except perhaps in the case of their obstruction of our purposes (for example, during the hostage crisis in Iran). And it seems that our journalists and others have not been able to explain what exactly it is that Islam finds so wrong about the Western influence, thus raising the issue of "use" to the level of "(mis)understanding." It is clear to most Americans who have studied the conflict that we have entered their territory because of its oil, and that our exploitation of their natural resources has been offensive to Muslims. But since their governments have wanted to keep control of their oil production, even fighting among themselves and their constituencies for such control, it does not seem to be enough to explain the adamant hostility and demand that we leave. Other journalists have mentioned aspects of our "liberal" cultures that conflict with Islamic culture, and the statements from the fundamentalists confirm that our social institutions, freedoms, and behavior offend them. But it is also the case that there does not seem to have been any consideration on the part of any of our "missionaries" concerning the consequences of our culture's confrontation with theirs, to say nothing of any understanding and appreciation for the cultural reasons Islamists have for resenting and resisting our presence and overt demands for compliance. No one has said that of course our incursion in another culture's territory violated a basic social interest rooted in its mythic grammar and mentality, a violation that could occur only because we were stronger, had guns, did not care, and saw ourselves as the masters of the situation.

That being the case, we need to ask ourselves whether our self-assurance as representatives of the American way, and our density in the face of another culture and its social logics, can be explained as a result of our Christian mentality. In my study *Myth and the Christian Nation* I traced such density to the logic of the Christian myth, with its intrinsic dualisms dividing Christians from non-Christians and its evaluation of the Other as "fallen" (if not worse) and thus in need of instruction and conversion, never appreciation and understanding. It is at least the case that we have not been interested in the cultures of the Islamic nations, only in their "friendship" at the level of cooperation with our industrial and financial interests. Whether there is any chance of appreciation, given the histories of both of us that come to mind, is another question. This question requires making some observations about the two religions and their myths, and that suggests some conversations that have not occurred.

THREE MONOTHEISMS

The history of religions and cultures interested in the civilizations of the Western traditions has often described and compared the three monotheistic religions of Judaism, Christianity, and Islam. The similarities were regularly emphasized, namely that all three are "religions of the book," that they all reach back into the Hebrew Scriptures to find the origin of their epic in common ("children/sons of Abraham"), and that each understands itself as a monotheism. The problem has been that each of the three gods is seen as the sole god of the universe, and the universe hardly needs three gods, much less three monotheistic religions in conflict. This conundrum has never caused the theologians of the three religions any anxiety. That is because their own mono-god is, of course, the only "real" god among the three. Still, in the case of Judaism and Christianity a compromise of sorts was inadvertently achieved when the Hebrew Scriptures became part of the Christian Bible. And in the case of Islam, it was possible to link Mohammed with a series of biblical prophets, including Jesus, and so claim to stand in the Jewish-Christian tradition. As a recent Egyptian general said about Islam under question, "Look here, Islam is one of the monotheistic religions." So that takes care of that.

Islam

Now the situation in the Near East is convoluted at several levels of social interest and mentality. Our descriptions of it in the media have hardly risen above the level of mentioning conflicts over natural resources and territories and the use of "strategies" to control access and ownership to those resources. Control has invariably had the military in mind, and the use of the military to solve such conflicts has actually destroyed cities and monuments of the indigenous cultures in order to say that another tribe (militia) or nation has taken control. It is clear that, in terms of military, industrial, and financial strengths, the Western nations have had the power to prevail for a period of time at this level of national conflict. But the ability to protect their establishments and interests in the Near East has become quite uncertain. That is because at the people level a veritable upsurge of insurgency has finally gotten its hands on Western weapons, and has called upon its religious mythology to marshal and rationalize "radical" rebellion. The signs say "Death to America"; the cries say "Allah is Great"; and the party leaders counsel "jihad." This is not merely a resurgence of rebellious insurgents. It is a cultural conflict of extraordinarily deep sensibilities. The articulations are not strategies. They are an appeal to their mythic history for insight into a cross-cultural situation in which their land, people, and religion have been violated. We have reduced the issue of the motivation for "terrorist" activity precisely to the level of strategies. The symbolism of the twin towers and Pentagon attacks in 2001 (commercial center, military center) has been noted but then overlooked in order to use 9/11 as *our* symbol of "terrorism" calling for war.

The authorization for radical insurgence and for "cleansing" their land of the corruption caused by an intruder is thoroughly understandable as an appeal to a mythic mentality with a social grammar that the West has violated. We need not think that the myth actually authorizes suicide bombing. That phenomenon is the horrible result of the extreme desperation of the people. But for both of us, Westerners and Islamists alike, the appeal to the myth needs to be seen as a rationalization called for by the social situation, not a reading of the inherent intention of the myth. What the appeal says, however, is that the myth is extremely important for the cultural self-understanding and the identity of the people, and that it can be interpreted in extreme ways if the situation is experienced as extremely problematic. We have not understood that, trying instead to explain the cultural clash at the social level, not at the mentality level, all the while using Western terms and logic. There is absolutely no way Western mentality and logic can explain the response to our incursions of social interests either as a military or logical conflict among nation-states, given our own interests for our incursions and rationalizing them in terms of our own good intentions ("nation building," "spreading democracy;" protecting our "friends"). The Near Eastern states are the creation of the Western nations, reaching back to the colonial era, not the product of Arabian, Persian, or Islamic configuration. The very notion of the "state" is a Western superimposition upon a tribal people who have for centuries organized their social formations as sheikhdoms.

Islam finds itself in the seams between the sheikhdoms and the Western nation-states by default. Whether its sense of social formation (sheikhdom) is an adequate model for Islamic nation building for the future, an experiment currently underway, remains to be seen. Were the West to back off and let the experiment run (hardly an option for us, given our interests in their oil), the new shape of an Islamic nation would already be a mixture of Arabic and Western social formations, their having learned to appreciate Western industry, oil production, nuclear science, and so forth. That is why we have tried to separate Islamic "terrorists" from the rest of Islamists by calling the insurgencies "radical" and "fundamentalist." We think those terms describe a conservative ideology to which not all Islamists adhere, just as the conservative coalition in the United States contains a fundamentalist Protestant ideology. In both cases, however, the similarity is that a social situation has resulted in the surfacing of a political ideology grounded in a cultural myth. That similarity might be enough to make the point that both cultural myths are at work, and thus help us see that Christian mentality is somehow involved in our own inability to understand the Islamic response to our treatment of their lands, people, and culture. But it would not get to the heart of the matter. The heart of the matter is that a culture's myth has a deep hold on a people's mentality and affects not only the thinking but also the practices of their society and its social interests. In the case of Islam, we are having trouble discerning the social logic of the Koran in ways similar to the social logic of the Christian myth. It may be that our categories of myth, mentality, and social formation are so beholden to the Western Christian cultural traditions that we cannot imagine other ways for myths to work at the social level of thinking, attitude, and practice. Our rational categories may simply be inadequate for understanding the Koran as it functions in Islam.

Jack Miles has addressed just this cross-cultural issue in *The Perils of Pluralism*. He uses the example of Salman Rushdie's *The Satanic Verses*, in which a satire on the Koran is written as a fiction and contains what the Islamic people found "disgusting," namely the subtle suggestions of parental sexual activity in his description of the encounter Muhammad had with Gibreel in a cave on the occasion of the oral revelation of the Koran. Miles examines the international furor to learn that the West's valorization of freedom of speech was hardly the reason for the Islamists' rage and the eventual *fatwa*. Rather, it was the gross depiction of parental sexual activity made public to the West in a fiction for money. The symbolisms stacked up. The Western reader saw the reason for the outrage as the "offense" intended by the book. But no, "offense" is the West's word for the grossness of the satire.

Islam did not have a literary tradition of fiction to understand this satire that way. Its response was leveled at the disgusting parade of cultural taboos before Westerners from an apostate Muslim. In the social logic of Islam, apostates are worthy of death.

But whether Rushdie's fiction was an offensive or disgraceful satire on the Koran, the response on the part of Islamists can be used to indicate the significance of a myth for a culture's mentality. In this case it is the nature of that mentality and its grounding in the myth (Koran) that we in the West have not been able to discern or understand. It might be approached by using our languages for divinity or sacrality, except for the fact that these terms are closely related to the Western notion of deity, and the Koran seems to have its own mystique apart from that attributed to Allah. In either case, however, it is the feature of the myth as untouchable, a deeply embedded articulation that cannot be dislodged without endangering the foundation of the culture that needs to be considered. It is the mentality thus created that is only partly similar to the piety of the Christian that marks the personal and social issues arising from a Christian-Islam encounter.

Judaism

Judaism is not a latecomer to the Western traditions of religion and culture. It was in fact the earliest, the religion of the Hebrews that provided the book, social model, mythology, and theology from which both Christianity and later Islam were derived. But present-day Israel as a modern nation-state clearly is a latecomer to Palestine and the Near East. The land of Palestine was chosen by the United Kingdom and the Western nations after the Second World War as the appropriate place for a

Jewish state, given the earlier history and the biblical mythology. The Holocaust was, of course, in everyone's minds as a grotesque image of Western civilization's treatment of the Jews. And Zionism had arisen from within the Jewish people as an answer to the European experience. Thus the carving out of a nation for Jews in Palestine took place on the colonial model in ways similar to much of the African and Indonesian marking of boundaries by the Western colonial powers. Whatever considerations there may have been at the time for the rights of the Palestinians who lived there, such considerations have not become part of the ways the Western nations continue to debate the issue.

From the immediate history of the Jewish immigration into Palestine in the early 1950s, however, it is clear that the ideology of repossession was put to work. The stories told by Palestinians who were forced to leave their villages and lands, often at gunpoint, are many and tragic. These stories have not been heard or rehearsed by the Western governments, all of which have agreed to support the Jewish nation-state as the solution to the European history of discrimination (and killing). The evacuation of the Palestinians must have been considered the necessary cost for the solution. At first, once the Palestinians were pushed out, the Jewish settlements caught the attention of Westerners who idealized their kibbutzim as a progressive and future-looking social formation. Unfortunately, it did not take long for the United States and American Jews to see Israel as the "friend" for American interests in the Near East and a barrier to communism. The current strength of the Israeli economy and military, to say nothing of its military victories over Islamic opponents, sets it apart as an outpost of Western (American) interests.

The curiosity has been that the state of Israel has been seen by Americans as a Western nation, not as a state rationalized by a religious mythology. Zionism as an ideology is now espoused by Prime Minister Netanyahu's administration. This thinking appears to be purely political, with its hard line against "terrorists," Palestinians, and any Islamic nation that opposes Israeli power and occupation (especially including the occupation of the West Bank beyond the agreed upon borders). Iran has emerged as the mortal enemy because of its nuclear research and schools for Shiite militants. But Zionism is basically a biblical mythology, not a political ideology. The Zionist appeal to the Bible is that Yahweh "gave" the "land of Israel" to the Jews, which means it is now their possession and property. Those who object to that count as enemies of Israel and Israel's god. Zionism is a modern-day example of just how serious a myth can become for a people and a nation. It is also an example of just how uncontestable such an appeal to the Bible can be. Who in the world would blow the whistle on this reading of the Bible as purely mythic thinking? Its effects in the structures and practices of a modern nation-state stand squarely in the way of debate at the level of literary (biblical) criticism and/or a theory of mythology according to the history of religions. The only thing the Western nations can suggest as a solution to the Palestinian "problem" and Netanyahu's reoccupation of the West Bank is a "two-state" proposal. Goodness. That persists at the level of Western thinking about the nation-state as the only viable model for modern social formations. That is understandable, of course, and it may be the only thinkable option available at this time. But it ignores the fact that both Israel and the Palestinians have mythic mentalities that resist political compromise. Where might there be another idea, a positively constructive idea of a society worth living in together that both could find attractive?

It is of course the case that the inability of the Western nations to criticize Israeli mythology and mentality is due to the fact that Western thinking is also beholden to biblical mythology. There has been some resistance in America to accepting the link between the Christian myth and the concept of the Christian Nation. That brings the topic of Christian mentality and culture much too close for comfort. But one does still hear reference to the "Judeo-Christian tradition" as the way to understand our support of Israel. This is not a statement about the current state of affairs. It is a statement about the history of Western civilization with its prehistory in the biblical epic, an epic mythology that both Judaism and Christianity have come to share. In my studies *Christian Nation* and *Christian Mentality* I focused only on the ways in which the legacy of Christendom continued to inform the popular mentality in America and its thinking about America itself. But now, having expanded the canvas for the worldwide view of Christianity among the nations, and having noticed aspects of biblical mentality at the political level in the Near East, where Western nations are pouring in arms and armies in the "national interests" of the United States and Israel, the links between social interests and mythic thinking are beginning to raise questions about basic human anthropology. If we stay at the level of biblical and Koranic mentality to debate the chances for peace in the Near East, the chances for a creative vision of life together seem to be quite dim.

Christianity

We might start with the famous line from George W. Bush to the effect that "we are not fighting a religious war in the Near East, we are fighting terrorists." Well, if you use the term *terrorist* to characterize your enemy, if you think of them as individuals, and if you can't find them or know why they have "attacked" you, you are declaring a very strange war. This war has gone on for more than fifteen years now and there is no end in sight. Judging from the media, most Americans accept the two reasons the administration gives for it. The one is that we have to find and eliminate the terrorists in order to protect the nation. The other is that we need the army to track them down. Neither of these reasons makes sense. But neither is easily dislodged, even though their deployment has made matters worse rather than better. And on the way a fairly large number of "crises" has shifted attention from terrorists to militias to nation-states throughout the entire spectrum of the North African/Levantine/Near Eastern theater. As I write, the war has focused on the Saudi-Yemen border, where both Iran and the United States have proxy militias. There may not be an Islamic country left in isolation from the shifting fronts as this ideological upheaval has surfaced in nation after nation as a result of our war on terrorists.

Americans do not think of this war as a war of religion, one that is driven by Christian interests and mentality. And it is true that Christianity as an establishment religion is not as obvious in the media descriptions of the Near Eastern battles as are Islam and Judaism. Yet the American presence is an offense to the Islamic people precisely because of its culture and the way that culture seeks to change the thinking and practices of the Islamic people. The cultures of the Western nations have their roots, as we know, in Christianity. But the culture of offense in the Near East is not Christianity per se but the modern and postmodern cultures of Western (Christian) nations, especially the United States. There is a penetration of videos, smart phones, and other electronic devices in the hands of the Islamists that seems innocent enough to American capitalism, whose proponents consider the attraction of its gadgets among the people of other nations "natural" at the people level, a sign of successful marketing at the corporation level. It is not, apparently, recognized as the vehicle for a transparent display of another culture's ways and values. From the conservative Islamist's point of view, however, such a display is offensive precisely because it serves as a constant reminder of the liberal and libertine values of the Christian West. This means that the United States has not been able to intrude into the Islamic nations merely to search for terrorists or to protect American oil interests. The American presence has become an intrusion into another culture as an alien culture, this time with guns.

Our problem at this point is that Americans do not think of the United States as having a culture. That is because of the particular social history of the United States, wherein the "separation of church and state" supposedly left each to its own devices. On the "state" side, society was open to the social interests of science and capitalism, while on the "church" side, religion became a matter for the private "belief systems" and "religious experiences" of individuals. Yet in my books *Christian Nation* and *Christian Mentality*, I was able to relate the self-understanding of American citizens to the social grammar and mentality of the Christian (biblical) myth. The history of the United States is full of commonly accepted terms that have functioned as a curious kind of symbolic conflation of religion and society, such as *manifest destiny, Moral Majority, American Century* (read "twenty-first century empire"), *Christian Coalition, Tea Party,* and so forth. What if we ponder the cultural conflict in the Near East in terms of the underlying mentality of the Western cultural tradition rooted in its religion? We know that in the United States the Christian myth is hardly still consciously in mind, and that the so-called mainline churches are in trouble holding on to their membership. Yet the mentality of the myth is still discernable. And the United States is not the only Western nation struggling with a national mentality rooted in the Christian tradition in the face of a large-scale immigration from other cultures with their religions. Recent studies of the "malaise" in France have traced its nostalgia back to periods of French history in which it was Christendom that provided the social and cultural framework for French culture and identity. Since that framework is now eroding in light of the influx of other peoples, the grand literary tradition of French culture and academy no longer seems to be in charge of the social issues resulting from Islamic immigration.

Thus the cultural formation of Christendom has not been completely erased by the social histories in Europe and the United States since the Enlightenment. And the marks of its mentality are clearly discernable in the thinking, practices, and attitudes of the Western nations as they intrude in the Near East. It is a posture of power, superiority, taking charge, and telling the "natives" what they must do, fortified by a sense of being right (righteous). This means that the cultural clashes in the Near East do not seem to have a chance of resolution except by military force. And since the use of military force is now completely out of hand, the failure of the United States to comprehend the reasons for the problem tells us that the reasons are apparently beyond its grasp. And part of the problem is that the United States has allowed its arms manufacturers, the Pentagon, and the diplomatic agencies to arm every one of the combatants with American weaponry as the solution to conflict. Now everybody has the power to kill opponents. And the opponents now include the United States, something of a practical policy irony that has to be left unacknowledged lest the whole house come tumbling down.

FLAWS IN THE FANTASY

The notion of a "big picture," as helpful as it may have been for the descriptions of ethnographic societies, and as innocent as it was in its application to the Western history and American scene, was actually an ideal fantasy. The innocence was possible because the "big picture" theory drew upon the shape of Christianity as the religion most familiar to Western scholars, the religion that gave scholars their first categories in the study of the history of religions. And the worldview of Christendom was a big picture. This worldview provided a universal scope to all of human history, forming a cosmic environment for human society on the model of the Roman-Catholic world. Society was thought of and structured as an ethical (religious) "community" whose ethos guaranteed obeisance to both the pope and the emperor, and whose submission to the Christian god was the definition of morality. And this big picture has survived a number of challenges in the course of Western history, right up until the notions of a "Christian Nation" and an "American Century" were used by the "Conservative Coalition" to celebrate and enhance American superiority and "leadership" in the larger world of nations. One might have thought that the expanding pictures of societies and the universe since the Renaissance would have tarnished if not challenged the worldview of Christendom, but they did not. A brief list of these historic events can help us see why the big picture theory, based as it is on a mythic worldview, needs now to be the object of criticism and revision.

The first challenge to this worldview was the rise of Islam in the seventh century resulting in the Crusades. This might have cautioned the European nations about wars for religious reasons, but it did not. The second major challenge was the discovery of the Americas in the late fifteenth century. This was a "new world" not mentioned on the older maps of the universe, and therefore disconcerting for scholars. This discovery reshaped the view of the world, but it did not rethink the Bible. The third challenge was the discovery of new peoples in the Western hemisphere, those not belonging to the family tree of peoples mentioned in the Bible. As Columbus said, they have no religion; send missionaries; they might be made good servants (slaves) for the queen. The fourth challenge was the realization that the entire world was available for colonization and missions. We are just now learning about the human costs of colonization, and about the extents to which both Christianity and trade can manage the changing of another culture. The fifth challenge has been the emergence of the material cultures of science and capitalism. This world has resulted in the organization of energies and motivations that can find little justification in the Christian myth. But the Christian world has not succumbed. And, as a sixth challenge, the American success in the development of the material cultures of science and capitalism *without* a controlling picture of a common-good society has created the international tensions and conflicts that describe the current global malaise as a secular world, not a Christendom. This malaise has been recognized by culture historians and critics as a sign of the ending of the "big picture" of the Western Christian tradition.

Now the lessons from America's "missions" to the Near East tell us that there are other religions producing mentalities that shape the thinking and behavior of their peoples in their own interests as collectives with their own cultures. They also tell us that Christian mentality is still at work subliminally in the interests of Western "missions," and that these interests have succeeded in creating conflicts with other cultures instead of conversions. This effort in exporting American "democracy" and its tragic consequences has been taken seriously by other nations as offensive, and by many intellectuals and journalists in the United States and Europe as counterproductive. The American administration and Congress have revealed their inability to cope with the situations abroad that they have created. Thus the time has come to recognize the reasons for the failure of the Western Christian tradition of culture and society in America, and for the failure of America's "missions" abroad.

I have touched upon and illustrated most of these reasons here, but without calling attention to any one of them as the cause of our malaise, much less suggesting a remedy. The first reason is that the internal logic of the Christian myth has been pervasive in America, and has been understood by our leaders as a mandate for reforming the rest of the world in our own image.

That is not working. The second is that the Christian myth and worldview has no mechanism or logic within it to contain or control the secular social interests of the post-Renaissance/post-Industrial revolutions that are now the major forces in our society. Social interests need to be in the big picture. It is this disconnect that has left the pursuits of the scientific and capitalistic age without much awareness on their part of the consequences for society. The third is that the attempt on the part of conservative Christians to project an American Empire for the Christian Nation for the next century (an "American Century") has already been found ridiculous. The fourth is that the global extent of Western missions, trade, and media has created a multicultural awareness among all the peoples on planet earth. But to use the term *multicultural* in America triggers offense as if the term suggests a critique of the traditional, united, "Christian" society as it is supposed to be in America. The fifth is that, since none of the mono myths can prevail as a picture for a global world of many cultures, it is not possible to project a big picture of the world based upon the values of one of them. And the sixth is that none of the mono myths has the resources to level the playing field so that cross-cultural interests and conflict can be addressed and/or adjudicated.

We therefore need a new picture of the world. We need to imagine a picture of the human enterprise of social formation that does not squash the pictures already there but shows their limits clearly as myths that support single cultures without the visions and logic necessary for living together on planet earth without violence. The question is whether such a picture is possible, whether the notion of a big picture can be painted as a rectification of the current global malaise created by the military and financial battles among nations. Big oil and other industrial/commercial enterprises have been picking up steam since the Second World War. These enterprises do not seem to have a clear picture of the future toward which they are hurtling, except for some kind of global monopoly. But now that the consequences of corporate capitalism in such matters as the threatening of the ecology of planet earth, the exploitation of lands and resources that "belong" to other nations, and the superimposition of markets at the expense of indigenous societies have become obvious, the social role of corporations is one of the questions and challenges for thinking about a new picture.

So we do need another picture of the world of people, interests, cultures, and nations. Without one it will be difficult to imagine the future without despairing. The news of the violence churning up the world has become so ugly it is horrific, and the sense of being powerless as an individual to change things leaves one stunned. Many of the voices calling for change are directed to our governments. But the stumbles of our politicians tell us that they, also, are stunned at the state of affairs and unable to imagine solutions. This means that the histories and traditions that have brought us to this point and resulted in the social structures that are not working have come to their end. Some are saying that the images of destruction and extinction are overwhelming, that there is little hope for Western civilization, to say nothing of planet earth, unless ways are found to alter our present course.

In the next chapter I engage this problem. There are resources available that can be used to address the current disease and project a future for a multicultural social democracy.

8 IMAGINING THE FUTURE

Drawing upon the conclusions from the preceding chapters, we can see that the mono myths are in trouble. The interconnectivity of the peoples of the world is such that the self-importance of a single Western institution, nation, or religion can no longer be successful as the dominant culture of the global world of nations, or even as the posture of an independent state caught in political turmoil with its neighbors. In Chapter 6 we explored the residue of the Christian myth and mentality in the United States. We discovered that the culture of late capitalism (Jameson's term) had supplanted Christian mentality among the people of the United States, with its videos that titillated personal and private aestheticisms. In Chapter 7 it became clear that the Christian mentality of "mission" was still at work in the thinking of the administration and military, but that this kind of "mission" was no longer working in the contemporary world of nations and nation-states. It was in fact creating havoc. This means that our questions about what happened to the "big picture" of the Western tradition and its culture have been answered. It was the history of industry since the Industrial Revolution that found a special place in the new nation-state called the United States and supplanted the erstwhile culture of the Western tradition. The worldview of Christendom can no longer provide a picture for the nation and its environments. And its myth can no longer support a mission to the world of nations in the interest of "the American way." Thus the residue of Christian mentality that is still discernable in aspects of our government's agencies and policies is not feasible. There may still be some features of Christian mentality among the people as a cultural lag that provides familiar ways of thinking about the world. But such ways of thinking can no longer call upon the big picture of Christendom in order to rationalize their authority. And the transcendent world of the Christian god is no longer the way to visualize the heavens for humans or the cosmos for the stars. Both the social arena and the imaginary world of the two environments have changed. The social world is now a multinational global universe. And the surrounding natural environment is the big picture of the universe that science has painted. As for the common language once used for civil and cultured discourse, it has been erased in the United States by a jumble of acronyms and metaphors that have popped up to negotiate the new world of disconnected images.

We might want to acknowledge that the "social interests" discussed in Chapter 4 have taken the lead and are now in control of our corporations, industries, and financial institutions. We might want to see them as the result of a past history of human interests and creativities for which we can be proud. According to our theory, social interests are the practices at the society level that become habitual and are taken up into a people's mythology. We might think that the new mythology for our current social interests has not yet appeared. We might also want to say that the "social issues" discussed in Chapter 5 are not problems but thoroughly understandable developments, given the complexities of the times. Social issues occur because of changes in the practices of a society, not necessarily because of devious behavior or mistaken designs. These assessments are certainly cogent, and they have allowed us to trace the history of the West since the Industrial Revolution in a descriptive format without finding fault. But neither assessment helps to explain the seriousness of the social situations that now pertain in the United States and the world. What we need to do, therefore, is to change the subject from mythic to practical mentalities.

What happened to the big picture of Christendom was that the new social interests, such as science and capitalism, became so successful as industries and businesses that they and their products filled the socialscape with their images and logics to the point where there was no longer need for the older mythic worldview. They did this by forming institutes and corporations for their productions and by mastering the art of financial and political thinking. This was an organization of energies for which the older feudal system had no preparation, and the church no myth for blessing or control. Eventually minor myths (stories of the founders, heroes, and histories of an organization) could begin to make self-reference possible and claim for the corporation a significant place in the larger society. None of this alone would have created the social consternations we are now experiencing. The social issues that have surfaced are the result of other developments. One is that the logic of capitalism called for "efficiency" and the expansion (growth) of an institution in the global marketplace. Thus the size of a corporation was no longer manageable for an individual to think of as a social entity to which one's contribution made a difference. Another is that there were now many such industries and institutions, all of which were competing with one another for dominance in the market. And a third was that the nation-state found itself beholden to the corporate world of finance and unable to control it in the interest of the quality of life for its people. The competition determined the speed of a project's practices and, once it was discovered that a TV ad did not need to be a minute in length, but could be successful even with a five-second flash, the twirls of the dancers and of the observers, to say nothing of the producers and consumers, spun faster and faster. And the dancing floor expanded to include every people and nation on the globe.

In Chapter 6 we consulted several culture critics for descriptions of the atmosphere and mentality that resulted from the breakdown of the grand Western tradition of society and culture. There was, they said, the loss of a sense of history, social context, and meaning at the personal and populace level. Because these are all related to large-scale issues having to do with the stability and health of the society as a whole, it was difficult to keep track of what the individual may have been thinking. But it does seem that myriad individuals have somehow "remembered" the residual "values" of social existence and identity from past times and found themselves distressed by the social conditions and issues in the present. This distress has contributed to the atmosphere and mood of the society itself. The voices of new movements and protests can be heard every day calling for the government to stop the injustices and the violations of common values. It is never clear whether the authorities addressed actually hear, understand, or care about the complaints. It is more the case that the unresolved distress settles into cynicism or despair, and that there seems to be nothing that anyone can do to change the social situation. The thrust and speed of energies has followed the "snatch and grab" approach to taking advantage of the new economic opportunities for the entrepreneur.

So it looks as if the Western tradition of industry and enterprise, coupled with the mentality of superiority that occurred by accident in the United States, has outfoxed itself by privileging the values of winning and supremacy as the ways to be important as individuals and strong as a government. It did not take long for the people of the United States to learn how to play the game of private enterprise. And sure enough, without any knowledge of capitalism as a system, or of Marx's caution about constraining its motivations for wild growth, the United States experienced an amazing period of economic growth after the Second World War. It was partly the success in the war, and partly the emerging economic prosperity after the war, that encouraged the politicians in Washington toward the end of the twentieth century to imagine the twenty-first century as the "American Century" and undertake our global missions. The astounding vision of the future for these politicians was that America was ready to gain the "leadership" of the nations and rule of the entire world in keeping with its own ideologies of "freedom" and "democracy." But instead of winning and ruling, the United States has exacerbated crass competition and promoted devastating domination. Thus the American people are currently dealing with a number of conundrums of the appreciation/distress variety. An example would be an appreciation of the promises of science coupled with distress about many of its applications and their destructive consequences for the natural and social worlds. Who would have thought in the eighteenth and nineteenth centuries that science would create a nuclear bomb capable of destroying civilization (and that the United States would use it to end the Second World War by destroying Hiroshima and Nagasaki)? Who would have imagined that industry would discover how to manufacture an electronic universe capable of spreading its net of connectivity over all the peoples in the world (and that the e-networks would become the world of virtual reality and displace personal, physical contact)? These and other issues are now being addressed in some way or other by individuals, small movements, journalists, academics, and other "voices in the wilderness," which have taken the lead at the local level because the nation-state does not seem able to address even the most obvious social issues in need of redress. The promise of science and capitalism, and the questionable consequences of some of their applications, have created a bind that is more than a matter of attitude and ambience. It has become an intellectual conundrum, a matter of not knowing what or how to think clearly about the energies at work in the painting of our big picture, a picture of tremendous scope and promise, but felt to be somehow out of control. The promise and the consequences are so often at odds that trying to analyze the social situation can lead to impasse. An example would be an appreciation for the constructive use of nuclear power against recognition of the distinct possibilities for nuclear war and the extinction of species, including the human kind. Both possibilities are the result of Western culture's own making. Thus the question of the sense of a future is no longer a matter just for cultural critics to explore, or for science fictions to project. As the Ehrlichs indicated, the nuclear threat needs to be recognized by our governments as the most important issue facing our civilizations.

This of course means that thinking clearly about religion and society for the future is no longer possible if our only categories for describing them are the categories given with Christendom's mythic worldview and the Aristotelian logics of the "classical" tradition of the Western academy. Neither is it possible if the current formulations of the conundrum stay in place as the only dialectics available for debate, a familiar popular level of discourse that does not have a chance of intellectual resolution. There are three formulations that can illustrate the problem of thinking clearly about the future in light of the issues created by the ending of Christian mentality and the current social situation. One is that the response to our social situation by "progressives," though laudable because of their projects and ethical sensibilities, is stymied by an understandable view of "government" as the problem. A second is the attempt to counter the progressives and project the ultimate solution to all social issues by means of science and the current form of capitalism. And a third is the turn to natural science to let a meditation on the wonders of geological time and evolutionary history caution the human species about its concerns of extinction. It will be helpful to ferret out the basic conundrum for each of these views of the future before suggesting another reason for our lack of clarity about our social issues, one that is not a conundrum but an embarrassing ideological problem that could actually be solved by intellectual and social-political means. I refer to the problem of America's resistance to the concepts of "social democracy" and "multiculturalism." But first, let us consider the conundrums.

GRASSROOTS THINKING

It has become exceedingly difficult to think clearly in the midst of the noise created by our electronic age since the breakdown and fragmentation of our Western societies and cultures. The media have only made matters worse for deliberation and thinking, beholden as all of them are to the notions of happening, crisis, wealth, guns, and entertainment. They look for the events of winning or losing some fight or competition, thinking that the reporting of such events constitutes the "news." A snapshot apparently can make it real. Our problem with the quest for clarity about the social interests and issues of the nation as a society is that their analyses require deliberation at the level of big picture theory and thinking. This level of discourse rarely appears in the media, and then only as an "opinion" article. The media are not interested in picking up on the insights of an opinion article as a theoretical statement needing deliberation, response, discussion, and action. Thinking is not considered news or action. That sort of thing is left to the intellectual elite, and their proposals are seldom taken up for discussion and action at the level of politics and legislation. So the populace is left out of the academic and intellectual arenas where the problem of our big pictures can be discussed.

Fortunately, according to Paul Hawken, world-renowned environmentalist, there is another level of thinking and action unreported by the media, a "social movement," as he calls it, that has grown to envelop the globe at the people level since it became clear during the past century that our corporate empires and economies were destroying the environment. He calls it a movement for lack of a better term, but it is not organized and consists only of the many small groups of people interested in particular local environmental issues. These groups often have leaders who have stepped forth to engage neighbors and others about cleaning up a waterway, developing an organic agriculture, putting a run-down village back together, keeping a medical facility going, working with teachers and local schools to find support, and the like. As a lecturer for several decades on the social justice and environmental issues facing the planet today, Hawken found himself compiling a long list of interested and active people addressing the inability of governments to provide for the needs of the people, especially the huge number of the poor who have been created by the "fair-trade" giants and who have no chance for jobs in the system in the new age. He finally started a research institute called Natural Capital Institute and created a database of thousands of nongovernmental organizations (NGOs) covering 243 countries. Just the catalogue of natural phenomena, social issues related to the environment, and social justice issues, along with the kinds of NGO activities under way, requires a hundred pages. It does not include names and numbers of the thousands of NGOs in their archives. These can be obtained from his web site (www.paulhawken.com). Hawken has published his findings as *Blessed Unrest: How the Largest Social Movement in History Is Restoring Grace, Justice, and Beauty to the World*.

Hawken's description of this "movement" is truly enlightening and hopeful, as he intends it to be. It gathers the voluntary efforts of "common" folk reported to him over a period of at least three decades and provides a profile of "what is right" in the world to counter the constant noise and outcries of what's wrong. The enlightening aspect is that, as Hawken emphasizes, this level of human activity is simply off the radar of the media, politics, and other forums, thus needs his institute and book to inform us. The hopeful aspect is the documentation of a sane and humanizing anthropology of which the Western world has lost track, a description of the human that has found meaning in common pursuits without the need for straining after more. I bring it to the reader's attention because it contains such an impressive documentation of the social problems facing the world today which Hawken cites as the background and context for the more positive energies he highlights.

The main problem, in Hawken's mind, is that the interests of government, industry, and global control have not paid any attention to "movements" such as these. Hawken describes the movement as distinct from all organizations, with their leaders, ideologies, action plans, and "isms." The movement is not organized and does not have an "ism." For Hawken this is its strength. Their actions and concerns are such that they do not need and do not develop an "ideology," a theory or plan that would lead to political engagements. He is right to see that ideologies and "isms" can conflict and divide an organization and thus frustrate a project. But he cannot claim that the movement shows the way to address the issues facing the nations that do have to do with questions of power, ideology, and governmental policies. These are the "big picture" issues with which I have here been concerned. It is therefore disappointing to find that Hawken has argued for a fundamental distinction between theory (his "ideology") and practice, a distinction that allows the movement to proceed without theory. Such a distinction could keep its leaders from thinking about their practices in relation to the big picture of the world and the issues on which they themselves are actually working. It is doubly disappointing because Hawken describes the "wrongs" of the big picture in the first chapter of his book. It is a remarkable summary of the social and environmental issues that have challenged the world and to which the movement has responded. If Hawken is right about the intelligence and wisdom of the movement's people, people who know why they are involved and what they are doing about it, there is no reason to discourage them from thinking deeply about the relations between their social justice concerns and the social reasons that have created the need for their concerns. That requires theory. And it would be wonderful to listen in to a collective forum of leaders in this "movement" talking about what they think is "wrong" with the current big picture of our nation-state and world, as well as what they think a better big picture of states and governance might look like.

CORPORATE CAPITALISM

Ian Frazier, author and columnist for the *New Yorker* magazine, found himself caught in the middle between these two ways of thinking about a social issue. In his case the issue was a public debate between conservationists and industry on how to counter carbon pollution. Frazier had been a bird lover for much of his life, thus tended to think about planet earth as a conservationist. But as a writer and thinker who was much at home in the civil and sophisticated society that the oil industry has made possible, he became troubled about the naïveté of the conservationists who thought that ending civilization's dependence on fossil fuels was the answer to saving the environment from destruction. The facts and figures did not add up for Frazier, who noted that reducing our "carbon footprint" would not stop global warming now that it had begun, or other kinds of environmental devastations that occur by human hands. He decided to have a look at some grassroots projects in conservation that were making a big difference in restoring forests, creating healthy agricultural production, and protecting bird habitat. He found many such projects and the people who were busy working on them. His interviews let the local reasons surface without being questioned. And the picture of people involved voluntarily in environmental projects provides a nice confirmation of Hawken's estimate of the sanity and capacity of the human spirit for addressing issues that the government overlooks. But in one case, a small successful organic farm and forest, a look over the fences revealed that the surrounding lands had been deforested and were now in the hands of gold miners. As Frazier comes to his conclusion, the question won't go away about what good the environmental movement is as an attempt by powerless people to address global issues and to try to stop corporate capitalism (big oil). He pays attention to the arguments of the conservationists and discovers that the final consideration for taking them seriously is the threat of the *extinction* of species. This leads him to a brief review of evolutionary history only to find that humans have extinguished species after species, mostly by gobbling them up. What should one make of this? he asks. It tells us that we are that species that learned how to "use" (destroy) the environment in the process of building great cities, magnificent industries, and now a luxuriant way of life. Bringing the birds back into the picture, Frazier says that were the tables turned around, the birds would not hesitate to eat us up. So we, not they, are those who "need life to have meaning." Punkt. My first response was, "Do we then need to exterminate other species in order to have life?" But that response plays into the unresolved dialectic of the conundrum, so cannot be the response that signifies.

PLANETARY FACETS

Our theory of myth says that the canvas on which a myth is painted is as vast as the combination of the two environments of a people, natural order and social history. For a tribal people neither of these environments had to be larger than their experience of their terrain. We have followed some stages in the course of Western civilization in which the discovery of writing and history allowed us to reconstruct the history of the Ancient Near East, Greece, Rome, and so forth. Now at the end of a certain social history cultivated by Christianity and its intellectual priests, we discover that this history is not great enough in scope or narrative to contain the world that has come into view. The world that has come into view is both global (a social concept) and astronomical (a scientific finding). What if we acknowledged that this new environment is much grander than the Christian worldview? For one thing, the astronomical expanse of space has resulted in concepts of time and place that are hardly comprehensible by the categories of Christian mentality. For another, the geological history of planet earth is a story of 4.5 billion years and still unfolding. Then there is the evolution of life-forms from trilobites to vertebrates. The late Harvard paleontologist Stephen Jay Gould became fascinated with the trilobite fossils of the Burgess

Shale, discovered the *Pikaia* as the first known chordate (our phylum), developed the theory of evolutionary "contingency," and wrote the book *Wonderful Life: The Burgess Shale and the Nature of History*. He ends the book with this paragraph:

> And so, if you wish to ask the question of the ages—why do humans exist?—a major part of the answer, touching those aspects of the issue that science can treat at all, must be: because *Pikaia* survived the Burgess decimation. This response does not cite a single law of nature; it embodies no statement about predictable evolutionary pathways, no calculation of probabilities based on general rules of anatomy or ecology. The survival of *Pikaia* was a contingency of "just history." I do not think that any "higher" answer can be given, and I cannot imagine that any resolution could be more fascinating. We are the offspring of history, and must establish our own paths in this more diverse and interesting of conceivable universes—one indifferent to our suffering, and therefore offering us maximal freedom to thrive, or to fail, in our own chosen way.

It has sometimes been thought that it was but a short step from the creation of the universe to the creation of "man." But now we know that humans have been on earth for only a tiny fraction of the planet's history, and that most hominid species have gone extinct without issue. Gould traces the many evolutionary options of the hominids to show that the distinctive thing about us is that, at some point, the human mind evolved, with its capacity for abstract thinking. Thus the worlds of nature, evolution, and human history can be celebrated as the knowledge humans have achieved by means of social interests—observation, thinking, and abstract reasoning. In Gould's view, this is our invitation to live and celebrate "the wonderful life."

If only we could account for the human enterprise of social formation in some such way. It is not yet clear to the scientific community, at least as far as I know, how and why humans became social creatures. But among the many attempts to explore possible scenarios and factors, one stands out for me. It is the relationship of the discovery and use of language to the experience of social formation (families, others, and so on) that seems to be the key. What if we notice that our theory of the two/three environments within which a people have oriented themselves to their world by painting their big picture might suggest that we pay attention to the astronomical and planetary facets of our modern scientific environment by giving them names as the active frames of reference for the production of a global, human culture?

It would mean shifting from theology to geology, of course, and that would make some religious people uneasy. But it would not mean that they would have to dispense with awe, wonderment, reverence, mystique, and mystery, much less history, heroes, honors, literature, and languages. The evolution of flora and fauna, and the surprising appearance of the human mind and its social interests, would be more than enough to keep all of us pondering the meaning of life on planet earth. We might even find the courage to ask about the significance of cultural formations. But it is not possible to entertain such a fantasy before our problems with sociology are answered. There are two problems still left unresolved. One is whether the changing demographics of our modern nation-states can paint a picture of an integrated society that need not privilege the Western traditions. The other is whether the current mentalities and practices of the Western peoples are capable of imagining and handling the transformations required for such an integration of peoples. At the intellectual level this may be the conundrum we have to parry. But at the level of praxis the answer is already in sight. It is the formation of a social democracy that can learn to accommodate a multicultural people.

A POLYCULTURAL PICTURE

So here we are with the remnants of an archaic myth that is no longer helpful to entertain a multicultural social democracy. What if we were to realize that we are in fact a multicultural people in a modern nation-state in need of a clearer picture of ourselves, our society, and our national interests? What if we allowed ourselves the thought that America might actually be an exceptional social experiment, not because of our accidental rise to leadership in the world since the Second World War, our frightening military power, the fantastic growth of our corporate and consumer economies, the results of our missions to spread democracy around the world, or our desire to be the biggest, strongest, and wealthiest nation in the world, but because we happen to have the necessary human ingredients for constructing a polycultural social democracy for the common good? That would be a novel notion to most Amercians, a single society composed of people from many cultures working together for the common good. We would need a new big picture that reflects social interests in human well-being. Just think of a people composed of many cultures painting a picture of one another and themselves as a polycultural nation.

In America there is resistance to both of these concepts—a multicultural nation, and a social democracy. And in each case the resistance is rooted in the residues of our Christian mentality and social history. We have noticed this mentality slowly coming to collective consciousness in the early civil histories of the European (white) Christians who immigrated to America and then, because circumstances called for it, founded the federal union, fought for independence, engaged in civil war, bought the Louisiana Territory, produced the westward movement as our Manifest Destiny, and decided to join the "Allies" in the Second World War. It was in the course of this brief history that the sense of superiority endemic to the Western Christian tradition took the form of resistance to thinking that the United States was multicultural or that multiculturalism was a good thing. This resistance has been documented over and over again in obvious practices and ways of thinking that treated other peoples as unacceptable: slavery, the treatment of the Native Americans, incarceration of Japanese Americans during the Second World War, and the current practices and plans about building walls against "foreign immigrants" and the deportation of "illegal immigrants." So how can the fact of actually being a polycultural people work as a resource for becoming a multicultural nation? Some have noticed that a breakdown of ethnic and cultural prejudices is already happening—clubs that have abolished exclusivity, mixed marriages, progressive civil rights laws. Others are saying that "living together" will eventually erase the prejudices related to cultural differences and create a more homogenous people in due time. Both of these observations are right and relevant. But the term *multicultural* has not yet surfaced as a resource of any kind for a common-good society. And the reason is that the many cultures have their myths and mentalities that provide big pictures packed with ideological and linguistic systems and signs for collective identities and orientation. The term *multicultural* is not easily reduced to the notion of the "many different peoples" among us. It signifies *cultural* differences rooted in traditional myths and mentalities that may determine subtle differences in social values and ways of thinking. This means that we might need to address the question of the myths (and religions) among us as features of the intellectual challenge that the idea of a multicultural nation presents.

The intellectual challenge is a matter of mentality, language, and meaning. Our theory has dared to name "language" as the "third environment" of a social formation. But we have not taken it up for analysis as such, given the more obvious and objective lists of social data that could more easily be recognized as indicators of the pervasive presence of Christian mentality. Now we have to recognize that a non-Christian culture in the United States presents its adherents and all of us with its own mentality rooted in its own myths and traditions. We have learned to handle some differences at the levels of attire and harmless habits. But at the levels of values, loyalties, and political philosophies, the negotiations need to proceed with great care. At the deeper levels of a sense of identity, meaning, and social logic, the cultural differences among us are much more difficult to acknowledge, talk about, analyze, and negotiate. That is because a mentality is rooted in mythic thought that resides at a subconscious level of cultural grammar, where the rhyme and reason of the social can be taken for granted. There is, however, a subtle link between this subliminal level of mythic logic and the language of myth at the articulate level of discourse. We have mentioned "language" as the "third environment" of a social formation, but we have not discussed its importance as a "social interest" belonging to the other features of interest in the big picture. We now need to see that among the many "social interests" of a people, "language" is as important as practical and political interests. Language functions as a social interest by means of its capacity to "name" features of a people's big picture that belong to their mythic world, and to make it possible to acknowledge its subliminal logics and grammars in the course of living together. Common discourse cannot afford to ask critical questions about one's myth and mentality. That is what makes it so difficult to imagine a multicultural collection of peoples forming a nation with a common structure of social formation.

It might be helpful to illustrate the problem of mythic and religious language by noticing that the term *god* is taken for granted as a reference to a generic entity, while never being investigated as a linguistic phenomenon or curiosity that has no ontological reference. As a matter of fact, there are many taboos against uses of the term and understandings of it that may threaten its mythic authority. In the Christian tradition this term can be used as a proper name as well as generic concept. This curious phenomenon, due in part by the merger of Hebrew and Greek concepts/configurations for the ultimate agent and point of reference for mythic reality, has intrigued and exercised the theologians of Christianity for hundreds of years. That it cannot be solved as an intellectual issue has not kept the quest from continuing. It is even the case that the oddness of the "concept" has been taken up by modern-day scientists in their metaphor of the "god parti-cle," revealing the extent to which the Christian myth is some-how taken for granted and accepted precisely because it cannot be used to describe the empirical world. We can understand the term *god* and its mythic function by recognizing that it "stands for" the extreme reach and limits of the human mind and imagi-nation when contemplating what we otherwise have thought of as the *ultimate* being, agent, or limit of our world. As such, the very concept is "beyond" definition.

That being the case, I would like to suggest that the conver-sations among cultures we need to have can start with compari-sons of their cultural codes and values and the reasons they may have for wanting to find a place in a multicultural society. But eventually, in light of the big picture that needs painting, we may want to ask about their "social interests" and values, and how they may fit into the big picture as a contribution to its quest for a basic social anthropology. It is, after all, the human values taken for granted in these traditional cultures that need to be surfaced and compared with other values from other cultures in order to consider the design of a multicultural society. If, as the postmodernists claim, the current world of social projects and interests is the result of human interests and practices, the design of the new multicultural society needs to be the work of human hands.

To help us clear the canvas for the big picture that needs to be painted I'd like to share a scenario I dared to include in *Myth and the Christian Nation*. I suggested that we might imagine for a moment putting all of the gods of all our cultures and all of the prophets of all of the gods of our erstwhile religions together into the same transcendent realm just as we are all together here in the real world. If we did this with a sense of humor to accompany the seriousness of the social situation we need to address, we might actually entertain the thought of the traditional gods in their traditional worlds unable to handle our multicultural world and our experiment in constructing a social democracy. If we had a healthy sense of humor, we might have some fun seeing what they might do with us and say to one another. Just think of Yahweh, Allah, the Christian God, Marduk, the Buddha, Moses, Muhammad, Jesus, Confucius, some Zen master, maybe a Shinto *kami* if we could catch one, and of course the Native American's trickster coyote, all in the same imaginary world together, just as all of their followers are together in the real world here on earth. What would they say to one another? Could we get them to talk? Would they recognize one another? And would they know what has happened in the human world since their followers first imagined them alone in their own imaginary worlds? If we could get them to talk, with all of us poised to listen in on the conversations, maybe we could have them explain themselves and their histories to one another. Maybe we could ask them to discuss human social interests, intellectual anthropology, and the transformation of religious grammars. It would be revealing to listen in on such a discussion. Yahweh might want to explain his many changes of mind in the course of his history, especially about temples, priests, and kings. Jesus might have to revise his notion of the kingdom of God and tell us that he had not intended a Roman Empire. The Christian God might have to wince about the "sacrifice" of his son and say that Mark, though innocent as a social critic, was far too romantic when writing about Jesus's resurrection, and that John's vision of the apocalypse was just too far out except for poetic types. The Buddha might be smiling and silent for most of that, but would probably not have too much trouble winking at the coyote, running around with its eyes wide open and ears perked. And Moses could chuckle about it all for a change, explaining that, as a fictional character, his intention in writing the five books was really that of an epic poem, not legislation for a people without a land. Muhammad would probably sniff, sneeze, and cough a bit when asked about jihad. Whether the *kami* could find his garments in the mix-up might be a problem. And of course, the very concepts of social formation and intellectual anthropology might seem so old hat to these denizens of human history that we would not learn anything new from them at all except for their wondering why it took us so long to figure it out. But at least we could imagine them all talking together instead of wanting to break up the conference and rush out to preside over their separate peoples and domains.

But then the question might be whether we need a *cosmic* canvas at all, with a transcendent world of the kind in which our erstwhile gods have ruled and cavorted, or whether, painting ourselves into a big picture on another kind of canvas with earthly scope would not be much better than any of the otherworldly realms of the cultural myths we now take for granted. If the gods are fading away, what about some focus on the humanities? What about our many human histories if the biblical and Western histories have lost their mythic promise? What about histories that reveal our inventions and creativities, as well as the mistakes we've made that do not have to be repeated? What about the pictures of the many peoples in our world filling up a global canvas of interesting geographical terrains with their villages, cities, machines, productions, economies, trips, literatures, festivals, and celebrations? Can a picture celebrate our differences as beautiful and constructive without ranking? Can small still be beautiful?

For the Aranda there were the churinga, lovely polished pieces of wood and bone, carved and painted with tribal designs. They symbolized clan identity and were used in clan transactions. "See, I am from the Big Rock tribe." For the Winnebago there were the feathers for the headdress, and the wigwams arranged to enhance the reciprocity between two centers of power. For the Tlingit of the Pacific Northwest there were the totem poles to remind the people of their ancestral leaders and tell the story of their place in the natural scheme of things. For the Greeks there were the painted bowls to surround their everyday culinary activities with their hero tales, and for the ancient Near Eastern peoples there were the grand portals and mosaics celebrating the builders of cities. Now that we find ourselves in a new social world and global situation, the question is whether the pictures of ourselves could celebrate a sane and sustainable society. The answer may lie not in the troubling picture that the United States has been painting of the global world of corporations and nations but in some of the nation-states of Europe that have created social democracies. They are those that have survived the existential and ideological furors of the political endings of the grand Western narrative, and have learned from them about social and political values in the interest of the well-being of their

nation-states and peoples. And they have become skilled diplomats in the governance of their social democracies. But first,
how is it that the United States cannot imagine itself as a social
democracy?

SOCIAL DEMOCRACY

The term *social democracy* is not a common concept in the
United States. We pride ourselves in being a *democracy,* of course,
and constantly remind the rest of the world that they too should
be like us and so become democracies. But although our democracy is supposed to be a government "of the people, by the people, and for the people," which would mean a social democracy,
it has taken some turns in the course of our history toward other
formations. To be sure, our politicians and media do not seem to
have noticed. They constantly pose as knowing what "the people" are thinking and what they want, as if saying that that is
all it takes to keep our democracy alive and well. But the issues
at stake in the minds of the politicians and media usually reveal that the voice of "the people" they have heard is little more
than the mimicry of their own political programs. And their own
political programs are little more than self-interests in issues of
power and money. So it is rather the case that our society is governed in the interests of the free-enterprise system, sometimes
called a "capitalistic democracy." The "freedoms" in mind are said
to be of benefit to individuals, of course, but in reality they are
more for the benefit of our businesses and industries. "Over the
last decade," according to Hedrick Smith, "Boeing rolled up more
than $35 billion in profits and paid no federal corporate taxes"
(*Los Angeles Times,* January 7, 2014). It is this kind of practice

that anchors our "democracy" in the logic of capitalism, a logic that has turned all relationships, encounters, and exchanges in our society into subtle forms of competition, conflict, or rankings. Thus the term *democracy* is misleading as a sufficient definition for our society and government. This is especially the case if we want to imagine our society as a social organization that works for the interest of values other than wealth accumulation. It needs the adjective *social* to give it content in keeping with its derivation in the American and French revolutions, with the intention of our Constitution, and with our erstwhile unreflected self-understanding as a people and a nation for more than two hundred years. We have not always had the term *social democracy* to signify our collective sense of living in the United States, but as a term it comes closest to that stream of self-understanding we have commonly called upon to imagine that all was working well in everyone's interests.

There are, of course, reasons for not thinking of our nation as a social democracy. One is that the term *social* has hardly ever been used in a positive sense in our public discourse. It has, on the contrary, frequently served as a red flag in common conversation as well as in the discussions of political policy in Washington. The post–Second World War conflicts with "communism" and "socialism" tarnished the concept of "the social" by association, and "the social" has frequently been thought to threaten the "rights" and "freedoms" of the individual. Thus the combination of the two problematic terms (*democracy* and *social*), a combination that should signify a remarkably clear concept of the society we thought we were building, has instead become an obstacle to thinking with clarity about what we stand for as a nation. It is true, of course, that the recent chapter of our history, overwhelmed by our failed ventures in "spreading democracy" throughout the world, and by the more recent surge of implacable domestic issues calling for attention, has muddied the political waters. This recent chapter has, in fact, fomented outbursts of anger and distress on the part of the people telling us that something has gone wrong. But these outbursts have hindered deliberative thinking because we do not know what it is that has "gone wrong" or what we might do to rectify the situation. The social factors and forces that have emerged in recent times are indeed confusing: the exaggerations of political purpose in the international arena by our nation, the burgeoning excitements about incredible scientific technologies, the worldwide expansion of global markets and financial institutions, the widespread patterns of immigration into all Western nation-states, and the repeated intrusions into other nations on the part of nations, businesses, and NGOs in the interest of exploitation, curtailing violence, and "advancing civilization." Our inability to respond in a reasonable and constructive manner to this recent chapter of our nation's history is understandable due to our lack of a clear picture about the kind of democracy we represent.

Thus we have been left with the term *democracy* as little more than an ideological shibboleth without definition or content. We should have been using the term *social democracy* as a concept capable of carrying a meaningful list of social values as its connotations, the values for which we have stood and might still stand as a people. Alas, our politicians and media have not been attracted to this concept in their discussions of social issues and policies. It sometimes seems that the vision of a common-good society is no longer in mind. It needs to be there, and the careful introduction of the term *social democracy* into these discussions could tip the debates in the right direction. At the present time, the debates in Washington and the media do not show signs of argument from or for social principles of any kind, whether as commitment to social values or as elements of a social vision. This book has been an attempt to think about the reasons for this lack of social vision, and to ask whether the outlines of a social democracy might still be there in the structures of our nation-state and so might function as a kind of vision or goal as we struggle to imagine our future.

How strange it is that we take the term *democracy* for granted, but shy away from the word *social*. It is the social fact of living in a society that should be taken for granted, not the fuzzy ideology of a "democracy" that has been tarnished by mantras. Societies have been with us for ages; democracies are a recent social experiment. And their emergence in the American and French revolutions tells a troubled history. Those invested in the structures of the erstwhile social formations challenged by the revolutions have never wanted a democracy. "How could the unlettered masses ever figure out how to govern a nation?" has been the common refrain. So as Christendom became empires, empires became kingdoms, kingdoms became nations, and nations became nation-states, the troubling experiment to find a workable social alternative to the medieval kingdoms finally found democracies wriggling around in the space between feudal aristocracies and fascist outbursts. We can be thankful for Anthony Giddens's study *The Nation-State*, which presents the nation-state as a contrast both to pre–Industrial Revolution medieval feudalism and to the various fascisms of the twentieth century that sprang up into the power vacancy left with the demise of the royal and aristocratic sovereignties. His detailed descriptions of the institutions constituting the nation-state, their interrelationships, and the dynamics of their workings together in the life of the nation-state make it possible to see them as the structural outline and promise for a social democracy. As he lays it out, article by article, the reader can chart the social changes that have taken place from the hierarchic structure of the aristocratic kingdoms to social formations that function at the level of the modern state. And many of the older ways of thinking about "traditional societies," as he calls them, have had to yield to new ways of understanding the dynamics of living together.

There are a few glitches to notice as the nation-state model established itself, such as the acceptance of "total surveillance" as the way to control the operations of the whole; the unfortunate lack of mechanisms against the rise of autocrats; the belief that the military is the only way to provide defense; and the inevitability of violence in defense of "national interests." One can see that most of these unfortunate features, all illustrated in the horrible histories of the twentieth century, are the results of continuing to think in terms of the older kingdom models of government, mentalities that the revolutionary experiments have not yet excised, and for which there are not adequate alternatives and constraints. Still, Giddens's studies count as a major description of the social changes that have taken place in Western history since the Enlightenment. His description is focused on the social function of state institutions and structures, and so does not engage questions about values cast in other terms. But we can see how the several transitions from kingdoms to nation-states occurred without destroying "the social" as an organism. And the more or less mechanical descriptions of the structures of "the social" only enhance the insight that it is society as an organism that persists even when cultural values change. A major example throughout all of this history is that kings came and went, and autocracies rose and fell, only to damage their societies as a temporary tragedy, not to destroy them. In course, we have almost learned that we do not need kings or autocrats in order to have a working society. This means that Giddens's studied outline of the institutions that structure the nation-state is a precious documentation, if not proof, of the fact that the sheer mechanical operation of society is a phenomenon we can count on, a kind of organism for which the collective has been responsible, the manifestation of a set of interests that are social. It won't go away, even when abused by unthinking politicians, dictators, and their wars. Looked at this way, Giddens's description of the organism also lets us see that it runs on intellectual energies and begs for common values to give it "meaning" and "motivation."

If so, why not take Giddens seriously and let the social structuration of the United States determine the politics of value for a change? The nation-state would not be crushed and go away were we to dispense with our guns and military. The huge financial disparities in our national budgets and in our distribution of wealth could easily be remedied were we to use our social structures for the production of a culture that celebrated the common good. And if our corporations found themselves intrigued by making contributions to the common good, we might not have to worry about senses of an ending in collapses and destructions.

If we managed to weave a coat of many colors for the collective to wear, we might not need to write so many scripts for the horror shows. And if we needed some help visualizing and producing a social democracy for the common good, there are the social democracies in Europe waiting in the wings. They are still there waiting for the United States to engage them in conversation about nation-states and social values. It is true that they are currently challenged by an influx of refugees and immigrants. But they will find a way to handle this problem, just as they have found ways to respond to the many political and ideological challenges of the past two or three centuries.

We can put these European nations with their social democracies together with their European Union and the United Nations as three examples of a positive ending to the long history of Western civilization. And none of the three examples has needed to parry the logic of the Christian myth in order to let its culture survive as an ingredient within the multicultural collectives. Were the people of the United States to do the same and join them in working together for a truly global world of social democracies, that would certainly lift our spirits and let us redirect our energies from destructive to constructive projects in the interest of a polycultural global civilization.

CONCLUSION

A Palliative Postscript

The concept of a big picture has been used as a theme to trace the history of mythmaking and social formation from tribal societies to nation-states. A theory has been used to link several social and mythic ingredients of the big picture. There are the three environments within which a people live: the social interests that motivate their productive activities, the myths and rituals that focus collective attention on fundamental activities, and language and symbols to create collective intelligence and cultural meaning. Under way, the Christian myth has focused our attention on the sweep of Western cultural history. It has been possible to analyze the social logic of the Christian myth, the manner of its authentication for the Christian church, and the reasons for its persistence at the level of cultural mentality. It has also been clear, however, that the social interests and energies of the Western nations since the Industrial Revolution have moved away from the Christian society and mythic world. The Christian myth and social formation (church and empire) no longer work to integrate the social interests of the modern nation-state or to solve the political issues that have developed among the modern nation-states in confrontation with the nations of the globe.

The perceptive reader will have been aware of a certain refusal throughout this book to entertain the topics of predation, war, and the abuse of power. These topics have been mentioned, of course, as the distasteful side of the anthropology under question. But the bright side has been preferred at every turn in the interest of a constructive social vision. Much of the ethnography has been read as if the human enterprise of social formation were thoroughly constructive, interested in the personal rewards of working together and the ethical awards of communal living. Myths and rituals seemed to underscore the values of social stability; symbols suggested a pervasive mentality that cultivated the positive meaning of community life for a people.

The turns to the long Western traditions of social history were also read in the interest of emphasizing their rational features and intentions in the construction of kingdoms, laws, texts, histories, myths, and rituals. As this social history took the shape of Christendom and then generated the intellectual movements we have called Renaissance, Enlightenment, science, Reformation, and industry, a more or less traditional sense of its sophistication determined the attempt to account for the social changes that came along almost as if they belonged to the logic of progress that used to be customary for making sense of the "classical tradition" and its "development" into modernity. The academics who write as if the collective can be described with having a mind-set and a logic rooted in the classical (Greek) tradition have not been criticized. Features of Western history that might be blamed for wrong turns have not been described. I have not explored the wars undertaken by Christian popes and kings, nor the relation between Christianity and the fascisms of the twentieth century.

Rather, the social changes from kingdoms to nation-states have been treated as struggles in the interest of establishing some kind of social democracy.

The treatment of the Western Christian traditions in the United States has allowed the American sensibilities concerning "freedom," "independence," and "manifest destiny" to stand for a mentality that has not been criticized. The nonaggressive ethic of the average American's thinking has been appreciated. From barn-raising to the Saturday markets and the Sunday churchgoings, the social activities of rural America seemed to indicate a world large enough and interesting enough for entire generations of families to live their lives fully engaged. And even the mentality of the conservative coalition, the very mentality considered to be the cause for much of the ugly social issues addressed, was treated rather as a grossly mistaken notion about both the nation's history and Christianity's continuing relevance and power. It was accounted for as a mark of the low level of education and thinking that had occurred in the United States.

However, the subtheme about social issues has also been constant throughout the book. And many of these issues have been described as if there were a popular common judgment about their ugliness among the people. Some of them have been offensive because business and corporate actions violated their own promises. Others seem to be grounded in older views of social values that have been violated or overlooked by patterns of behavior. Few have been offensive because they violated basic principles of a moral social model. We have traced many of these social issues to conflicts among major social interests as institutions that have no built-in system of self-criticism, as if once they were aware of the problem, they would change course. And most of the public outcries and critical responses to these social issues seem to have assumed that the underlying reasons for an offense surely must be understood by everyone. But then the phenomena of social issues began to focus on the trio of power abuse, violence, and predation that seemed somehow to be justified by an unconscious Christian mentality.

We have followed the social history of the Christian myth and worldview into the modern period, when the traditional cultural dominance of Christianity was in erosion. We discovered that what was left of Christendom's big picture was not the memory of an epic narrative couched in a cosmic universe but only a mentality that gave privilege to Western attitudes of superiority and power. Now even that collection of assumptions has run its course. Instead, what we have before us are the pictures of the violence inadvertently unleashed by the postures of power in the United States both at home and abroad. These postures and actions of the United States are now creating anger on the part of those mistreated. There are many movements, intellectuals, and local groups in the United States calling for the rectification of our social issues, and for the restructuring of our society. And those presumed to be in charge of affairs are constantly being asked to do something about these situations. But we now realize that those in charge do not know what to do. The media and their journalists are being asked what they make of the situation. We are impressed with their control of the data and history of events, and their ability to render telling criticisms of the social agencies that should be able, or should have been able, to do something about an issue on their own terms. This does tell us that many know how our society has been assumed to operate according to this or that set of social principles, and that it should be expected to perform according to those principles. But alas, the pace at which the issues evolve is faster than that at which rectifications can happen. There are very few answers being proposed for the resolution of our social issues.

So the thesis of our study has been the need for another big picture, one that imagines the polycultural people we in fact are, learning to live together without violence. However, such a picture of the future is nowhere in sight. Yet "the sense of the future" has been a rather consistent topic at many levels of thoughtful commentary among leaders, journalists, and academics. Several scenarios have become rather common in public discourse. One is that if the United States and its industries do not change course, the future for society and the planet is bleak. The references are frequently to nuclear war, ecological disasters, and the probable extinction of species including humankind. Another scenario is the exact opposite, namely the continuing confidence in the ultimate victory of scientific and corporate capitalism to turn the globe into a glorious world city. This vision is glorious in some pictures of the luxurious cities that have been built around the world, but disgusting when one realizes that corporate capitalism has also created the conditions for the predation, violence, and destruction that characterize the current social world.

So here we are with little to show for our haunting memories of the Christian big picture, as faded as it may be, or for our naïve visions of a future in our own hands. It seems that the entire history of Western civilization came tumbling into the United States just to see what might be made of its people in the "new world," a continent considered vacant and available for experimentation. There was no need for these immigrants to go to school to learn what to do or think about society and culture. The know-how, skills, and confidence came along with the peoples in their crossings. There was the land for the taking, and both the land and the future were wide open, stretching as far as the Pacific Ocean. With such a backdrop, some culture historians, such as Tocqueville, have let the American people think that they did very well.

There was no time for deep reflections on the meaning of life at the beginning of our national history, or on the way west, or during the wars. Families mourned their losses, of course. And monuments could be raised. But all of that was in the interest of getting on with it, learning to live in this land, devising practical solutions, and always starting over. We were thoroughly engaged in the building of a society out of stalwarts and can-dos. Now we see that the self-confidence and self-interest of the American individual, though glorious in some ways as the character of a frontier people, is not enough to manage the global world our clever corporations have created. There is much twisting and turning, but little insight in how to proceed. And so our study may have answered our questions about what happened to the big picture of Christendom. But it did not find another big picture of that kind in the making, and it has not found a substitute for the Christian myth and mentality that still resides among the interests and energies driving an active world. This meant that our questions needed to be refocused to ask whether there was any modern social formation good enough for the future.

The answer, however, was already at hand. It was the concept and model of a social democracy. A social democracy does not need a big picture of the cosmic kind in order to know its place and importance among the histories of peoples and civilizations. And it does not need myths and rituals of the traditional kind in order to celebrate its practices. A social democracy can cultivate the significance of its social interests in the production of honors, rewards, and meaningful experiences of human social existence. It does require a level of interest and education among the people in general who are invested in the formation of their society and culture. But the big picture in view needs only to let the experience of the human species fill the canvas for review, invite reflection and critical thinking, and so provide the topics for significant political and cultural projects. The modern nation-state can provide the structure for a people's projects in the interest of collective well-being, as well as the supports for its common-good endeavors, and the constraints necessary when energies are in danger of violating the welfare.

In the previous chapter we discussed the reasons for the resistance to the term *social democracy* in the United States, how those reasons were rooted in an outworn Christian mentality, and why those reasons were insufficient to reject the concept. It was suggested that a social democracy would be the way to counter the many social issues that have inadvertently been created by the "capitalistic democracy" our conservative leaders have put in place. A social democracy would go a long way toward answering many of the social issues that are creating the problematic picture we have been painting. We would do well to use the concept of a social democracy as the vision for the future we need. A social democracy is what we were working on before we got sidetracked after the Second World War and found ourselves fascinated with the thoughts of power and leadership among the nations. Since acting out that fantasy has led the world not to peace but to enmity, we might pause long enough to think about our nation building before these recent times. The governmental structures that produced our strengths and virtues are still there. We could use them again to work for a common-good society in which the well-being of the people suggested a picture of ourselves of which we could be proud. To realize that a social democracy is the very form of a society within which the virtues of pride, honor, and achievement can flourish without violence or predation would be a way of remembering our marvelous past. It could also be the way to think about our future.

AUTHORS AND WORKS CITED

Augustine of Hippo. *The Confessions of St. Augustine* (A.D. 397–400). Introduction and translation by David Vincent Mecon. New York: Ignatius, 2012.

Boas, Franz. *Race, Language, and Culture*. New York: Macmillan, 1940; Free Press, 1966.

Bourdieu, Pierre. *Esquisse d'une théorie de la pratique*. Geneva: Droz, 1972. Trans. as *Outline of a Theory of Practice*, Richard Nice. Cambridge Studies in Social Anthropology 16. Cambridge: Cambridge University Press, 1977.

Bronowski, J. *The Ascent of Man*. Boston: Little, Brown, 1973.

———. *A Sense of the Future: Essays in Natural Philosophy*. Cambridge: MIT Press, 1977.

Cameron, Ron, and Merrill Miller. *Redescribing Christian Origins*. Symposium Series 28. Atlanta: Society of Biblical Literature, 2004.

———. *Redescribing Paul and the Corinthians*. Early Christianity and Its Literature, no. 5. Atlanta: Society of Biblical Literature, 2011.

Carlson, Jennifer. "The NRA's Hidden Power." *Los Angeles Times*, January 3, 2013.

Durkheim, Émile. *Les Formes élémentaire de la view religieuse*. Paris: F. Alcan, 1912.

Ehrlich, Paul, and Anne Ehrlich. "Can a Collapse of Global Civilization Be Avoided?" *Proceedings of the Royal Society*, January 8, 2013.

Frazer, Sir James George. *The Golden Bough: A Study in Magic and Religion*. Abridged ed. London: Macmillan, 1963. (Various editions from 1890 to 1922).

Giddens, Anthony. *The Nation-State and Violence*. Vol. 2 of *A Contemporary Critique of Historical Materialism*. Berkeley: University of California Press, 1987.

Gould, Stephen Jay. *Wonderful Life: The Burgess Shale and the Nature of History*. New York: Norton, 1989.

Harvey, David. *The Condition of Postmodernity*. Oxford: Blackwell, 1990, 1995.

Hawken, Paul. *Blessed Unrest: How the Largest Social Movement in History Is Restoring Grace, Justice, and Beauty to the World*. New York: Penguin, 2005.

Hedges, Chris. "The Myth of Human Progress." *Truthdig*, January 10, 2013.

Heidegger, Martin. *Sein und Zeit*. Tübingen: Max Niemeyer, 1927.

Hertsgaard, Mark. "Adapting to Change." *New Yorker*, February 4, 2013.

Hultkranz, Ake. *The Religions of the American Indians*. Trans. Monica Setterwall. Berkeley: University of California Press, 1979.

Jameson, Fredric. *The Political Unconscious: Narrative as a Socially Symbolic Act*. Ithaca, NY: Cornell University Press, 1981.

———. *Postmodernism; or, The Cultural Logic of Late Capitalism*. Durham: Duke University Press, 1991.

———. *Archaeologies of the Future: The Desire Called Utopia and Other Science Fictions*. London: Verso, 2005.

Lepore, Jill. "The Force: How Much Military Is Enough?" *New Yorker*, January 28, 2013.

———. "Richer and Poorer." *New Yorker*, March 16, 2015.

Lévi-Strauss, Claude. *Introduction to a Science Mythology*, 3 vols. Trans. John and Doreen Weightman. New York: Harper and Row, 1975–78.

Mack, Burton. *The Christian Myth: Origins, Logic, and Legacy*. New York: Continuum, 2003.

———. *Myth and the Christian Nation: A Social Theory of Religion*. London: Equinox, 2008.

———. *Christian Mentality: The Entanglements of Power, Violence, and Fear*. London: Equinox 2011; Acumen, 2013.

Malinowski, Bronisław. *Magic, Science, and Religion and Other Essays*. Boston: Beacon, 1948; Garden City, NY: Doubleday, 1955.

Marx, Karl. *Communist Manifesto: Socialist Landmark*. London: Labour Party, 1848.

———. *Das Kapital.* Vol 1. Hamburg, 1867.

Mauss, Marcel. *Essai sur le don, forme archaique de l'echange.* Paris, 1925. Trans. as *The Gift: Forms and Functions of Exchange in Archaic Societies,* Ian Cunnison. New York: Norton, 1967.

McGowan, John. *Postmodernism and Its Critics.* Ithaca: Cornell University Press, 1991.

McKibben, Bill. "Time Is Not on Our Side." *TomDispatch,* January 6, 2013.

Miles, Jack. *The Perils of Pluralism: In Quest of a Common Literary Culture.* Center for the Humanities Studies, Monograph 4. Claremont, CA: Claremont McKenna College, 1990.

Morozon, Evgeny. "Only Disconnect: Boredom Reconsidered." *New Yorker,* October 23, 2013.

Petrarch, Francesco. *De secreto conflictu cumarum mearum* (ca. 1347–53; first published, 1470). Trans. and ed. as *Petrarch's Secretum: With Introduction, Notes, and Critical Anthology,* Davy A. Carozza and H. James Shey. New York: P. Lang, 1989.

Prichard, James B., ed. *Ancient Near Eastern Texts Relating to the Old Testament,* 3rd ed. Princeton: Princeton University Press, 1955, 1969.

Radin, Paul. *The Winnebago Tribe.* Lincoln: University of Nebraska Press, 1970.

Rifkin, Jeremy. *Entropy: A New World View.* New York: Bantam, 1980.

Runions, Erin. "Theologico-Political Resonance: Carl Schmitt between the Neocons and the Theonomists." *Differences: A Journal of Feminist Cultural Studies* 18, no. 3 (2007): 43–80.

Sahlins, Marshall. *Historical Metaphors and Mythical Realities: Structure in the Early History of the Sandwich Islands Kingdom.* Association for Social Anthropology in Oceania, Special Publications no. 1. Ann Arbor: University of Michigan Press, 1987.

Sanchez, David. *From Patmos to the Barrio: Subverting Imperial Myths.* Minneapolis: Fortress, 2008.

Saussure, Ferdinand de. *Course in General Linguistics* (1916). Trans. W. Barkin. New York: Duckworth.

Schell, Jonathan. *The Unconquerable World: Power, Nonviolence, and the Will of the People.* New York: Metropolitan, 2003.

Schmitt, Carl. *Political Theology: Four Chapters on the Concept of Sover-*

eignty. Trans. George Schwab. Chicago: University of Chicago Press, 1985.

Sharlet, Jeff. *The Family: The Secret Fundamentalism at the Heart of American Power.* New York: HarperCollins, 2008.

Smith, Hedrick. "Boeing Rolled Up 35 Million." *Los Angeles Times,* January 7, 2015.

Smith, Henry Nash. *Virgin Land: The American West as Symbol and Myth.* Cambridge: Harvard University Press, 1950.

Smith, Jonathan Z. *Imagining Religion: From Babylon to Jonestown.* Chicago: University of Chicago Press, 1982.

———. *To Take Place: Toward Theory in Ritual.* Chicago: University of Chicago Press, 1987. Pages 42–45 contain Smith's views on the Winnebago's village.

Spanos, William V. "The Apollonian Investment of Modern Humanist Education: The Examples of Matthew Arnold, Irving Babbitt, and I. A. Richards," part 1. *Cultural Critique,* no. 1, Fall 1985, 7–72.

Specter, Michael. *Denialism: How Irrational Thinking Hinders Scientific Progress.* New York: Penguin, 2009.

Stowers, Stanley K. "Greeks Who Sacrifice and Those Who Do Not: Toward an Anthropology of Greek Religion." In *The Social World of the First Christians: Essays in Honor of Wayne A. Meeks.* Ed. Michael White and O. Larry Yarbrough. Minneapolis: Fortress, 1995.

Tainter, Joseph. *The Collapse of Complex Societies.* New York: Cambridge University Press, 1988, 1990.

Teresi, Dick. *Lost Discoveries: The Ancient Roots of Modern Science—From the Babylonians to the Maya.* New York: Simon and Schuster, 2002.

Tocqueville, Alexis de. *Democracy in America.* New York: Mentor, 1956.

Trilling, Lionel. *The Liberal Imagination: Essays on Literature and Society.* Garden City, NY: Doubleday Anchor, 1957.

Williams, Raymond. *Culture and Society: 1780–1950.* New York: Columbia University Press, 1958, 1983.

———. *Keywords: A Vocabulary of Culture and Society.* New York: Oxford University Press, 1976, 1983.

Wright, Will. *Six Guns and Society: A Structural Study of the Western.* Berkeley: University of California Press, 1975.

INDEX

Marx's analysis of, 105–11,
113–14; mentality of, 103, 112;
myth of, 169; pattern to, 218;
permeating collective mentality, 151; postmodernism and,
219; predation and, 176–77; as
revolutionary force, 220; social
interests and, 123, 194, 196;
social issues and, 115–17; structural defect in, 172; success of,
114–15, 253; system of, 109; as
worldview, 104
capitalistic democracy, 274–75, 287
Carlson, Jennifer, 134
cathedrals, 30–31, 33–34
Catholic Church, 69, 80
causes, consideration of, 55
Cheney, Dick, 12, 167
Christendom, 10, 12, 13–14,
26–31, 58, 66–70; big picture of, 96–97; challenges to,
246–48; cultural formation of,
244; culture and, 93, 97–98;
imagery of, 97; mythic worldview of, 67–69; residual elements of, 33–34, 35; social construction of, 67; social interests
and, 58, 69–70, 93; transformed
into Protestant culture, 72;
worldview of, 87, 245
Christ event: Protestants and, 77;
reenactment of, 67
Christian Coalition, 161, 193, 244
Christianity: Ancient Near Eastern
myths and, 6; authority of, in

nation-states, 100; Bible Belt,
99; big-picture mythology
of, 13; as cultural tradition
in United States, 160; early
authors of, 205; familiarity of,
245; influence of, 229; interest of, in society, 192; loyalty
to, 192–93; migrants and, 3,
169, 229–30; myths of, 8–9;
origins of, 5, 9, 62, 66, 71,
96–97; as religion of the book,
233–34; response of, to post-
Renaissance history, 98; social
concerns of, 1; social dis-ease
and, 193; social interests of, 66;
worldview of, 4, 98, 99–100,
145–46, 184
Christian logos, 81
Christian mentality, 79–84, 100,
160; capitalism and, 196; coming to collective consciousness,
267; cultural critique of, 174;
and denialism of science, 192;
endarkenment and, 148; gun
violence and, 135; narrative
logic in, 225; pervasiveness of,
193; social thinking of, 174;
survival of, 227–28, 252
Christian Mentality (Mack), 14, 99,
160, 227, 241, 243–44
Christian myth: and the American mental atmosphere, 169;
belief in, 5, 8–9; biblical form
of, 77, 84; colonialism and,
170; cosmology of, 68, 87;

Frazer, James George, 70
Frazier, Ian, 261–63
freedom, 221, 283; in capitalistic democracy, 274; negative, 215; postmodernists' quest for, 214–15; U.S. embrace of, 76, 101
Freud, Sigmund, 215
From Patmos to the Barrio (Sánchez), 83–84
Funk, Robert, 8
future: scenarios for, 285; sense of, 169–82, 285

Galileo, 92
Gast, John, 83
Gates agencies, 164
Gehry, Frank, 223–24
genealogy, importance of, 46
Giddens, Anthony, 31, 32, 207, 277–79
Gill, Ted, 4, 5
Girard, René, 10
global collapse, 145–47, 150
globalization, 82, 102, 109, 169, 172, 194–95, 218–19
global warming, 94, 152
god, concept of, 269–70
God: kingdom of, 26–27, 58, 62, 65; monarchical power of, 97
Golden Bough, The (Frazer), 70
Gospels: belief in, 29; reception of, 62; reenactment of, 67; stories in, reasons for telling, 62; writing of, 62
Gould, Stephen Jay, 263–65

government: attitude toward, 221; as social unit, 117–18
grand narrative, 14, 215, 220
grassroots movements, 116. *See also* social movements
Greece, ancient, 20–22, 205
growth, economic goal of, 108–9
gun control: debate over, 130–31; legislation for, 131–32, 139–42; social democracy and, 141
guns: acceptability of, 133; sales of, 131–32. *See also* arms manufacturing
gun violence, 129–42

Habitat for Humanity, 164
habitus, 96
Hamilton, Clive, 143
Hamilton, Neal Q., 5
Hammurabi's Code (Hammurabi), 204
Harrington, Michael, 207
Harvard University, 210–11, 220
Harvey, David, 113, 166–67, 216–20
Hawken, Paul, 116, 151, 258–61, 262
Hebrew epics, 204–5
Hebrews, 25–26
Hedges, Chris, 143
Hegel, G. W. F., 215
Heidegger, Martin, 81
Heracles of Tiryins, 21
heroes, 20–22, 137–38
Hertsgaard, Mark, 152

historical materialism, 219–20
history: central event of, 87–88; language and, 42; loss of, 217
history of religions, 5–6, 20
holism, 215
Holocaust, 239
Holy Spirit, 1
Hultkranz, Ake, 11, 46
humanisms, 82, 89
humanities, history of, 90
humans: behavior of, 56; community of, interest in, 114; divine plan for, 79–80; evolution of, 187, 264–65; labor of, exploitation of, 108; motivations for, 123; painting pictures, 17; scientific analysis of, 95; social formation of, 174–75, 186, 197, 248, 265; violence by, social pattern of, 175–76
Hurricane Sandy, 151–52

IAC. *See* Institute for Antiquity and Christianity
identity, 52, 64
imagination, 43, 54
imperialism, 214
independence, 283. *See also* individualism
indigenous tribes, myths of, 11
individual: construction of, 57; discovery of, 88, 90; experience of, 224; interest in, 95, 189; mystique of, 137 (*see also* individualism); psychology of, 189;

salvation of, 170; spirituality and, 193; value of, 189; values of, 254
individualism, 123, 138, 215, 286
industrial economies, 102–3
Industrial Revolution, 31–32, 86, 194, 207; effects of, 105–9, 111–12, 142; Marx's analysis of, 105, 109
industry, supplanting culture, 251–52
Institute for Antiquity and Christianity (IAC), 7–8
intellection, 48–49
intellectuals: anxiety of, 215; history of, 203–8, 214, 224; self-consciousness of, 203; traditions of, analysis of, 225
interests, 47–48, 148–49; conflict between, 188; fragmentation of, 150; individual, 186. *See also* national interests; social interests; special interests, as ideologies
invention, as motivation, 198
Islam, 89, 158; cultural conflict of, with the West, 232–33, 235–36, 242–45; literary tradition of, 237–38; militant, 231, 236; as religion of the book, 233–34; rise of, 246; social formation of, 236; Westerners' difficulty in understanding, 237–38; Western policy toward, 231–32
isolationism, 163

Israel: epic of, 25–26, 29, 65; present-day, 238–41

Jameson, Fredric, 113, 215, 220–27
Jaspers, Karl, 5
Jefferson, Thomas, 136, 137
Jesuits, recasting biblical account of creation, 98
Jesus: Christ as name for, 65; as founder figure, 63; interest in, 62, 65; linked to Judaic and Greek myths, 61; martyrological myth of, 66–67; as messiah, 64–65; myths about, 61–64; teachings of, 27
Jesus schools, 27, 61–62, 65; and governance in the Roman Empire, 66; identity of, 64, 65–66; interests of, 63–64; as public state institutions, 67; social formations of, 63; social networks of, 65–66; transformed into myth-ritual religion, 66–67
Jesus Seminar, the, 7
John, Prologue to Gospel of, 6, 13
Judaism, 233, 238–39

Kant, Immanuel, 215
Kerry, John, 128
kerygma, 5
Keywords: A Vocabulary of Culture and Society (Williams), 207
Khomeini, Ruhollah, 231–32

Kierkegaard, Søren, 5
kingdom of God, 26–27, 58, 62, 65
kingdoms, 71, 73, 107
kings, 22
Kings County (CA) Migrant Ministry, 3
Koran: satire on, 237–38; social logic of, 237
Küng, Hans, 11

Lacanale, Bob, 2
Laertes of Ithaca, 21
land, attachment to, 46
language: Aristotelian theory of, 81; as environment, 41; significance of, 42; social formation and, 265, 268–69; social interests and, 49–50, 269
last supper, memorial ritual for, 67
Lepore, Jill, 152–53
Lévi-Strauss, Claude, 11, 46, 49
liberal imagination, 90
Liberal Imagination, The (Trilling), 96, 209
literary criticism, 212
literary culture, 209, 228
literature, study of, 90–91
logics, within social segments, 149–50
logos, 6, 213
Lone Ranger, The, 138
Los Angeles Times, 222
Lost Discoveries (Teresi), 92
Loudon, John, 9
Luther, Martin, 71–72

mythmaking: pre-Christian experiments in, 12; social formation and, 12

Myth of Innocence, A (Mack), 8, 11

myths, 41; affecting practice and social interests, 237; belief in, 5; common understanding of, 11; creating big picture of imaginary worlds, 147; ethnographic theory of, 61; ethos of, 54; function of, 51–54, 93; idealism of, 56; mentality and, 78–79; narrative grammar of, 54; narrative logic of, 55–56; occasions for, 51; as pictures, 17; as religious mechanism, 96; rituals and, 93; setting of, 53–54; significance of, 49; social interests and, 48; social theory of, 39; studies of, 40; tribal societies and, 46; for Western civilization, 147–48

narrative grammar, 54, 96

nation: connotations of, 121–22, 124; as social interest, 197. *See also* nation-states

National Climate Assessment and Development Advisory Committee, 143

national identity, 64

national interests, 117–25, 154, 157, 230

National Rifle Association, 132, 133–36, 178

nation-building, 14, 159, 230, 236, 288

Nation-State and Violence, The (Giddens), 31, 277–79

nation-states, 31–33, 70, 73, 74, 88; Christianity's authority in, 100; corporations and, 254; demographics of, 265–66; evolution of, 277–78, 282–83; and the Industrial Revolution, 106–7; as misnomer, 118; national interests and, 118; social democracy and, 278; social interests and, 187; structure of, 187

Native Americans, conflict with, 137–38

Natural Capital Institute, 259

natural environment, 41, 42, 252; exploitation of, 108; extension of, 190; knowledge of, 191; study of, to address human interests, 95

natural order: individual in, discovery of, 90; manipulation of, 92; origins of, 44; study of, 92–93

Near East: insurgency in, 235; U.S. involvement in, 154, 157–59, 165–68, 231–45. *See also* Ancient Near East

negative freedom, 215

Netanyahu, Benjamin, 240

Netanyahu administration, 240

Netherlands, climate change adaptation and the, 152

New American Century, 167–68. *See also* American Century

ism and, 123, 194, 196; changes
in, 48; Christendom and, 58,
69–70, 93; Christian myth and,
248; conceptualizing, 47–48;
conflicts among, 184, 199, 200;
culture and, 57; defined, 93;
ethnography and, 46; features
of, 49–50; histories of, 124;
language and, 49–50, 269; as
motivations, 189, 198; mythic
thinking and, 58, 241; nations
and, 120–21, 124, 187, 197;
new mythology for, 252–53;
power of, 197–98; production
of, 86; rituals and, 48; science
as, 91, 95, 123; self-criticism
and, 198; social formation
and, 185–86; social issues and,
129; society's infrastructure
and, 183; symbols and, 201;
in traditional society, 95–96;
tradition of, 91; tribal societies
and, 47, 49–50, 185; of the
United States, 195; Western,
81–82, 185
socialism, 275
social issues, 38, 94, 124–25,
253; capitalism and, 115–17;
common judgment about,
283–84; engagement with, 174;
evolution of, 285; as intellectual issues, 14–15; intensity of,
increasing, 226; science and,
95; social interests and, 129;
solutions to, 257

social media, 179–81, 222–23
social movements, 258–61
social practices, interests of, 186
social projects, 36–38, 100–101,
117
social science, 147
social situations, critical thinking
and, 225
social system: civilization as,
144–45; motivations of, 125
social theory, 8; of myth, 39; of
religion, 11, 39–40
social vision, lack of, 277
social world, 44, 252
society: dis-ease in, 183–84, 187,
193, 198–99, 203, 254–55;
evolution of, 55; mentality of,
202; mythic anchorage of, 202;
as network of interests, 248–49;
operation of, 54–55; as totality,
222–23; vocabulary of, 207–8;
Western, cultural productions
of, 202–3
Society of Biblical Literature
(SBL), 7
Socrates, 64
Sophia-Chokma, 6
space: compressed, 219; expansion
of, 42; merged with time, 52;
place and, 217
Spanos, William V., 211–13
special interests, as ideologies, 177
Specter, Michael, 191–92
spirituality, 193
stand your ground, 100, 135

in, 252; economy of, 101–3; European roots of, 76; foreign policy of, 162–69, 230, 234–45; formation of, 119; freedom and, 101, 148; future vision of, 169–82; globalization and, 82; as global power, 154–59, 161–69; gun-friendly history of, 132, 133–34, 136; gun violence in, 129–42; hero stories in, 137–38; hostilities against, 121; House Un-American Activities Committee, 156–57; humanitarian aid by, 163–64; incoherence in, 192; inequities in, 102; isolationism of, 163; leadership of, 120, 128–29, 163, 167, 172–73, 209, 230, 247, 255; literary culture of, 209; losing big picture, 140; manifest destiny and, 172–73 (see also manifest destiny); mentality gap in, 191; mentality of, 88, 255; military involvement of, 154–59, 161–68, 170; military of, 120; military spending in, 152–54; missions of, 38, 82, 120, 161–62, 164, 181, 228, 229, 247–48, 255; mistaken turn in, 210; motivation in, 195–96; multiculturalism and, 257, 266–71; myths and, 169–70; national interests of, 120–21, 157–58, 162, 165–66, 230; national mentality of, rooted in Christian tradition, 244; national story of, 119–20; Near East involvement of, 165–68, 231–45; new social vision for, 181–82; non-Christian culture in, 268–69; obsession of, with freedom, 76; origins of, 34–35; patriotism in, 120; political ideology of, 165; politics of value in, 279–80; post–World War II changes in, 110, 122, 159; Protestantism traveling to, 99; relations with Russia, 165; religion in, 39, 244; role of, in international affairs, 56; rural social activities in, 283; as secular nation, 76; self-understanding of, 243–44; social democracy and, 257, 266–71, 273–80, 287–88; social history of, 243; social interests of, 195; social situation in, 208–9; standing army in, 153; superiority of, 110–11, 167; Western Christian tradition in, failure of, 247–48; western expansion of, 136–37, 286; world wars and, 119–20

University of Göttingen, 5–6

vaccinations, 191
values, 94, 179; changes in, 105–6; conflict of, 188
violence: entertainment and, 138–39; motivation for, 140; social pattern of, 175–76